WORKBOOK IN LATIN FIRST YEAR

By **CHARLES I. FREUNDLICH**

Author of
Latin for the Grades, Books I, II, III
Latin Two Years
Latin Three and Four Years

Dedicated to serving

AMSCO

our nation's youth

When ordering this book, please specify:
either **R 58 W** *or*
WORKBOOK IN LATIN FIRST YEAR

AMSCO SCHOOL PUBLICATIONS, INC.

315 Hudson Street   New York, N. Y. 10013

ISBN 0-87720-553-1

PRINTED IN THE UNITED STATES OF AMERICA

PREFACE

Workbook in Latin First Year is a valuable supplement to any first-year Latin textbook. Replete with copious and varied exercises, it provides the teacher with handy assignments, and the student with a means of drill and self-evaluation.

Starting with a unit on verbs, the most important element in any sentence, the Workbook takes up in progressive lessons other parts of speech, idioms, grammar, passages for comprehension, derivation and word study, culture, vocabularies, and finally specimen examinations. Review and mastery exercises permit the teacher to pause at strategic places and test large areas. The optional lessons deal with verb forms omitted in some first-year textbooks, and may be used at the discretion of the teacher.

In keeping with the modern trend to stress the audio-lingual approach in foreign languages, the author has incorporated in the Workbook a section on oral classroom conversation with exercises. This section can profitably be used both for motivation and as a teaching device. The enterprising teacher, with this material at hand, will be able to create interest in the classroom, to bring life to Latin, and at the same time to teach proper pronunciation, vocabulary, Latin word order, and grammatically correct sentences.

The Workbook is so designed that the teacher may assign any topic in which the class needs drill, without following strictly the order of the units. The perforated pages permit the student to do the exercises directly in the Workbook and hand them in as homework. Of particular interest to New York State teachers are the new-type Regents questions which have been incorporated in the book.

Perhaps the greatest value of the Workbook lies in the organization of the material. Most textbooks have the forms, grammar, culture, derivation, etc., scattered throughout the book. The Workbook has assembled all this material into convenient units, subdivided into lessons, each an entity in itself. The table of contents permits the teacher to find instantly any topic in its entirety.

The teacher of a second-year Latin class also will find this book a very convenient means of reviewing the first-year work, particularly after a summer vacation.

For drilling, for assigning work, for reviewing, for testing, for oral work—for all these purposes the teacher will find this Workbook a veritable thesaurus.

—C. I. F.

CONTENTS

Unit I—Verbs, Active Voice

Unit XII—Roman Civilization and Culture

Unit XIII

Unit XIV

Unit XV

Unit I—Verbs, Active Voice

Lesson 1—PRESENT TENSE ACTIVE OF FIRST AND SECOND CONJUGATION VERBS

FIRST CONJUGATION

port*āre,* to carry; present stem, **portā–**

SINGULAR		PLURAL	
port*ō*	I carry	port*āmus*	we carry
port*ās*	you carry	port*ātis*	you carry
port*at*	he or she carries	port*ant*	they carry

SECOND CONJUGATION

doc*ēre,* to teach; present stem, **docē–**

SINGULAR		PLURAL	
doc*eō*	I teach	doc*ēmus*	we teach
doc*ēs*	you teach	doc*ētis*	you teach
doc*et*	he or she teaches	doc*ent*	they teach

Note

1. The present stem of a verb is found by dropping the ending **-re** of the infinitive.

2. The present tense is formed by adding to the stem the personal endings **-ō, -s, -t, -mus, -tis, -nt.** (Note that in the form **portō** the final **ā** of the stem is dropped.)

3. The present tense may be translated in several ways:

> **portās,** you carry, you are carrying, you do carry
> **docēmus,** we teach, we are teaching, we do teach

4. Although there are personal pronouns in Latin, they are generally not used as subject, since the personal endings indicate the person.

-ō = I	**-mus** = we
-s = you (sing.)	**-tis** = you (pl.)
-t = he, she, it	**-nt** = they

Aquam port*ō.*	*I* am carrying water.
Port*ant* togam.	*They* carry the toga.
Fīliās doc*ētis.*	*You* are teaching your daughters.

5. The verb in Latin generally comes at the end of a sentence. However, for emphasis it may appear earlier.

Puerōs **monet.**	He is warning the boys.
Monet puerōs.	*He is warning* the boys.

NEGATIVE FORM OF VERBS

A verb may be made negative by placing **nōn** before it.

Mārcus gladium **nōn** portat.	Marcus does not carry a sword.
Nāvigāre **nōn** dubitō.	I do not hesitate to sail.

INTERROGATIVE FORM OF VERBS

A verb may be made interrogative by attaching the enclitic **-ne** to the verb and placing the verb at the beginning of the sentence.

Docent*ne* magistrī hodiē?	Are the teachers teaching today?
Habet*ne* suum librum?	Does he have his book?

The enclitic **-ne,** however, is unnecessary if a sentence contains an interrogative word.

Quid agit Mārcus? What is Marcus doing?
Ubi sunt īnsulae? Where are the islands?

COMMON VERBS OF THE FIRST CONJUGATION

amāre, to love
appellāre, to name
appropinquāre, to approach
comparāre, to prepare
cōnfīrmāre, to strengthen
cōnservāre, to keep
dare, to give
dēmōnstrāre, to show
dubitāre, to hesitate
ēnūntiāre, to proclaim

exīstimāre, to think
exspectāre, to wait for, expect
labōrāre, to work
laudāre, to praise
līberāre, to free
nāvigāre, to sail
nūntiāre, to report, announce
occupāre, to seize
parāre, to prepare
portāre, to carry

pugnāre, to fight
putāre, to think
renūntiāre, to report, to bring word back
servāre, to save
spectāre, to look at
superāre, to defeat, surpass
temptāre, to try
vocāre, to call
vulnerāre, to wound

COMMON VERBS OF THE SECOND CONJUGATION

commovēre, to alarm
continēre, to hold together
dēbēre, to owe, ought
docēre, to teach
habēre, to have
iubēre, to order
manēre, to stay, remain

monēre, to advise, warn
movēre, to move
obtinēre, to obtain, hold
permovēre, to arouse
perterrēre, to frighten
pertinēre, to extend
prohibēre, to prevent, keep from

removēre, to withdraw
respondēre, to reply
sustinēre, to uphold, withstand
tenēre, to hold
terrēre, to frighten
timēre, to fear
vidēre, to see

EXERCISES

A. Complete the English translation.

1. Ad terram nāvigant. _____ to the land.

2. Servus victōriam nūntiat. The slave _____ the victory.

3. Dēbēmus manēre diū. _____a long time.

4. Amāsne patrem? _____ your father?

5. Hostēs nōn timeō. _____ the enemy.

6. Quis populum permovet? Who _____ the people?

7. Vidētisne montem? _____ the mountain?

8. In agrīs nōn labōrant. _____ in the fields.

9. Oppidum occupāre temptāmus. _____ the town.

10. Cīvēs pecūniam dant. The citizens _____ money.

B. Write the correct form of the verb in the present tense active.

1. Sextus aquam _____. (obtinēre)

2. Quid agricolae _____? (parāre)

3. Nōs (*We*) equōs _____. (tenēre)

4. Iūlius et Mārcus amīcōs _____. (vocāre)

5. Ego (*I*) iniūriam _____. (prohibēre)

6. _____ puer? (appropinquāre)

2

7. Tū (*You*, sing.) nōn _____. (respondēre)

8. Hominēs lēgem _____. (sustinēre)

9. Vōs (*You*, pl.) hostēs _____. (superāre)

10. Servōs _____ dēbēmus. (līberāre)

C. Make each sentence negative.

1. Puellae viam dēmōnstrant. _____

2. Castra movēmus. _____

3. Cūr librum spectās? _____

4. Quīntus respondēre dubitat. _____

5. Gladium habeō. _____

D. Make each sentence interrogative.

1. Agricolam exspectant. _____

2. Puellās perterret. _____

3. Dux bellum ēnūntiat. _____

4. In agrīs docēmus. _____

5. Frūmentum comparātis. _____

E. Write the present tense active of the following verbs in the form indicated:

1. *exīstimāre* and *terrēre:* third person plural _____

2. *removēre* and *amāre:* second person singular _____

3. *monēre:* first person singular and plural _____

4. *servāre* and *habēre:* second person plural _____

5. *iubēre* and *putāre:* third person singular _____

F. Translate into Latin.

1. he carries _____

2. we are strengthening _____

3. are they fighting? _____

4. I do not wound _____

5. you (sing.) praise _____

6. it extends _____

7. I am trying to think _____

8. is Marcus working? _____

9. the girl doesn't see _____

10. are you (pl.) staying? _____

Lesson 2—PRESENT TENSE ACTIVE OF THIRD CONJUGATION VERBS

dūcere, to lead; present stem, dūce-

dūcō	I lead	dūcimus	we lead
dūcis	you lead	dūcitis	you lead
dūcit	he or she leads	dūcunt	they lead

Note

In forming the present tense of third conjugation verbs, the final **e** of the stem is dropped in the first person singular, changed to **u** in the third person plural, and to **i** in all the other persons.

COMMON VERBS OF THE THIRD CONJUGATION

addūcere, to lead to, influence
agere, to drive, do
āmittere, to send away, lose
cēdere, to yield
cōgere, to collect, compel
cognōscere, to learn, find out
committere, to join, entrust
cōnscrībere, to enlist
cōnstituere, to decide
contendere, to strive, hasten, fight
dēfendere, to defend
dēligere, to choose
dīcere, to say, tell

dīmittere, to send away
discēdere, to leave
dūcere, to lead
excēdere, to depart
expōnere, to set forth, explain
gerere, to carry on, wage
īnstruere, to draw up
intermittere, to interrupt, stop
legere, to read, choose
lūdere, to play
mittere, to send
ostendere, to show
pellere, to drive

permittere, to allow
petere, to seek
pōnere, to put
praemittere, to send ahead
premere, to press
prōdūcere, to lead forth
prōpōnere, to set forth, propose
reddere, to give back, return
relinquere, to abandon, leave
remittere, to send back
scrībere, to write
trādere, to surrender
vincere, to conquer

EXERCISES

A. Add the correct ending of the present tense active.

1. Puerī librōs leg _____.

2. Mīles ad castra contend _____.

3. Nōs (*We*) servōs praemitt _____.

4. Dūc _____ vir equōs ad flūmen?

5. Vōs (*You*, pl.) bellum cum hostibus ger _____.

6. Quis librum scrīb _____?

7. Ego (*I*) oppidum fortiter dēfend _____.

8. Līberī in viīs lūd _____.

9. Tū (*You*, sing.) aciem nōn īnstru _____.

10. Pet _____ pācem hominēs?

B. Translate into English the sentences in Exercise A.

1. _____

2. _____

3. _____

4. _____

5. ---

6. ---

7. ---

8. ---

9. ---

10. ---

C. Translate the English words into Latin.

1. Cōpiās *I am collecting*. ---

2. *He tells* cōnsilium puellae. ---

3. *Are they choosing* ducem? ---

4. Ratiōnem *to show* cōnstituit. ---

5. Cūr *are you (sing.) leaving?* ---

6. Praemium *we are sending back*. ---

7. Sextus *does not influence* puerōs. ---

8. Mīlitēs hostibus *are surrendering*. ---

9. Quis oppidum *is not abandoning?* ---

10. Dēbēmus *to send away* barbarōs. ---

D. Write the present tense active of the following verbs in the form indicated:

1. *pellere:* third person singular ---

2. *cēdere:* third person plural ---

3. *permittere:* first person plural ---

4. *prōdūcere:* second person singular ---

5. *cōnscrībere:* first person singular ---

E. Complete the Latin translation.

1. The Romans are conquering the Gauls. Rōmānī Gallōs ------------------------------.

2. He joins battle with the enemy. Proelium cum hostibus ------------------------.

3. Are you (pl.) putting the grain on the ship? ------------------------- frūmentum in nāve?

4. We learn the plan of the horsemen. Cōnsilium equitum ------------------------.

5. Who is interrupting the speech? Quis ōrātiōnem ------------------------?

6. I am giving back the sword. Gladium ------------------------.

7. We are trying to propose laws. Lēgēs ------------------------ temptāmus.

8. You (sing.) are not deciding to reply. ------------------------ respondēre.

9. What are you doing, boys? Quid ------------------------, puerī?

10. Are they sending the slaves to the river? ------------------------ servōs ad flūmen?

Lesson 3—PRESENT TENSE ACTIVE OF -IŌ THIRD AND FOURTH CONJUGATION VERBS

-IŌ THIRD CONJUGATION

capere, to take; present stem, cape-

capiō	I take	capimus	we take
capis	you take	capitis	you take
capit	he or she takes	capiunt	they take

FOURTH CONJUGATION

audīre, to hear; present stem, audī-

audiō	I hear	audīmus	we hear
audīs	you hear	audītis	you hear
audit	he or she hears	audiunt	they hear

Note

1. The present tense endings of -iō third and fourth conjugation verbs resemble each other closely.

2. In -iō third conjugation verbs, the final e of the stem is changed to i before the personal endings are added. In the third person plural, the ending is -unt instead of -nt.

3. In fourth conjugation verbs, the ending of the third person plural is also -unt instead of -nt.

COMMON VERBS OF THE -IŌ THIRD CONJUGATION

accipere, to receive
capere, to take, capture, seize
cōnficere, to finish
conicere, to throw

cupere, to wish, want
dēficere, to fail, revolt
facere, to make, do
iacere, to throw

incipere, to begin
interficere, to kill
perficere, to accomplish

COMMON VERBS OF THE FOURTH CONJUGATION

audīre, to hear
circumvenīre, to surround
convenīre, to come together

invenīre, to find
mūnīre, to fortify
pervenīre, to arrive

scīre, to know
sentīre, to feel, perceive
venīre, to come

EXERCISES

A. Complete the English translation.

1. Scīmus potestātem hostium. _____ the power of the enemy.

2. Ōrātiōnem cōnficere nōn potest. He is not able _____ the speech.

3. Venītisne ad fīnēs nostrōs? _____ to our territory?

4. Oppidum nōn mūniunt. _____ the town.

5. Cūr sagittās iacis? Why _____ arrows?

6. Signum ducis audiō. _____ the leader's signal.

7. Imperātor castra circumvenit. The general _____ the camp.

8. Incipitne lūcem vidēre? _____ to see light?

9. Prīncipēs nōn conveniunt. The chiefs _____.

10. Rēgem monēre cupimus. _____ to warn the king.

B. Write the present tense active of each verb for the subjects indicated.

1. dēficere: mīlitēs_____   nōs (we)_____

2. sentīre: quis_____   māter_____

6

3. *facere:*   ego (*I*) nōn _____   Gaius _____

4. *pervenīre:*   tū (*you,* sing.) _____   puella _____

5. *interficere:*   vōs (*you,* pl.) _____   cīvēs _____

C. Complete the Latin translation.

1. The soldier receives the award.   Mīles praemium _____

2. We do not find the ship.   Nāvem _____

3. Are you (sing.) accomplishing the task?   _____ negōtium?

4. They are taking arms.   Arma _____

5. We wish to hear our leader.   _____ nostrum ducem.

6. Cicero is beginning the speech.   Cicerō ōrātiōnem _____

7. What are you (pl.) doing?   Quid _____?

8. The boys are throwing swords.   Puerī gladiōs _____

9. I am arriving at that time.   Eō tempore _____

10. Is Caesar fortifying the camp?   _____ castra Caesar?

D. Write the present tense active of the following verbs in the form indicated:

1. *incipere* and *mūnīre:* third person plural   _____

2. *sentīre* and *dēficere:* first person singular   _____

3. *conicere* and *scīre:* third person singular   _____

4. *venīre:* second person singular and plural   _____

5. *facere* and *audīre:* first person plural   _____

E. Change each verb to the plural.

1. Cupit discēdere.   _____ discēdere.

2. Audiō bene.   _____ bene.

3. Mūnīsne castra?   _____ castra?

4. Puella nōn pervenit.   Puellae nōn _____

5. Auxilium accipiō.   Auxilium _____

Coins were made of copper, tin, brass, silver, and gold. Their designs give us an insight into Roman social, religious, and military life.

Roman Coins

7

Lesson 4—REVIEW OF THE PRESENT TENSE ACTIVE

A. Complete the English translation.

1. Gallī unam partem obtinent.   The Gauls ----------------- one part.
2. Īnsulās magnās spectātis.   ------------------------------ the large islands.
3. Quid dīcit puer?   What --------------------------------------?
4. Rēgnum circumveniunt.   ------------------------------- the kingdom.
5. Audīsne magistrum?   ------------------------------ the teacher?
6. Victōriam ēnūntiāmus.   ------------------------------ the victory.
7. Pertinet ad īnferiōrem partem.   ------------------------ to the lower part.
8. Auxilium mittere incipiunt.   ----------------------------------- aid.
9. Urbem nōn relinquimus.   --------------------------------- the city.
10. Gaius hostēs timet.   Gaius ------------------- the enemy.
11. Dēbeō respondēre hodiē.   ------------------------------- today.
12. Ubi līberōs dūcunt?   Where ----------------------- the children?
13. Aciem īnstruere nōn cupiō.   ------------------------ the battle line.
14. Scrībitne Cicerō litterās?   --------------------------- a letter?
15. Ad Galliam contendimus.   ----------------------------- to Gaul.
16. Cōnsul haec videt.   The consul --------------- these things.
17. Satis labōrāre nōn temptās.   ------------------------------- enough.
18. Cūr cīvēs nōn monētis?   Why ----------------------- the citizens?
19. Multum frūmentum habēmus.   ----------------- much grain.
20. Etiam in senātum venit.   ----------------- even into the senate.

B. Translate into Latin.

1. he orders
2. I am sailing
3. are they surrendering?
4. you (pl.) know
5. Marcus does not wish
6. who is trying?
7. we show
8. to defeat
9. why does he not give?
10. you (sing.) feel
11. the girls hear
12. they are making
13. it arouses

8

14. is Lesbia staying?   --
15. the man enlists   --
16. do we seek?   --
17. you (sing.) are not collecting   --
18. I carry on   --
19. do you (pl.) yield?   --
20. they do accomplish   --

C. Write the English meaning and the Latin infinitive of each of the following verbs:

	ENGLISH MEANING	INFINITIVE
1. dēficiunt	----------------------------------	----------------------------------
2. conveniuntne?	----------------------------------	----------------------------------
3. premō	----------------------------------	----------------------------------
4. habēs	----------------------------------	----------------------------------
5. dubitāmus	----------------------------------	----------------------------------
6. amātis	----------------------------------	----------------------------------
7. nōn sustinet	----------------------------------	----------------------------------
8. respondēsne?	----------------------------------	----------------------------------
9. expōnō	----------------------------------	----------------------------------
10. cognōscimus	----------------------------------	----------------------------------
11. lūdunt	----------------------------------	----------------------------------
12. remittitne?	----------------------------------	----------------------------------
13. pervenītis	----------------------------------	----------------------------------
14. coniciunt	----------------------------------	----------------------------------
15. nōn excēdis	----------------------------------	----------------------------------
16. perterreō	----------------------------------	----------------------------------
17. cōnservantne?	----------------------------------	----------------------------------
18. prohibet	----------------------------------	----------------------------------
19. dēligimus	----------------------------------	----------------------------------
20. nōn dēfendunt	----------------------------------	----------------------------------

D. Underline the correct verb form.

1. Rōmānī (iubet, iubent, iubēre) Gallōs discēdere.
2. Mārcus librum (reddit, reddere, reddō).
3. Nōs (*We*) iam (dēficitis, dēficiunt, dēficimus).
4. Ego (*I*) patriam (amāre, amō, amat).
5. Tū (*You*, sing.) fortiter (pugnās, pugnātis, pugnat).
6. (Dēligitne, Dēliguntne, Dēligisne) mīlitēs ducem?
7. Vōs (*You*, pl.) nōn (convenītis, convenīre, convenīs).
8. Quid (cōgis, cōgimus, cōgit) Iūlia?

9

9. Nōs (*We*) diū (manent, manēmus, maneō).

10. Puerī frūmentum (comparant, comparat, comparātis).

E. Write the present tense active of the following verbs in the form indicated:

1. *gerere:* third person singular and plural   --

2. *superāre:* first person singular and plural   --

3. *tenēre:* second person singular and plural   --

4. *scīre* and *nūntiāre:* third person plural   --

5. *facere* and *continēre:* third person singular   --

Chariot Racing

Chariot racing was as popular among the ancient Romans as baseball is in the United States. Chariots drawn by a team of from two to six horses raced around the Circus Maximus, which could accommodate more than 200,000 spectators. Harness racing is the modern sport most closely paralleling chariot racing.

Lesson 5—IMPERFECT ACTIVE OF ALL CONJUGATIONS

FIRST CONJUGATION

portāre, to carry

I was carrying, I carried,
I used to carry, I did carry

SECOND CONJUGATION

docēre, to teach

I was teaching, I taught,
I used to teach, I did teach

THIRD CONJUGATION

dūcere, to lead

I was leading, I led,
I used to lead, I did lead

portā*bam*	docē*bam*	dūcē*bam*
portā*bās*	docē*bās*	dūcē*bās*
portā*bat*	docē*bat*	dūcē*bat*
portā*bāmus*	docē*bāmus*	dūcē*bāmus*
portā*bātis*	docē*bātis*	dūcē*bātis*
portā*bant*	docē*bant*	dūcē*bant*

-IŌ THIRD CONJUGATION

capere, to take

I was taking, I took,
I used to take, I did take

FOURTH CONJUGATION

audīre, to hear

I was hearing, I heard,
I used to hear, I did hear

capiē*bam*	audiē*bam*
capiē*bās*	audiē*bās*
capiē*bat*	audiē*bat*
capiē*bāmus*	audiē*bāmus*
capiē*bātis*	audiē*bātis*
capiē*bant*	audiē*bant*

Note

1. The endings of the imperfect tense are the same for all conjugations.

–bam	–bāmus
–bās	–bātis
–bat	–bant

These endings are attached to the present stem. However, in –iō third conjugation verbs an **i** is inserted before the final **e** of the stem, and in fourth conjugation verbs an **ē** is added to the stem, before the endings of the imperfect are attached.

2. The personal endings of the imperfect are the same as those of the present, except in the first person singular where the ending is **–m** instead of **–ō**.

USES OF THE IMPERFECT

The imperfect is used:

1. To express continuous or progressive action in past time.

Servus **labōrābat** tōtum diem.   The slave worked (was working) all day.

11

2. To express repeated action in past time.

    Cōpiās prō castrīs saepe **īnstruēbat.**   He often drew up his forces in front of the camp.

3. To express customary or habitual action in past time.

    Librōs dē bellō **legēbam.**   I used to read books about war.
    Dūcēbāsne exercitum?   Did you use to lead the army?

EXERCISES

A. Complete the English translation.

1. Ex castrīs equōs removēbant. _____ the horses from camp.

2. In agrīs lūdēbāmus. _____ in the fields.

3. Docēbatne Mārcus in Italiā? _____ in Italy?

4. Cūr oppidum nōn dēfendēbātis? Why _____ the town?

5. Bellum gerere nōn temptābās. _____ to carry on war.

6. Aestāte labōrābam. _____ in summer.

7. Frūmentum portābat. _____ grain.

8. Cōnsulēs praesidium petēbant. The consuls _____ protection.

9. Cōpiās cōgere incipiēbāmus. _____ to collect troops.

10. Dēmōnstrābāsne virtūtem? _____ courage?

B. Fill in the required form of the imperfect active and translate it into English.

	IMPERFECT ACTIVE	MEANING
1. *vulnerāre:* vōs (*you,* pl.)		
2. *interficere:* mīlitēs		
3. *relinquere:* Iūlius		
4. *prohibēre:* tū (*you,* sing.)		
5. *sentīre:* ego (*I*)		
6. *nūntiāre:* pater et fīlius		
7. *conicere:* nōs (*we*)		
8. *praemittere:* Germānī		
9. *tenēre:* servus		
10. *convenīre:* vōs (*you,* pl.)		

C. Change from the present to the imperfect.

1. Semper bellum gerunt. _____

2. Spectatne homō flūmen? _____

3. Omnēs rēs nōn cognōscitis. _____

4. Dēbēmus vidēre prīncipem. _____

5. Ad urbem perveniō. _____

6. Cupisne populum addūcere? _____

7. Reliquōs Gallōs superant. ---------------------------------

8. Optimus dux dēficit. ---------------------------------

9. Cūr exercitum prōdūcis? ---------------------------------

10. Iubēmus equitēs trādere. ---------------------------------

D. Translate the English words into Latin.

1. *He was setting forth* condiciōnēs pācis. ---------------------------------

2. *You (sing.) used to know* omnia. ---------------------------------

3. *They were throwing* rēs. ---------------------------------

4. *Were you (pl.) calling* servōs? ---------------------------------

5. *I did not hesitate* dare auxilium. ---------------------------------

6. *We stayed* diū. ---------------------------------

7. Quid *were you (sing.) showing* puerīs? ---------------------------------

8. Gallī *used to carry on* bellum. ---------------------------------

9. *Was* Cornēlia *playing* in viā? ---------------------------------

10. *I was beginning* petere praesidium. ---------------------------------

E. Write the imperfect active of the following verbs in the form indicated:

1. *dīmittere:* second person singular and plural ---------------------------------

2. *mūnīre:* third person singular and plural ---------------------------------

3. *exīstimāre:* first person singular and plural ---------------------------------

4. *habēre* and *capere:* third person singular ---------------------------------

5. *reddere* and *putāre:* third person plural ---------------------------------

Lesson 6—FUTURE ACTIVE OF FIRST AND SECOND CONJUGATION VERBS

FIRST CONJUGATION	SECOND CONJUGATION
portāre, to carry	**docēre**, to teach
I shall (will) carry	I shall (will) teach

portā*bō*	portā*bimus*	docē*bō*	docē*bimus*
portā*bis*	portā*bitis*	docē*bis*	docē*bitis*
portā*bit*	portā*bunt*	docē*bit*	docē*bunt*

Note

1. The endings of the future tense of first and second conjugation verbs are:

-bō   -bimus
-bis   -bitis
-bit   -bunt

These endings are attached to the present stem.

2. The personal endings are the same as those of the present tense.

EXERCISES

A. Underline the correct Latin translation of the English verb.

1. he will give — (dabat, dabit, dat)
2. you will see — (vidēbis, vidēbit, vidēbimus)
3. they will prevent — (prohibent, prohibēbunt, prohibēbant)
4. I shall wait — (exspectābō, exspectō, exspectābam)
5. we shall prepare — (parābitis, parābātis, parābimus)
6. will you save? — (servābitisne? servābātisne? servātisne?)
7. she will obtain — (obtinēbis, obtinēbitis, obtinēbit)
8. will he have? — (habēbatne? habēbitne? habetne?)
9. they will name — (appellant, appellābuntne, appellābunt)
10. we shall praise — (laudābāmus, laudābimus, laudāmus)

B. Change to the future.

1. Arma portat. --
2. Equī puellās perterrent. --
3. Manētisne in Italiā? --
4. Nōn sustineō perīculum. --
5. Ducem bellī vidēs. --
6. Temptābāmus lūdere. --
7. Appropinquantne ad oppidum? --
8. Cōnsul hostem discēdere iubet. --
9. Breviter respondeō. --
10. Spectatne pontem rēx? --

C. Complete the English translation.

1. Diū manēbimus.   _____ a long time.
2. Servōs līberābunt.   _____ the slaves.
3. Puer legere temptābit.   The boy _____ to read.
4. Iubēbisne eōs convenīre?   _____ them to come together?
5. Eī fīliam suam dabit.   _____ his daughter to him.
6. Populum posteā permovēbō.   _____ the people afterwards.
7. Hostēs facile superābitis.   _____ the enemy easily.
8. Ad Britanniam nōn nāvigābunt.   _____ to Britain.
9. Quis frūmentum comparābit?   Who _____ the grain?
10. Auxilium nōn obtinēbis.   _____ aid.

D. Write the future active of the following verbs in the form indicated:

1. _dēbēre:_ third person singular and plural   _____
2. _cōnservāre:_ first person singular and plural   _____
3. _amāre:_ second person singular and plural   _____
4. _vulnerāre_ and _commovēre:_ third person plural   _____
5. _habēre_ and _pugnāre:_ third person singular   _____

The Torch

The earliest torches were made of pine splinters bound together and saturated with pitch, asphalt, or resin. They were used outdoors to light the way, since there was no street lighting. The torch has always denoted that which enlightens or illuminates, such as the torch of knowledge. A classic example of the burning torch as a symbol of freedom is the one seen on the Statue of Liberty in New York Harbor.

Lesson 7—FUTURE ACTIVE OF THIRD, -IŌ THIRD, AND FOURTH CONJUGATION VERBS

THIRD CONJUGATION	-IŌ THIRD CONJUGATION	FOURTH CONJUGATION
dūcere, to lead	capere, to take	audīre, to hear
I shall (will) lead	I shall (will) take	I shall (will) hear

dūc*am*	cap*iam*	aud*iam*
dūc*ēs*	cap*iēs*	aud*iēs*
dūc*et*	cap*iet*	aud*iet*
dūc*ēmus*	cap*iēmus*	aud*iēmus*
dūc*ētis*	cap*iētis*	aud*iētis*
dūc*ent*	cap*ient*	aud*ient*

Note

1. The endings of the future of third, -iō third, and fourth conjugation verbs are:

-am	-ēmus
-ēs	-ētis
-et	-ent

These endings are attached to the present stem. However, in third conjugation verbs the final **e** of the stem is dropped, and in **-iō** third conjugation verbs the final **e** of the stem is changed to **i,** before the endings of the future are attached.

2. The personal endings are the same as those of the imperfect.

3. The future of third conjugation verbs is often confused with the present of second conjugation verbs in all forms exept the first person singular.

THIRD CONJUGATION		SECOND CONJUGATION	
FUTURE		PRESENT	
dīcēs,	you will say	docēs,	you teach
dīcet,	he will say	docet,	he teaches
dīcēmus,	we shall say	docēmus,	we teach
dīcētis,	you will say	docētis,	you teach
dīcent,	they will say	docent,	they teach

EXERCISES

A. Write the verb in the future active.

1. agere: Puer equōs ad flūmen _____.

2. mittere: Gallī equitēs _____.

3. venīre: _____ tū (*you*, sing.) ad senātum?

4. cupere: Nōs (*We*) nōn _____ manēre.

5. scrībere: Quid _____ cōnsul?

6. premere: Rōmānī hostēs _____.

7. sentīre: Ego (*I*) _____ rem esse gravem.

8. accipere: _____ vōs (*you*, pl.) amīcōs vestrōs?

9. pellere: Imperātor barbarōs ab oppidō _____ .

10. dēligere: Mārcus Iūliusque ducem _____ .

    B. Complete the English translation.

1. Ad campōs contendent. _____ to the plains.

2. Ratiōnem nōn āmittet. _____ the plan.

3. Interficiētisne barbarōs? _____ the foreigners?

4. Cum Gallīs bellum gerēmus. _____ war with the Gauls.

5. Cūr oppidum circumvenient? Why _____ the town?

6. In Italiam exercitum dūcēs. _____ the army into Italy.

7. Hodiē incipiam labōrāre. Today _____ to work.

8. Condiciōnēs pācis faciet. _____ terms of peace.

9. Scientne auctōritātem ducis? _____ the influence of the leader?

10. Aciem īnstruet. _____ the battle line.

    C. Translate the English words into Latin.

1. *We will learn* potestātem hostium. _____

2. Diē septimō *he will arrive.* _____

3. *They will not throw* sagittās. _____

4. Posteā *I shall decide.* _____

5. *Will you collect* tuam familiam? _____

6. Y*ou (pl.) will put* equōs in nāve. _____

7. Quis *will want* togam? _____

8. Agricolae *will come together.* _____

9. Caesar *will enlist* omnēs mīlitēs. _____

10. Praemium *we shall send back.* _____

    D. Write the future active of the following verbs in the form indicated:

1. *reddere:* second person singular and plural _____

2. *interficere:* third person singular and plural _____

3. *pervenīre:* first person singular and plural _____

4. *dēfendere* and *conicere:* third person plural _____

5. *audīre* and *relinquere:* third person singular _____

A. Write the present, imperfect, and future active of each verb in the form indicated. (This is known as a *synopsis*.)

	PRESENT	IMPERFECT	FUTURE
1. *tenēre:* third singular			
2. *vincere:* third plural			
3. *exīstimāre:* first singular			
4. *invenīre:* second singular			
5. *dēficere:* first plural			
6. *dare:* second plural			
7. *continēre:* third plural			
8. *committere:* first plural			
9. *facere:* third singular			
10. *mūnīre:* second singular			

B. In the space before each verb in column *A*, write the letter of the Latin equivalent in column *B*.

	Column A	*Column B*
____	**1.** we were praising	*a.* laudābimus
____	**2.** he will yield	*b.* audit
____	**3.** you hear	*c.* coniciēbant
____	**4.** to throw	*d.* laudāmus
____	**5.** I see	*e.* audīsne
____	**6.** we are praising	*f.* cēdet
____	**7.** to see	*g.* laudābāmus
____	**8.** they are throwing	*h.* vidēbō
____	**9.** he yielded	*i.* cēdit
____	**10.** he hears	*j.* audīs
____	**11.** I shall see	*k.* vidēre
____	**12.** we shall praise	*l.* coniciunt
____	**13.** they were throwing	*m.* cēdēbat
____	**14.** do you hear?	*n.* videō
____	**15.** he yields	*o.* conicere

C. Underline the correct English translation.

1. audiēbat   (he will hear, he heard, he hears)

2. pertinet   (it extends, it will extend, it extended)

3. contendunt   (we strive, he strives, they strive)

4. nāvigābō (I sail, I shall sail, I was sailing)

5. petēsne? (are you seeking? will you seek? do you seek?)

6. cōnficiēmus (we shall finish, we finish, we were finishing)

7. trādēbātis (he was surrendering, they surrendered, you were surrendering)

8. occupābuntne? (are they seizing? will they seize? were they seizing?)

9. incipit (he begins, he began, he will begin)

10. temptāmus (we were trying, we are trying, we did try)

D. Change each verb to the plural.

1. trādet _____   6. dabam _____

2. incipiō _____   7. accipiam _____

3. audiēbās _____   8. quid agit? quid _____

4. movēbit _____   9. dēfendēbās _____

5. labōrāsne? _____   10. vincetne? _____

E. Complete the English translation.

1. Suīs fīnibus eōs prohibent. _____ them from their territory.

2. Magnum numerum servōrum habēbat. _____ a large number of slaves.

3. In Italiam contendēmus. _____ to Italy.

4. Faciēbatne impetum in eōs? _____ an attack upon them?

5. Ibi duās legiōnēs cōnscrībam. _____ two legions there.

6. Appellābisne eum Mārcum? _____ him Marcus?

7. Nōn audītis bene. _____ well.

8. Incipiēbant discēdere. _____ to leave.

9. Quō nāvigābimus? Where _____?

10. Eōs vōce nōn vulnerō. _____ them with my voice.

11. Ducem hostium vidētis. _____ the leader of the enemy.

12. In fīnēs Gallōrum perveniet. _____ in the territory of the Gauls.

13. Gallī partem ūnam obtinēbant. The Gauls _____ one part.

14. Pācem cōnfīrmāre cōnstituunt. _____ to establish peace.

15. Reliquōs Gallōs superābis. _____ the rest of the Gauls.

F. Draw a line through the form that does *not* belong with the others in each group.

1. nūntiat, audiet, monet, capit

2. habēmus, incipiēmus, vocābimus, agēmus

3. legēbam, sentiēbam, exspectābam, scrībam

4. cēdēbātis, cupiēbātis, perveniēbās, vidēbātis

5. iubent, venient, vincunt, laudant

6. pugnābis, petēs, accipiēs, dēbēs

7. respondēbat, dēligēbant, sciēbat, servābat

8. renūntiāre, mūnīre, līberāsne, pertinēre

9. removēbō, cōnficiam, amābō, prohibeō

10. monetne, vincisne, audīsne, putāsne

G. Place a check in the proper column to indicate whether each verb is present or future. Then translate the verb into English.

	PRESENT	FUTURE	TRANSLATION
1. iubet	-----	-----	---
2. petet	-----	-----	---
3. relinquēmus	-----	-----	---
4. obtinēmus	-----	-----	---
5. excēdēs	-----	-----	---
6. movēs	-----	-----	---
7. scrībent	-----	-----	---
8. vincent	-----	-----	---
9. perterrētis	-----	-----	---
10. sustinētis	-----	-----	---

Lesson 9—PRESENT, IMPERFECT, AND FUTURE OF *SUM* AND *POSSUM*

esse, to be			posse, to be able		
PRESENT	IMPERFECT	FUTURE	PRESENT	IMPERFECT	FUTURE
I am	I was	I shall (will) be	I am able, I can	I was able, I could	I shall (will) be able
su*m*	er*am*	er*ō*	pos*sum*	pot*eram*	pot*erō*
e*s*	er*ās*	er*is*	pot*es*	pot*erās*	pot*eris*
es*t*	er*at*	er*it*	pot*est*	pot*erat*	pot*erit*
su*mus*	er*āmus*	er*imus*	pos*sumus*	pot*erāmus*	pot*erimus*
es*tis*	er*ātis*	er*itis*	pot*estis*	pot*erātis*	pot*eritis*
su*nt*	er*ant*	er*unt*	pos*sunt*	pot*erant*	pot*erunt*

Note

1. The third person of **esse** may sometimes be translated as follows:

est, there is	**sunt,** there are
erat, there was	**erant,** there were
erit, there will be	**erunt,** there will be

2. **Possum** is a compound of **sum.** Its base is **pot-** when it is followed by a vowel and **pos-** when it is followed by the letter **s.**

3. Other compounds of **esse** are:

> **abesse,** to be away, to be absent
> **adesse,** to be near, to be present
> **praeesse,** to be in charge

EXERCISES

A. Change each verb to the plural.

1. cōnsul erat   cōnsulēs _____

2. praeerās   _____

3. absum   _____

4. potest scrībere   _____ scrībere

5. erit cōpia   _____ cōpiae

6. esne līber?   _____ līberī?

7. erō amīcus   _____ amīcī

8. poteratne dūcere?   _____ dūcere?

9. puella nōn poterit   puellae nōn _____

10. cūr est malus?   cūr _____ malī?

B. Complete the English translation.

1. Fortissimī sunt Belgae.   The bravest _____ the Belgians.

2. Erantne sociī?   _____ allies?

3. Legere nōn potest.   _____ to read.

21

4. Estisne semper parātī? _____ always prepared?

5. Poterimus excēdere. _____ to depart.

6. Cūr absunt? Why _____?

7. Eram cupidus victōriae. _____ desirous of victory.

8. Nōn poterant respondēre. _____ to reply.

9. Eritne prīmus? _____ first?

10. Cum hostibus erās. _____ with the enemy.

11. Pugnāre poteritis. _____ to fight.

12. Esse aut nōn esse. _____ or _____.

13. Castra sunt in Italiā. _____ a camp in Italy.

14. Possumusne esse līberī? _____ free?

15. Imperātor praeerat. The general _____.

C. Translate into Latin.

1. they are able _____
2. you (sing.) are _____
3. he will be _____
4. we could _____
5. were they? _____

6. I am in charge _____
7. will they be able? _____
8. were you (pl.)? _____
9. we shall be _____
10. he was present _____

D. In the space before each verb in column *A*, write the letter of the Latin equivalent in column *B*.

	Column A	Column B
_____	1. you were	a. poterāmus
_____	2. we shall be able	b. erō
_____	3. to be able	c. poterās
_____	4. they can	d. eritne?
_____	5. I shall be	e. adesse
_____	6. we could	f. poterant
_____	7. he was in charge	g. erātis
_____	8. will he be able?	h. aberam
_____	9. you were able	i. possunt
_____	10. will he be?	j. estne?
_____	11. is there?	k. poterat
_____	12. they were able	l. posse
_____	13. he could	m. poteritne?
_____	14. I was absent	n. praeerat
_____	15. to be near	o. poterimus

22

Lesson 10—PERFECT ACTIVE OF FIRST AND SECOND CONJUGATION VERBS

FIRST CONJUGATION

portāre, to carry; perfect stem, **portāv-**

I carried, I have carried, I did carry

SECOND CONJUGATION

docēre, to teach; perfect stem, **docu-**

I taught, I have taught, I did teach

portāv*ī*	portāv*imus*	docu*ī*	docu*imus*
portāv*istī*	portāv*istis*	docu*istī*	docu*istis*
portāv*it*	portāv*ērunt*	docu*it*	docu*ērunt*

Note

1. The perfect tense of all verbs is formed by adding to the perfect stem the following endings:

-ī = I   **-imus** = we

-istī = you   **-istis** = you

-it = he, she, it   **-ērunt** = they

2. The perfect stem varies in formation. However, there are certain guides that help in learning the stems of verbs. In the first conjugation, most verbs form their perfect stem by adding the letter **v** to the present stem.

PRESENT INFINITIVE	PRESENT STEM	PERFECT STEM
amāre	**amā-**	*amāv-*
portāre	**portā-**	*portāv-*
vocāre	**vocā-**	*vocāv-*

By exception, the perfect stem of the verb **dare** is **ded-.**

3. In the second conjugation, most verbs form their perfect stem by changing the final **ē** of the present stem to **u.**

PRESENT INFINITIVE	PRESENT STEM	PERFECT STEM
docēre	**docē-**	*docu-*
monēre	**monē-**	*monu-*
timēre	**timē-**	*timu-*

4. The following second conjugation verbs do not follow the pattern given above:

PRESENT INFINITIVE	PRESENT STEM	PERFECT STEM
iubēre	**iubē-**	*iuss-*
manēre	**manē-**	*māns-*
movēre (and its compounds)	**movē-**	*mōv-*
respondēre	**respondē-**	*respond-*
vidēre	**vidē-**	*vīd-*

5. Both the imperfect and perfect represent action in past time. The perfect tense should generally be used unless the action was in progress, repeated, or customary, in which case the imperfect is preferred.

Ad Graeciam **nāvigāvit.** (perfect)	He sailed to Greece.
Ad Graeciam **nāvigābat.** (imperfect)	He was sailing to Greece.

23

EXERCISES

A. Complete the following sentences using the perfect tense of the verbs in italics:

1. *timēre:*   Gallī Rōmānōs _____.

2. *superāre:*   Puer _____ reliquōs celeritāte.

3. *nūntiāre:*   Ego (*I*) victōriam populō _____.

4. *vidēre:*   _____ tū (*you*, sing.) nāvēs novās?

5. *dare:*   Nōs (*We*) agricolīs equōs _____.

6. *cōnfīrmāre:*   Quis animōs mīlitum _____?

7. *temptāre:*   Vōs (*You*, pl.) _____ lūdere.

8. *manēre:*   Puellae nōn _____ diū.

9. *dēbēre:*   _____ mīlitēs pugnāre?

10. *vulnerāre:*   Eques prīncipem _____.

B. Write the perfect active of the following verbs in the form indicated:

1. *appellāre* and *tenēre:* third person plural   _____

2. *iubēre* and *exīstimāre:* first person singular   _____

3. *docēre* and *portāre:* second person singular   _____

4. *occupāre* and *habēre:* second person plural   _____

5. *sustinēre* and *dubitāre:* third person singular   _____

C. Complete the English translation.

1. Cum Germānīs pugnāvērunt.   _____ with the Germans.

2. Meōs amīcōs vīdī.   _____ my friends.

3. Respondistīne iam?   _____ already?

4. Omnēs servōs docuimus.   _____ all the slaves.

5. Victōrem nōn laudāvistis.   _____ the victor.

6. Quis ad Britanniam nāvigāvit?   Who _____ to Britain?

7. Populum permōvit.   _____ the people.

8. Monuēruntne cōnsulem?   _____ the consul?

9. Virtūtem dēmōnstrāvimus.   _____ courage.

10. Socium tuum nōn vulnerāvistī.   _____ your comrade.

D. Translate into Latin.

1. they seized   _____

2. did they seize?   _____

3. I have prepared   _____

4. you (sing.) did not see   _____

5. we feared   _____

6. it extended   _____

7. did you (pl.) prevent?   _____

8. has he worked? --

9. we did not try --

10. they have approached --

Baths of Caracalla

Built in the third century A.D., the baths covered an area of a mile in circumference. Used as a sort of club in Roman days, the baths serve today as a setting for opera. Pennsylvania Station in New York City is modeled after the Baths of Caracalla.

25

Lesson 11—PERFECT ACTIVE OF THIRD CONJUGATION VERBS

dūcere, to lead; perfect stem, **dūx-**

I led, I have led, I did lead

dūx*ī*	dūx*imus*
dūx*istī*	dūx*istis*
dūx*it*	dūx*ērunt*

Note

The perfect stem of third conjugation verbs varies considerably. However, there are a few patterns into which many verbs fit.

1. The perfect stem of the following verbs ends in **s**:

PRESENT INFINITIVE	PRESENT STEM	PERFECT STEM
lūdere	**lūde-**	*lūs-*
mittere (and its compounds)	**mitte-**	*mīs-*

2. The following verbs have a double **s** in the perfect stem:

PRESENT INFINITIVE	PRESENT STEM	PERFECT STEM
cēdere (and its compounds)	**cēde-**	*cess-*
gerere	**gere-**	*gess-*
premere	**preme-**	*press-*

3. The perfect stem of the following verbs ends in **x**: (The **x** often takes the place of **cs** or **gs**.)

PRESENT INFINITIVE	PRESENT STEM	PERFECT STEM
dīcere	**dīce-**	*dīx-* (dīcs-)
dūcere (and its compounds)	**dūce-**	*dūx-* (dūcs-)
īnstruere	**īnstrue-**	*īnstrūx-*

4. The perfect stem of the following verbs ends in **d**:

PRESENT INFINITIVE	PRESENT STEM	PERFECT STEM
contendere	**contende-**	*contend-*
dēfendere	**dēfende-**	*dēfend-*
ostendere	**ostende-**	*ostend-*

5. The perfect stem of the following verbs must be learned separately:

PRESENT INFINITIVE	PRESENT STEM	PERFECT STEM
agere	**age-**	*ēg-*
cōgere	**cōge-**	*coēg-*
cognōscere	**cognōsce-**	*cognōv-*
cōnstituere	**cōnstitue-**	*cōnstitu-*
dēligere	**dēlige-**	*dēlēg-*
legere	**lege-**	*lēg-*
pellere	**pelle-**	*pepul-*
petere	**pete-**	*petīv-*
pōnere (and its compounds)	**pōne-**	*posu-*
reddere	**redde-**	*reddid-*
relinquere	**relinque-**	*relīqu-*
scrībere (and its compounds)	**scrībe-**	*scrīps-*
trādere	**trāde-**	*trādid-*
vincere	**vince-**	*vīc-*

26

A. Write the correct form of the verb in the perfect.

1. Mīlitēs --- castra.   (pōnere)
2. Nōs (*We*) -- ducem.   (dēligere)
3. Caesar -- Gallōs.   (vincere)
4. Cūr -- puellae?   (discēdere)
5. Hostēs nōn --.   (trādere)
6. Ego (*I*) in viīs --.   (lūdere)
7. Quis īnsulam --?   (petere)
8. Tū (*You*, sing.) aciem --.   (īnstruere)
9. Vōs (*You*, pl.) bellum --.   (gerere)
10. Puer -- librōs.   (remittere)

B. Write the perfect active of the following verbs in the form indicated:

1. *pellere:* first person singular and plural   ---
2. *relinquere:* third person singular and plural   ---
3. *addūcere:* second person singular and plural   ---
4. *dēfendere* and *agere:* third person plural   ---
5. *cognōscere* and *scrībere:* third person singular   ---

C. Translate into English.

1. praemīsit   ---
2. coēgistī   ---
3. ostendērunt   ---
4. dīxistis   ---
5. reddidimus   ---
6. vīcī   ---
7. cessitne?   ---
8. nōn intermīsistī   ---
9. prōposuēruntne?   ---
10. mīsimus   ---

D. Change the verbs to the perfect tense.

1. Suam familiam cōgit.   ---
2. Virōs ad eum mittunt.   ---
3. Diem cōnstituis.   ---
4. Hōs ego videō.   ---
5. Litterās scrībēmus.   ---
6. Equōs pellebātis.   ---
7. Dīmittitne amīcōs suōs?   ---

8. Ubi excēdunt?

9. Nōn trādēmus.

10. Premis hostēs.

A Street in Pompeii

When Vesuvius erupted in 79 A.D., Pompeii was one of the cities completely buried by volcanic ash. Today, through expert excavation, one can again see the city restored to life with everything intact. Many modern shops in Italy resemble those of ancient Pompeii.

Lesson 12—PERFECT ACTIVE OF -IŌ THIRD AND FOURTH CONJUGATION VERBS

-IŌ THIRD CONJUGATION

capere, to take; perfect stem, **cēp-**

I took, I have taken, I did take

cēpī	cēpimus
cēpistī	cēpistis
cēpit	cēpērunt

FOURTH CONJUGATION

audīre, to hear; perfect stem, **audīv-**

I heard, I have heard, I did hear

audīvī	audīvimus
audīvistī	audīvistis
audīvit	audīvērunt

Note

1. Most **-iō** third conjugation verbs form their perfect stem by changing the **a** or **i** of the present stem to **ē.**

PRESENT INFINITIVE	PRESENT STEM	PERFECT STEM
capere	cape-	cēp-
facere	face-	fēc-
iacere	iace-	iēc-
accipere	accipe-	accēp-
cōnficere	cōnfice-	cōnfēc-
conicere	conice-	coniēc-
dēficere	dēfice-	dēfēc-
incipere	incipe-	incēp-
interficere	interfice-	interfēc-
perficere	perfice-	perfēc-

The perfect stem of the verb **cupere** is **cupīv-.**

2. In the fourth conjugation, many verbs form their perfect stem by adding the letter **v** to the present stem.

PRESENT INFINITIVE	PRESENT STEM	PERFECT STEM
audīre	audī-	audīv-
mūnīre	mūnī-	mūnīv-
scīre	scī-	scīv-

3. The verbs below do not follow the pattern given above.

PRESENT INFINITIVE	PRESENT STEM	PERFECT STEM
sentīre	sentī-	sēns-
venīre (and its compounds)	venī-	vēn-

4. Note the difference between

venit, he comes
vēnit, he came

venīmus, we come
vēnimus, we came

29

EXERCISES

A. Complete the English translation.

1. Vēnistī in senātum. _____ into the senate.
2. Eius vōcem audīvimus. _____ his voice.
3. In fīnēs hostium pervēnit. _____ in the enemy's territory.
4. Sēnsistisne eās rēs? _____ these things?
5. Condiciōnēs pācis scīvī. _____ the terms of peace.
6. Omnēs captīvōs interfēcērunt. _____ all the prisoners.
7. Cupīvitne mē vidēre? _____ to see me?
8. Iter magnum fēcērunt. _____ a forced march.
9. Negōtium cōnfēcimus. _____ the task.
10. Domum meam mūnīvī. _____ my house.

B. Write the perfect active of the following verbs in the form indicated:

1. *iacere:* third person singular and plural _____
2. *invenīre:* second person singular and plural _____
3. *incipere:* first person singular and plural _____
4. *facere* and *venīre:* third person plural _____
5. *mūnīre* and *accipere:* third person singular _____

C. Translate into Latin.

1. they began _____
2. did you (sing.) hear? _____
3. we have taken _____
4. he did not wish _____
5. has he arrived? _____
6. I received _____
7. you (pl.) have thrown _____
8. they did surround _____
9. did they surround? _____
10. we finished _____

D. Underline the correct verb form.

1. Puer (cupīvit, cupere, cupīvistī) discēdere.
2. Hominēs (sēnsistis, sēnsimus, sēnsērunt) idem.
3. Nōs (*We*) imperātōrem (audīre, audīvī, audīvimus).
4. Tū (*You*, sing.) togam (fēcistī, fēcistis, fēcī).
5. (Convēnitne, Convēnēruntne, Convēnistisne) sociī?
6. Vōs (*You*, pl.) oppidum (mūnīvērunt, mūnīvimus, mūnīvistis).
7. Ego (*I*) labōrāre (incipere, incēpī, incēpistī).

30

8. Mārcus et Sextus ad oppidum (vēnērunt, vēnimus, vēnistis).

9. Quid (iēcistī, iēcit, iēcērunt) mīles?

10. Caesar causam bellī (scīre, scīvī, scīvit).

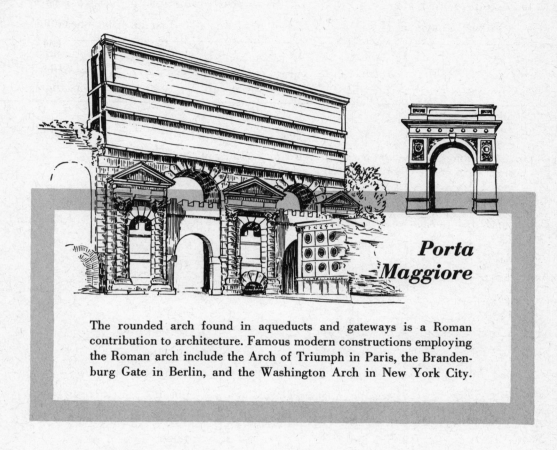

Porta Maggiore

The rounded arch found in aqueducts and gateways is a Roman contribution to architecture. Famous modern constructions employing the Roman arch include the Arch of Triumph in Paris, the Brandenburg Gate in Berlin, and the Washington Arch in New York City.

Lesson 13—PERFECT OF *SUM* AND *POSSUM*

esse, to be; perfect stem, **fu-**

I was, I have been

posse, to be able; perfect stem, **potu-**

I was able, I could, I have been able

fu*ī*	fu*imus*	potu*ī*	potu*imus*
fu*istī*	fu*istis*	potu*istī*	potu*istis*
fu*it*	fu*ērunt*	potu*it*	potu*ērunt*

Note

1. The perfect endings of **esse** and **posse** are the same as those of regular verbs.
2. The perfect stem of the compound verb **abesse** is **āfu-**.

EXERCISES

A. In the space before each verb in column *A*, write the letter of the Latin equivalent in column *B*.

	Column A		Column B
_____	**1.** he could	*a.*	āfuit
_____	**2.** were they?	*b.*	fuit
_____	**3.** were they able?	*c.*	potuistī
_____	**4.** it was away	*d.*	potuēruntne?
_____	**5.** you were able	*e.*	fuērunt
_____	**6.** he was	*f.*	adfuit
_____	**7.** was he in charge?	*g.*	potuit
_____	**8.** we have been	*h.*	potuērunt
_____	**9.** I could	*i.*	fuistī
_____	**10.** it was near	*j.*	potuimus
_____	**11.** they have been able	*k.*	fuēruntne?
_____	**12.** was he present?	*l.*	potuī
_____	**13.** they have been	*m.*	adfuitne?
_____	**14.** we have been able	*n.*	fuimus
_____	**15.** you were	*o.*	praefuitne?

B. Complete the English translation.

1. Fuērunt nōbilēs. _____ noble.
2. Potuimus docēre. _____ to teach.
3. Potuitne nāvigāre? _____ to sail?
4. Fuistisne amīcī? _____ friends?
5. Cicerō fuit cōnsul. Cicero _____ consul.
6. Omnēs līberī adfuērunt. All the children _____.
7. Āfuēruntne longē castra? _____ the camp far _____?

32

8. Respondēre nōn potuī. _____ to reply.

9. Cupidī pācis fuimus. _____ desirous of peace.

10. Tū, Caesar, praefuistī. You, Caesar, _____.

    C. Write the perfect of the following verbs in the form indicated:

1. *esse:* second person singular and plural _____

2. *posse:* third person singular and plural _____

3. *abesse:* first person singular and plural _____

4. *praeesse:* first and third person singular _____

5. *adesse:* second and third person plural _____

    D. Translate into Latin.

1. I have been _____

2. we could _____

3. they were able _____

4. you (sing.) were _____

5. he has been able _____

6. has he been in charge? _____

7. were we? _____

8. you (pl.) were present _____

9. he was absent _____

10. have they been? _____

Lesson 14—REVIEW OF THE PERFECT ACTIVE OF ALL CONJUGATIONS

A. Translate into English.

1. dīxistī _____

2. servāvit _____

3. potuērunt _____

4. sēnsimus _____

5. petīvistis _____

6. obtinuī _____

7. vocāvitne? _____

8. nōn iēcērunt _____

9. fuimus _____

10. audīvistīne? _____

11. praefuit _____

12. circumvēnistis _____

13. prohibuēruntne? _____

14. relīquimus _____

15. vēnī, vīdī, vīcī _____

B. In the space before each verb in column A, write the letter of the Latin equivalent in column B.

	Column A	Column B
_____	1. did you begin?	a. fēcēruntne?
_____	2. we knew	b. adfuērunt
_____	3. they made	c. scīvistis
_____	4. he tried	d. cōnfīrmāvit
_____	5. I have been	e. invēnimus
_____	6. has he begun?	f. incēpistīne?
_____	7. they were near	g. reddiditne?
_____	8. did they make?	h. scīvimus
_____	9. he did strengthen	i. temptāvit
_____	10. has he surrendered?	j. potuī
_____	11. you knew	k. incēpitne?
_____	12. did he give back?	l. āfuērunt
_____	13. we found	m. fuī
_____	14. they were absent	n. trādiditne?
_____	15. I could	o. fēcērunt

34

C. Write the perfect active of each verb in the form indicated:

1. *mūnīre* and *esse:* third person plural _____

2. *perficere* and *posse:* third person singular _____

3. *dubitāre* and *timēre:* first person plural _____

4. *remittere:* second person singular and plural _____

5. *agere:* first person singular and plural _____

D. Underline the correct verb form.

1. Caesar hostēs (vīcērunt, vīcit, vīcistī).

2. Cōnsulēs (praefuērunt, praeesse, praefuimus).

3. Tū (*You,* sing.) senātum (relīquī, relīquistis, relīquistī).

4. Nōs (*We*) sōlem (vīdimus, vīdī, vidēre).

5. (Lūsistīne, Lūsistisne, Lūsitne) vōs (*you,* pl.) in viīs?

6. Ego (*I*) lēgēs (scrīpsimus, scrīpsī, scrīpsistī).

7. Quis togam (āmīsērunt, āmittere, āmīsit)?

8. Servī labōrāre (potuērunt, potuit, posse).

9. (Fuitne, Fuistīne, Fuīne) gladius gravis?

10. Sextus sororque (contendērunt, contendit, contendere).

E. Complete the English translation.

1. Cīvium iūra tenuērunt. _____ the rights of citizens.

2. Mē petīvistī. _____ me.

3. Quis āfuit? Who _____?

4. Fortūna tē servāvit. Fortune _____ you.

5. Mīlitēs cēdere iussit. _____ the soldiers to yield.

6. Potuistisne audīre? _____ to hear?

7. Fuimus frātrēs. _____ brothers.

8. Eum vidēre nōn cupīvī. _____ to see him.

9. Collem occupāvērunt. _____ the hill.

10. Oppidum circumvēnit. _____ the town.

Lesson 15—MASTERY EXERCISES ON VERBS, ACTIVE VOICE

A. Write a synopsis (four tenses active) of the following verbs in the form indicated:

		PRESENT	IMPERFECT	FUTURE	PERFECT
1. tenēre:	3rd., sing.	-----------	-----------	-----------	-----------
2. dūcere:	1st., pl.	-----------	-----------	-----------	-----------
3. esse:	2nd., pl.	-----------	-----------	-----------	-----------
4. pugnāre:	3rd., pl.	-----------	-----------	-----------	-----------
5. mūnīre:	2nd., sing.	-----------	-----------	-----------	-----------
6. posse:	1st., sing.	-----------	-----------	-----------	-----------
7. facere:	3rd., pl.	-----------	-----------	-----------	-----------
8. vulnerāre:	3rd., sing.	-----------	-----------	-----------	-----------
9. habēre:	1st., pl.	-----------	-----------	-----------	-----------
10. gerere:	2nd., sing.	-----------	-----------	-----------	-----------

B. Underline the correct English translation.

1. petēbat   (he will seek, he was seeking, he seeks)

2. coniciunt   (they are throwing, they did throw, they will throw)

3. sciēs   (you know, you knew, you will know)

4. potuī   (I could, I am able, I can)

5. vocābimus   (we were calling, we shall call, we do call)

6. dabātis   (you were giving, you will give, you give)

7. vidēsne?   (did you see? will you see? do you see?)

8. erant   (they are, they have been, they were)

9. dīcetne?   (is he saying? will he say? did he say?)

10. cēpimus   (we took, we are taking, we shall take)

C. Draw a line through the form that does *not* belong with the others in each group.

1. iaciēbat, sentiēbam, respondēbit, dubitābam

2. superābunt, vincent, iubēbunt, fuērunt

3. convēnimus, pōnimus, petunt, possunt

4. appellās, erās, estis, docuistī

5. incipiēbant, audiunt, permovēbat, erunt

6. posse, erit, cōnficere, scīre

7. expōnetne, habētisne, dabantne, cōgēbāmus

8. poteram, fuī, prōpōnō, gessistī

9. laudāvī, nāvigāvistis, relinquunt, cupimus

10. scrīpsimus, sēnsimus, trādimus, vīcimus

36

D. In the space before each verb in column *A*, write the letter of the English translation in column *B*.

	Column A		Column B
-------	**1.** venit	*a.*	you have saved
-------	**2.** cōgent	*b.*	we are throwing
-------	**3.** cōgunt	*c.*	he came
-------	**4.** iacimus	*d.*	I was obtaining
-------	**5.** servāvistī	*e.*	you were saving
-------	**6.** vēnit	*f.*	they will collect
-------	**7.** obtinēbō	*g.*	you did read
-------	**8.** legitis	*h.*	he is coming
-------	**9.** iēcimus	*i.*	he was
-------	**10.** poterat	*j.*	they are collecting
-------	**11.** erat	*k.*	he will be able
-------	**12.** servābās	*l.*	he could
-------	**13.** poterit	*m.*	you are reading
-------	**14.** lēgistis	*n.*	I shall obtain
-------	**15.** obtinēbam	*o.*	we have thrown

E. Change each verb to the plural.

1. īnstruit	_____	**6.** premēs	_____
2. scīvī	_____	**7.** pertinēbit	_____
3. prohibēbās	_____	**8.** temptābam	_____
4. erit	_____	**9.** fēcistī	_____
5. ēnūntiō	_____	**10.** potestne	_____

F. Write the English meaning and the Latin infinitive of each of the following verbs:

	MEANING	INFINITIVE
1. perficiam	_____	_____
2. cupiēbās	_____	_____
3. habuit	_____	_____
4. manēmus	_____	_____
5. sēnsistis	_____	_____
6. posuitne	_____	_____
7. spectābis	_____	_____
8. labōrābam	_____	_____
9. nōn cognōscit	_____	_____
10. fuērunt	_____	_____
11. vidēbitis	_____	_____
12. poterant	_____	_____

13. līberābō --- ---

14. perveniēmus --- ---

15. gessit --- ---

16. pepulēruntne --- ---

17. coniciētis --- ---

18. āmīsī --- ---

19. īnstruit --- ---

20. perterrēbās --- ---

G. Translate into Latin.

1. we were seeking ---

2. to reply ---

3. you (sing.) made ---

4. they are putting ---

5. he could ---

6. you (pl.) have heard ---

7. will he seize? ---

8. I shall collect ---

9. they did not write ---

10. does he lead? ---

11. we have been ---

12. I was calling ---

13. did you (sing.) see? ---

14. they do praise ---

15. he will order ---

38

Lesson 16—PLUPERFECT ACTIVE (Optional)

portāre, to carry; perfect stem, **portāv-**
I had carried

portāv**eram**	portāv**erāmus**		
portāv**erās**	portāv**erātis**		
portāv**erat**	portāv**erant**		

dūcere, to lead; perfect stem, **dūx-**
I had led

dūx**eram**	dūx**erāmus**
dūx**erās**	dūx**erātis**
dūx**erat**	dūx**erant**

esse, to be; perfect stem, **fu-**
I had been

fu**eram**	fu**erāmus**
fu**erās**	fu**erātis**
fu**erat**	fu**erant**

posse, to be able; perfect stem, **potu-**
I had been able

potu**eram**	potu**erāmus**
potu**erās**	potu**erātis**
potu**erat**	potu**erant**

Note

1. The pluperfect active of all verbs is formed by adding to the perfect stem the following endings:

-eram	**-erāmus**
-erās	**-erātis**
-erat	**-erant**

2. These endings are exactly the same as the imperfect of the verb **esse**.

3. The pluperfect tense, representing time completed before another past time, is always translated by the auxiliary verb *had* plus the past participle.

EXERCISES

A. In each group of verbs there is one verb in the pluperfect tense. Underline the verb and then translate it into English.

1. dūxit, dūxerat, dūcēbat, dūcit   _____

2. cēperāmus, cēpimus, capiēbāmus, capiēmus   _____

3. mūnītis, mūniēbātis, mūnīvistis, mūnīverātis   _____

4. pugnāvistī, pugnābās, pugnāverās, pugnābis   _____

5. tenuērunt, tenēbant, tenuerant, tenēbunt   _____

6. pōnēbam, posueram, pōnam, posuī   _____

7. erat, fuit, erit, fuerat   _____

8. poterant, possunt, potuerant, potuērunt   _____

9. nāvigāvit, erāmus, iēcērunt, fēceram   _____

10. ēgerās, gessit, poterāmus, scīvērunt   _____

B. Change each singular verb to the plural, and each plural verb to the singular.

1. pervēnerat   _____
2. pepulerāmus   _____
3. mīserātis   _____

4. potuerant   _____
5. exspectāveram   _____
6. interfēcerās   _____

39

7. fuerat ----------------------------   **9.** sēnserant ----------------------------

8. iusserāsne ----------------------------   **10.** cupīveram ----------------------------

   C. Write the pluperfect active of the following verbs in the form indicated:

1. *agere:* first person singular and plural --

2. *mūnīre:* third person singular and plural --

3. *amāre:* second person singular and plural --

4. *manēre* and *posse:* third person plural --

5. *esse* and *capere:* third person singular --

   D. Translate the English words into Latin.

1. *He had ordered* virōs pugnāre. ----------------------------------

2. *They had given* auxilium oppidō. ----------------------------------

3. *We had been* in marī. ----------------------------------

4. *Had you (sing.) heard* perīculum? ----------------------------------

5. *I had not read* librum. ----------------------------------

6. *You (pl.) had been able* cōnscrībere. ----------------------------------

7. Rōmānī Gallōs *had conquered.* ----------------------------------

8. Quis *had seen* montem? ----------------------------------

9. Homō sē *had killed.* ----------------------------------

10. Mortem *we had feared.* ----------------------------------

The Fasces

The Roman fasces, a bundle of rods and an ax all tied together, were a symbol of supreme authority. The Italian dictator Mussolini revived the symbol in founding the system of fascism. The fasces, as a symbol of unity, are stamped on the American dime.

Lesson 17—FUTURE PERFECT ACTIVE (Optional)

portāre, to carry; perfect stem, **portāv-**
I shall (will) have carried

portāv*erō*	portāv*erimus*
portāv*eris*	portāv*eritis*
portāv*erit*	portāv*erint*

dūcere, to lead; perfect stem, **dūx-**
I shall (will) have led

dūx*erō*	dūx*erimus*
dūx*eris*	dūx*eritis*
dūx*erit*	dūx*erint*

esse, to be; perfect stem, **fu-**
I shall (will) have been

fu*erō*	fu*erimus*
fu*eris*	fu*eritis*
fu*erit*	fu*erint*

posse, to be able; perfect stem, **potu-**
I shall (will) have been able

potu*erō*	potu*erimus*
potu*eris*	potu*eritis*
potu*erit*	potu*erint*

Note

1. The future perfect active of all verbs is formed by adding to the perfect stem the following endings:

-erō	-erimus
-eris	-eritis
-erit	-erint

2. These endings are the same as the future of the verb **esse,** with the exception of the third person plural where the ending is **-erint** instead of **-erunt.**

3. The future perfect tense, representing time completed before some future time, is always translated by the auxiliary verb *shall have* or *will have* plus the past participle.

4. Distinguish carefully between verbs ending in **-ērunt, -erant,** and **-erint.**

audīvē**ru**nt, they heard
audīver**a**nt, they had heard
audīver**i**nt, they will have heard

EXERCISES

A. Write the future perfect active of the following verbs in the form indicated:

1. *spectāre:* second person singular and plural ....

2. *dēfendere:* third person singular and plural ....

3. *posse:* first person singular and plural ....

4. *pervenīre* and *esse:* third person singular ....

5. *facere* and *monēre:* third person plural ....

B. The following verbs are all in the future perfect. Identify the person and number of each verb, and then translate into English.

	PERSON AND NUMBER	MEANING
1. mōverimus	....	....
2. scīverit	....	....
3. cōnfēcerint	....	....

41

4. temptāverō _____ _____

5. dūxeris _____ _____

6. fueritis _____ _____

7. coēgeritne? _____ _____

8. potuerint _____ _____

9. nōn cesserimus _____ _____

10. vīcerisne? _____ _____

C. Translate into Latin.

1. he will have seen _____

2. I shall have heard _____

3. they will have prepared _____

4. we shall have called _____

5. you (pl.) will have been _____

6. will they have conquered? _____

7. you (sing.) will have been able _____

8. will he have sought? _____

9. we shall not have surrendered _____

10. I shall not have begun _____

Lesson 18—PRESENT ACTIVE IMPERATIVE (Optional)

INFINITIVE	PRESENT STEM	IMPERATIVE SINGULAR	IMPERATIVE PLURAL
portāre	portā-	portā	portāte
docēre	docē-	docē	docēte
vincere	vince-	vince	vincite
capere	cape-	cape	capite
audīre	audī-	audī	audīte

Note

1. With few exceptions, the imperative singular is the same as the present stem. The imperative plural is formed by adding **-te** to the singular form. However, in third and **-iō** third conjugation verbs, the final **e** of the singular form is changed to **i** before adding **-te**.

2. The following common verbs drop the final **e** in the imperative singular:

INFINITIVE	PRESENT STEM	IMPERATIVE SINGULAR	IMPERATIVE PLURAL
dīcere	dīce-	dīc	dīcite
dūcere	dūce-	dūc	dūcite
facere	face-	fac	facite

3. The imperative is used in the second person to express a command. The singular form is used when addressing one person, the plural when addressing more than one.

Tē *dēfende,* Caesar.	Defend yourself, Caesar.
Occupāte oppidum, mīlitēs.	Soldiers, seize the town.

EXERCISES

A. Complete the English translation.

1. Līberā rem publicam. _____ the republic.

2. Dūc omnēs amīcōs ex urbe. _____ all your friends from the city.

3. Quam ob rem discēdite. Therefore _____.

4. Appropinquāte, sociī. _____, friends.

5. Incipe negōtium, Iūlia. _____ the task, Julia.

6. Dēfendite pontem. _____ the bridge.

7. Pugnāte fortiter. _____ bravely.

8. Gere bellum. _____ war.

9. Prohibēte perīculum. _____ the danger.

10. Convenīte, mīlitēs. _____, soldiers.

B. Write the imperative singular and plural of the following verbs:

	SINGULAR	PLURAL
1. exspectāre	----------------------	----------------------------
2. dūcere	----------------------	----------------------------
3. relinquere	----------------------	----------------------------

43

4. obtinēre   ----------------------------   ----------------------------

5. mūnīre   ----------------------------   ----------------------------

    C. Translate the English words into Latin.

1. *Call* tuam mātrem, Cornēlia.   ----------------------------

2. *Hear* magistrum, puerī.   ----------------------------

3. *Speak* mihi, puella.   ----------------------------

4. *Stay* diū, amīcī.   ----------------------------

5. *Conquer* hostēs, hominēs.   ----------------------------

    D. Change the singular imperative to the plural.

1. vulnerā   ----------------------------

2. fac   ----------------------------

3. iace   ----------------------------

4. pōne   ----------------------------

5. mitte   ----------------------------

Glassware

The Romans had no superiors in ornamental glassmaking. The vases found in Pompeii are excellent examples of delicate beauty and superb workmanship. Today most glassware is made by machine, but the original Roman designs are still sometimes reproduced.

Unit II—Verbs, Passive Voice

Lesson 19—PRESENT PASSIVE OF ALL CONJUGATIONS

FIRST CONJUGATION

portāre, to carry; present stem, **portā-**

I am carried, I am being carried

port*or*	port*āmur*
port*āris*	port*āminī*
port*ātur*	port*antur*

SECOND CONJUGATION

docēre, to teach; present stem, **docē-**

I am taught, I am being taught

doc*eor*	doc*ēmur*
doc*ēris*	doc*ēminī*
doc*ētur*	doc*entur*

THIRD CONJUGATION

dūcere, to lead; present stem, **dūce-**

I am led, I am being led

dūc*or*	dūc*imur*
dūc*eris*	dūc*iminī*
dūc*itur*	dūc*untur*

-IŌ THIRD CONJUGATION

capere, to take; present stem, **cape-**

I am taken, I am being taken

cap*ior*	cap*imur*
cap*eris*	cap*iminī*
cap*itur*	cap*iuntur*

FOURTH CONJUGATION

audīre, to hear; present stem, **audī-**

I am heard, I am being heard

aud*ior*	aud*īmur*
aud*īris*	aud*īminī*
aud*ītur*	aud*iuntur*

Note

1. The passive personal endings are:

-r	-mur
-ris	-minī
-tur	-ntur

2. These endings are substituted for the active endings of the present tense. However, in the first person singular, the final **o** is kept, making the ending **-or**.

3. In the second person singular of third and **-iō** third conjugation verbs, the final **e** of the present stem is kept and not changed to **i** as in the active voice. Thus, dūc*eris*, cap*eris*.

4. In the active voice, the subject performs some action. In the passive voice, the subject is acted upon.

ACTIVE VOICE	PASSIVE VOICE
Vir puerum **portat.**	Puer ab virō **portātur.**
The man is carrying the boy.	The boy is carried by the man.
Puerōs perīculō **prohibēmus.**	Perīculō **prohibēmur.**
We keep the boys from danger.	We are kept from danger.
Līberantne servōs?	**Līberantur**ne servī?
Are they freeing the slaves?	Are the slaves being freed?

A. Change the following verbs from the active to the passive, and then translate the passive forms into English:

ACTIVE	PASSIVE	TRANSLATION
1. nūntiant	....	....
2. tenēmus	....	....
3. petit	....	....
4. capiō	....	....
5. pellis	....	....
6. audītisne?	....	....
7. relinquimus	....	....
8. superat	....	....
9. monentne?	....	....
10. nōn iubeō	....	....

B. Write the present passive of the following verbs in the form indicated:

1. *movēre:* third person singular and plural ....

2. *agere:* first person singular and plural ....

3. *laudāre:* second person singular and plural ....

4. *interficere* and *circumvenīre:* third person singular ....

5. *vincere* and *superāre:* third person plural ....

C. Complete the English translation.

1. Tenēris, Catilīna. ...., Catiline.

2. In castrīs exspectātur. .... in camp.

3. Mīlitēs vulnerantur. The soldiers ....

4. Ab hostibus circumvenīmur. .... by the enemy.

5. Ā cōnsule accipiminī. .... by the consul.

6. Relinquorne in oppidō? .... in the town?

7. Fortiter dēfenduntur. .... bravely.

8. Frūmentum nōn parātur. Grain ....

9. Prohibērisne ab urbe? .... from the city?

10. Ab puerō intermittimur. .... by the boy.

D. Write the proper form of the verb in the present passive.

1. dēligere Ducēs ....

2. mūnīre Oppidum ....

3. spectāre Tū (*You*, sing.) ....

4. monēre Nōs (*We*) ab imperātōre ....

5. capere Ego (*I*) ab hostibus ....

6. servāre   ------------------------------ fēminae?

7. remittere Vōs (*You*, pl.) ad populum ------------------------------.

8. invenīre Dominus nōn ------------------------------.

9. docēre Puer puellaque ------------------------------.

10. cōnficere ------------------------------ negōtium?

Jupiter, or Jove, identified by the Romans with the Greek Zeus, was king of the gods. He was worshipped as the god of rain, storms, thunder, and lightning. His name was usually associated with the words "Optimus Maximus," signifying that he was the highest and most powerful among the gods.

Lesson 20—IMPERFECT PASSIVE OF ALL CONJUGATIONS

FIRST CONJUGATION

portāre, to carry; present stem, **portā-**

I was carried, I was being carried

portā*bar*	portā*bāmur*
portā*bāris*	portā*bāminī*
portā*bātur*	portā*bantur*

SECOND CONJUGATION

docēre, to teach; present stem, **docē-**

I was taught, I was being taught

docē*bar*	docē*bāmur*
docē*bāris*	docē*bāminī*
docē*bātur*	docē*bantur*

THIRD CONJUGATION

dūcere, to lead; present stem, **dūce-**

I was led, I was being led

dūcē*bar*	dūcē*bāmur*
dūcē*bāris*	dūcē*bāminī*
dūcē*bātur*	dūcē*bantur*

-IŌ THIRD CONJUGATION

capere, to take; present stem, **cape-**

I was taken, I was being taken

capiē*bar*	capiē*bāmur*
capiē*bāris*	capiē*bāminī*
capiē*bātur*	capiē*bantur*

FOURTH CONJUGATION

audīre, to hear; present stem, **audī-**

I was heard, I was being heard

audiē*bar*	audiē*bāmur*
audiē*bāris*	audiē*bāminī*
audiē*bātur*	audiē*bantur*

Note

1. The endings of the imperfect passive for all conjugations are:

-bar	-bāmur
-bāris	-bāminī
-bātur	-bantur

2. These endings are substituted for the active endings of the imperfect.

EXERCISES

A. Change the following verbs from the present to the imperfect, and then translate the new forms into English:

PRESENT	IMPERFECT	TRANSLATION
1. petitur		
2. timentur		
3. cōnfīrmāris		
4. vocor		
5. capimur		
6. audīminī		

48

7. vidēturne? _____ _____

8. nōn occupantur _____ _____

9. cōgimur _____ _____

10. pellerisne? _____ _____

B. Write the imperfect passive of the following verbs in the form indicated:

1. *cōnscrībere:* second person singular and plural _____

2. *interficere:* third person singular and plural _____

3. *commovēre:* first person singular and plural _____

4. *appellāre* and *scīre:* third person plural _____

5. *relinquere* and *audīre:* third person singular _____

C. Complete the English translation.

1. Bellum gerebātur.   War _____.

2. Omnēs servī capiēbantur.   All the slaves _____.

3. Ab cōnsule laudābāmur.   _____ by the consul.

4. Ab amīcīs sustinēbar.   _____ by friends.

5. Ad proelium prōdūcēbāminī. _____ to battle.

6. Ab omnibus audiēbāris.   _____ by all.

7. Reddēbāturne liber?   _____ the book _____?

8. Ā duce nōn petēbāris.   _____ by the leader.

9. Iubēbanturne manēre?   _____ to stay?

10. Signum dabātur.   The signal _____.

D. Translate into Latin.

1. they were prevented _____

2. was he being freed? _____

3. I was loved _____

4. you (sing.) were being surrounded _____

5. we were received _____

6. you (pl.) were taught _____

7. he used to be called _____

8. were they set forth? _____

9. we were strengthened _____

10. they were not being drawn up _____

Lesson 21—FUTURE PASSIVE OF ALL CONJUGATIONS

FIRST CONJUGATION

portāre, to carry; present stem, **portā-**

I shall (will) be carried

portā*bor*	portā*bimur*
portā*beris*	portā*biminī*
portā*bitur*	portā*buntur*

SECOND CONJUGATION

docēre, to teach; present stem, **docē-**

I shall (will) be taught

docē*bor*	docē*bimur*
docē*beris*	docē*biminī*
docē*bitur*	docē*buntur*

THIRD CONJUGATION

dūcere, to lead; present stem, **dūce-**

I shall (will) be led

dūc*ar*	dūc*ēmur*
dūc*ēris*	dūc*ēminī*
dūc*ētur*	dūc*entur*

-IŌ THIRD CONJUGATION

capere, to take; present stem, **cape-**

I shall (will) be taken

capi*ar*	capi*ēmur*
capi*ēris*	capi*ēminī*
capi*ētur*	capi*entur*

FOURTH CONJUGATION

audīre, to hear; present stem, **audī-**

I shall (will) be heard

audi*ar*	audi*ēmur*
audi*ēris*	audi*ēminī*
audi*ētur*	audi*entur*

Note

1. The endings of the future passive are as follows:

1ST AND 2ND CONJUGATIONS		3RD, -IŌ 3RD, AND 4TH CONJUGATIONS	
-bor	-bimur	-ar	-ēmur
-beris	-biminī	-ēris	-ēminī
-bitur	-buntur	-ētur	-entur

2. These endings are substituted for the active endings of the future.

3. In third conjugation verbs, a long **e** distinguishes the future passive from the present passive in the second person singular.

PRESENT	FUTURE
dūc*e*ris, you are led	dūc*ē*ris, you will be led

4. The future passive of third conjugation verbs is often confused with the present passive of second conjugation verbs in all forms except the first person singular.

THIRD CONJUGATION	SECOND CONJUGATION
FUTURE	PRESENT
dūcēris, you will be led	docēris, you are taught
dūcētur, he will be led	docētur, he is taught
dūcēmur, we shall be led	docēmur, we are taught
dūcēminī, you will be led	docēminī, you are taught
dūcentur, they will be led	docentur, they are taught

50

EXERCISES

A. Write the English meaning and Latin infinitive of each of the following verbs:

		MEANING	INFINITIVE
1. parābuntur			
2. audiēmur			
3. interficiētur			
4. iubēberis			
5. dēligar			
6. dēfendēminī			
7. nōn līberābimur			
8. perterrēbiturne?			
9. dīmittentur			
10. īnstruenturne?			

B. Write the future passive of the following verbs in the form indicated:

1. *ostendere:* third person singular and plural
2. *prohibēre:* first person singular and plural
3. *capere:* second person singular and plural
4. *superāre* and *mittere:* third person plural
5. *invenīre* and *docēre:* second person singular

C. Translate the English words into Latin.

1. *He will be seen* ab omnibus.
2. Signum posteā *will be given.*
3. Mīlitēs in castra *will be led.*
4. *Will you (sing.) be received* ab duce?
5. *We shall be praised* ā cōnsule.
6. Hodiē *you (pl.) will be freed.*
7. Castra *will not be fortified.*
8. Quis *will be sent back?*
9. Ab oppidō *I will not be driven.*
10. *It will be finished* facile.

D. The verbs in the following list are either in the present or the future. Indicate the tense of each verb, and then translate into English.

	TENSE	MEANING
1. cōgeris		
2. tenētur		
3. permoventur		
4. pōnēmur		

51

5. dēfendēris   ------------------   --

6. docēminī   ------------------   --

7. timēris   ------------------   --

8. petenturne?   ------------------   --

9. nōn sustinētur   ------------------   --

10. relinquētur   ------------------   --

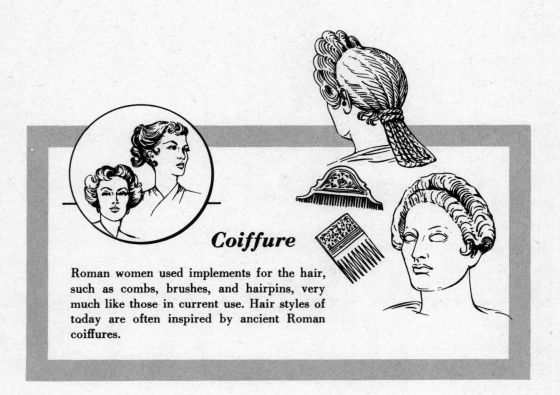

Coiffure

Roman women used implements for the hair, such as combs, brushes, and hairpins, very much like those in current use. Hair styles of today are often inspired by ancient Roman coiffures.

Lesson 22—PERFECT PASSIVE OF FIRST AND SECOND CONJUGATION VERBS

FIRST CONJUGATION	SECOND CONJUGATION
portāre, to carry; participial stem, **portāt-**	**docēre**, to teach; participial stem, **doct-**
I was (have been) carried	I was (have been) taught

portāt*us*, -a, -um	{ *sum* *es* *est*	portāt*ī*, -ae, -a	{ *sumus* *estis* *sunt*	doct*us*, -a, -um	{ *sum* *es* *est*	doct*ī*, -ae, -a	{ *sumus* *estis* *sunt*

Note

1. The perfect passive consists of two parts. The first part is the participial stem plus the endings **-us, -a, -um** for the singular, and **-ī, -ae, -a** for the plural. The second part is the present of the verb **esse**.

2. The first part is called the *perfect passive participle*. Like an adjective, the participle agrees in gender, number, and case with the subject.

Puer doct*us* **est.**	The boy was taught.
Puerī doct*ī* **sunt.**	The boys were taught.
Puella doct*a* **est.**	The girl was taught.
Puellae doct*ae* **sunt.**	The girls were taught.

3. The perfect passive participle of verbs of the first conjugation ends in **-ātus, -a, -um**.

4. The perfect passive participle of verbs of the second conjugation ends in **-tus** or **-sus**. However, the spelling of the participial stem varies, as shown in the following list of verbs:

INFINITIVE	PERFECT PASSIVE PARTICIPLE
dēbēre	*dēbitus*
docēre	*doctus*
habēre	*habitus*
monēre	*monitus*
movēre (and its compounds)	*mōtus*
prohibēre	*prohibitus*
tenēre (and its compounds)	*tentus*
terrēre (and its compounds)	*territus*
iubēre	*iussus*
respondēre	*respōnsus*
vidēre	*vīsus*

5. Some verbs lack a perfect passive participle and therefore cannot be used in the perfect passive. Two such verbs are **manēre** and **timēre**.

EXERCISES

A. Complete the perfect passive of each verb by supplying the correct ending of the participle and the proper form of the verb *esse*.

1. Sociī territ _____   _____

2. Perīculum vīs _____   _____

3. Īnsula occupāt _____   _____

4. Homō permōt _____   _____

5. Oppida līberāt _____   _____

6. Fēminae monit _____   _____
7. Ego (*I*) servāt _____   _____
8. Puella et māter doct _____   _____
9. Nōs (*We*) vocāt _____   _____
10. Tū (*You*), Caesar, prohibit _____   _____

B. Write the perfect passive of the following verbs in the form indicated:

1. *movēre:* third person singular and plural

_____

2. *cōnservāre:* first person singular and plural

_____

3. *appellāre:* second person singular and plural

_____

4. *continēre* and *superāre:* third person plural

_____

5. *dare* and *respondēre:* third person singular

_____

C. Complete the English translation.

1. Līberī laudātī sunt.   The children _____.
2. Quis perterritus est?   Who _____?
3. Ab duce iussī sumus.   _____ by the leader.
4. Vulnerātusne es gladiō?   _____ by a sword?
5. Nōn līberātī estis, servī.   _____, slaves.
6. Ā magistrō monitus sum.   _____ by the teacher.
7. Animī eōrum cōnfīrmātī sunt.   Their minds _____.
8. Prōvincia nova obtenta est.   A new province _____.
9. Perīculum prohibitum est.   The danger _____.
10. Arma occupāta sunt.   The arms _____.

D. Change each verb to the plural.

1. Terra vīsa est.   Terrae _____.
2. Auxilium remōtum est.   Auxilia _____.
3. Hostis exspectātus est.   Hostēs _____.
4. Ab servīs amātus es.   Ab servīs _____.
5. Iussus sum discēdere.   _____ discēdere.

Lesson 23—PERFECT PASSIVE OF THIRD CONJUGATION VERBS

dūcere, to lead; participial stem, **duct-**

I was (have been) led

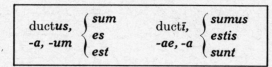

Note

The perfect passive participle of verbs of the third conjugation ends in **-tus** or **-sus**. However, the spelling of the participial stem varies, as shown in the following list of verbs:

INFINITIVE	PERFECT PASSIVE PARTICIPLE
agere (and its compounds)	*āctus*
cognōscere	*cognitus*
cōnstituere	*cōnstitūtus*
contendere	*contentus*
dīcere	*dictus*
dūcere (and its compounds)	*ductus*
gerere	*gestus*
īnstruere	*īnstrūctus*
legere (and its compounds)	*lēctus*
ostendere	*ostentus*
petere	*petītus*
pōnere (and its compounds)	*positus*
reddere	*redditus*
relinquere	*relictus*
scrībere (and its compounds)	*scrīptus*
trādere	*trāditus*
vincere	*victus*
cēdere (and its compounds)	*cessus*
dēfendere	*dēfēnsus*
lūdere	*lūsus*
mittere (and its compounds)	*missus*
pellere	*pulsus*
premere	*pressus*

EXERCISES

A. Write the perfect passive of the following verbs in the form indicated:

1. *cognōscere:* third person singular and plural

----

2. *premere:* first person singular and plural

----

3. *pellere:* second person singular and plural

----

4. *agere* and *dēfendere:* third person singular

55

5. *mittere* and *relinquere:* second person plural

   B. Change each verb to the singular.

1. Bella gesta sunt.   Bellum _____ .

2. Ab hostibus petītī sumus. Ab hostibus _____ .

3. Ad castra ductī estis.   Ad castra _____ .

4. Rēs cōnstitūtae sunt.   Rēs _____ .

5. Equī remissī sunt.   Equus _____ .

   C. Translate into English.

1. dīmissī sunt   _____

2. dēlēctus est   _____

3. nōn adductus es   _____

4. victī sumus   _____

5. positus sum   _____

6. coāctī estis   _____

7. redditīne sunt?   _____

8. pulsae sumus   _____

9. relicta es   _____

10. nōn petītus est   _____

   D. Change the following forms to the gender and number indicated:

1. prōpositus est   masculine plural   _____

2. dēlēctī sumus   feminine singular   _____

3. victus es   feminine plural   _____

4. commissī sunt   neuter singular   _____

5. dēfēnsī estis   masculine singular _____

Lesson 24—PERFECT PASSIVE OF *-IŌ* THIRD AND FOURTH CONJUGATION VERBS

-IŌ THIRD CONJUGATION	FOURTH CONJUGATION
capere, to take; participial stem, **capt-**	**audīre,** to hear; participial stem, **audīt-**
I was (have been) taken	I was (have been) heard

capt*us,* -a, -um	{ sum es est	capt*ī,* -ae, -a	{ sumus estis sunt	audīt*us,* -a, -um	{ sum es est	audīt*ī,* -ae, -a	{ sumus estis sunt

Note

1. The perfect passive participle of verbs of the **-iō** third conjugation ends in **-tus.** However, the spelling of the participial stem varies, as shown in the following list of verbs:

INFINITIVE	PERFECT PASSIVE PARTICIPLE
capere	*captus*
cupere	*cupītus*
facere	*factus*
iacere	*iactus*

2. Compounds of **capere, facere,** and **iacere** change the **a** of the stem to **e** in the perfect passive participle.

captus	*but*	ac**ce**ptus
factus	*but*	cōnf**e**ctus
iactus	*but*	coni**e**ctus

3. The perfect passive participle of most fourth conjugation verbs ends in **-ītus.** Note the exceptions included in the list below.

INFINITIVE	PERFECT PASSIVE PARTICIPLE
audīre	*audītus*
mūnīre	*mūnītus*
scīre	*scītus*
sentīre	*sēnsus*
venīre (and its compounds)	*ventus*

EXERCISES

A. Change each verb to the plural.

1. Oppidum circumventum est.   Oppida _____
2. Ab barbarīs capta sum.   Ab barbarīs _____
3. Ab omnibus audītus es.   Ab omnibus _____
4. Homō interfectus est.   Hominēs _____
5. Urbs mūnīta est.   Urbēs _____

B. Complete the English translation.

1. Cōnsilium inceptum est.   The plan _____
2. Spēs sēnsa est.   Hope _____
3. Rēs scītae sunt.   The things _____

57

4. Arma iacta sunt. Arms _____.

5. Cūr nōn acceptus es? Why_____?

6. Ab prīncipe captī sumus. _____ by the chief.

7. Ā magistrō nōn audīta sum. _____ by the teacher.

8. Ab equitibus circumventī estis. _____ by the cavalry.

9. Quis factus est cōnsul? Who _____ consul?

10. Cōnfectumne est negōtium? _____ the task _____?

C. Write the perfect passive of the following verbs in the form indicated:

1. *cupere:* third person singular and plural

----

2. *convenīre* and *capere:* second person plural

----

3. *conicere* and *invenīre:* third person plural

----

4. *accipere:* first person singular and plural

----

5. *audīre:* second person singular and plural

D. Translate into Latin.

1. he was killed _____

2. they were found _____

3. we have been received _____

4. you (sing.) were taken _____

5. she has been heard _____

6. it was known _____

7. you (pl.) were not surrounded _____

8. I was found _____

9. they (fem.) were made _____

10. they (n.) have been finished _____

58

Lesson 25—MASTERY EXERCISES ON VERBS, PASSIVE VOICE

A. Write a synopsis (four tenses passive) of the following verbs in the form indicated:

1. līberāre: 2nd., sing.   *Pres.* _____   *Imp.* _____

   Fut. _____   *Perf.* _____

2. terrēre: 1st., pl.   *Pres.* _____   *Imp.* _____

   Fut. _____   *Perf.* _____

3. invenīre: 3rd., pl.   *Pres.* _____   *Imp.* _____

   Fut. _____   *Perf.* _____

4. interficere: 3rd., sing.   *Pres.* _____   *Imp.* _____

   Fut. _____   *Perf.* _____

5. pellere: 1st., sing.   *Pres.* _____   *Imp.* _____

   Fut. _____   *Perf.* _____

6. superāre: 2nd., pl.   *Pres.* _____   *Imp.* _____

   Fut. _____   *Perf.* _____

7. vidēre: 3rd., sing.   *Pres.* _____   *Imp.* _____

   Fut. _____   *Perf.* _____

8. īnstruere: 3rd., pl.   *Pres.* _____   *Imp.* _____

   Fut. _____   *Perf.* _____

9. audīre: 1st., pl.   *Pres.* _____   *Imp.* _____

   Fut. _____   *Perf.* _____

10. accipere: 2nd., sing.   *Pres.* _____   *Imp.* _____

   Fut. _____   *Perf.* _____

B. Draw a line through the form that does *not* belong with the others in each group.

1. vincēbātur, audiēbāmur, laudāberis, vocābantur
2. vulnerātus est, mūniēbantur, cōgor, timēberis
3. pōneris, capiēris, docēberis, agēris
4. vidēmur, servāmur, relinquēmur, accipimur
5. sciuntur, dēligēbāminī, parābimur, appellātus es
6. monitus est, iussus es, redditus, vīsus sum
7. līberātī estis, prohibitus est, cōnfīrmāris, tenēbāminī
8. datum est, remōta sunt, iactum est, occupātī sunt
9. dēligitur, territī sumus, dēfendēbantur, petētur
10. amāta sunt, commōta est, coāctae sunt, facta est

C. Underline the correct English translation.

1. cōnfectum est   (it is finished, it was finished, it will be finished)
2. vincētur   (he will be conquered, he is conquered, he was conquered)
3. audiēbāris   (you will be heard, you are heard, you were being heard)
4. terrentur   (they were frightened, they will be frightened, they are frightened)
5. superābiminī   (you were defeated, you will be defeated, you are defeated)
6. parāmur   (we are prepared, we were prepared, we shall be prepared)
7. commovēbar   (I have been alarmed, I am alarmed, I was alarmed)

59

8. relictī sunt   (they were abandoned, they are abandoned, they were being abandoned)
9. iaciturne?   (was it thrown? will it be thrown? is it thrown?)
10. dēlēcta sunt   (she was chosen, he was chosen, they were chosen)

D. In the space before each verb in column *A*, write the letter of the English translation in column *B*.

Column A	*Column B*
_____ **1.** accipiētur	*a.* you are praised
_____ **2.** timentur	*b.* he was being freed
_____ **3.** ostenderis	*c.* they were heard
_____ **4.** vocātus sum	*d.* he is received
_____ **5.** laudāmur	*e.* I am called
_____ **6.** līberābātur	*f.* you are shown
_____ **7.** accipitur	*g.* they will be feared
_____ **8.** monēmur	*h.* we shall be advised
_____ **9.** audītī sunt	*i.* we are praised
_____ **10.** timēbuntur	*j.* you will be shown
_____ **11.** vocor	*k.* they were being freed
_____ **12.** monēbimur	*l.* he will be received
_____ **13.** ostendēris	*m.* we are advised
_____ **14.** līberābantur	*n.* I have been called
_____ **15.** laudāminī	*o.* they are feared

E. Change each verb to the passive.

1. capiunt _____
2. mūniēbat _____
3. posuimus _____
4. parābō _____
5. docēs _____

6. dēfendētis _____
7. mīsit _____
8. accipis _____
9. cōnfīrmābant _____
10. prohibuī _____

F. Translate into English.

1. permōtī sunt _____
2. addūcēbāmur _____
3. audīminī _____
4. vocābitur _____
5. sustentus sum _____
6. relinquēris _____
7. timēturne? _____
8. nōn pellēbantur _____
9. datum est _____
10. circumveniuntur _____

11. laudāberisne? --

12. lēctae sunt --

13. victī sumus --

14. praemittēminī --

15. nōn interficitur --

G. Change each verb to the plural.

1. incipiēbātur ---------------------- 6. audīta sum ----------------------

2. prōductus es ---------------------- 7. cōnficiētur ----------------------

3. monēbar ---------------------- 8. renūntiātum est ----------------------

4. redditurne ---------------------- 9. docērisne ----------------------

5. līberāberis ---------------------- 10. cōnscrībēbātur ----------------------

H. Translate into Latin.

1. they were being carried on --

2. he was killed --

3. you (sing.) are named --

4. I shall be carried --

5. we have been frightened --

6. you (pl.) are being sought --

7. was he being sent away? --

8. they will be drawn up --

9. will you (sing.) be chosen? --

10. we were not being conquered --

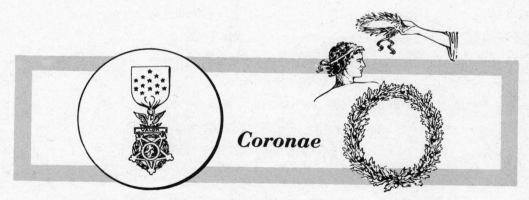

Coronae

Awards in Roman times usually took the form of crowns or wreaths made of acorns, oak leaves, laurel leaves, or olive leaves. The corōna cīvica, corresponding roughly to the Congressional Medal of Honor, was given as a reward for saving a citizen's life in battle. Similar crowns were awarded for excellence in the arts, literature, and athletics.

Lesson 26—PLUPERFECT AND FUTURE PERFECT PASSIVE (Optional)

PLUPERFECT PASSIVE

portāre, to carry; participial stem, **portāt-**   **dūcere**, to lead; participial stem, **duct-**

I had been carried   I had been led

portāt*us*, -a, -um	{ *eram* *erās* *erat*	portāt*ī*, -ae, -a	{ *erāmus* *erātis* *erant*	duct*us*, -a, -um	{ *eram* *erās* *erat*	duct*ī*, -ae, -a	{ *erāmus* *erātis* *erant*

FUTURE PERFECT PASSIVE

I shall (will) have been carried   I shall (will) have been led

portāt*us*, -a, -um	{ *erō* *eris* *erit*	portāt*ī*, -ae, -a	{ *erimus* *eritis* *erunt*	duct*us*, -a, -um	{ *erō* *eris* *erit*	duct*ī*, -ae, -a	{ *erimus* *eritis* *erunt*

Note

1. The pluperfect passive of all verbs consists of the perfect passive participle plus the imperfect of the verb **esse**.

2. The future perfect passive of all verbs consists of the perfect passive participle plus the future of the verb **esse**.

EXERCISES

A. Underline the correct English translation of the following Latin verbs:

1. positus erit   (he will have been put, he had been put)

2. inventī erant   (they had been found, they will have been found)

3. līberātus eram   (I had been freed, I shall have been freed)

4. monitī eritis   (you will have been advised, we shall have been advised)

5. captī erāmus   (we shall have been taken, we had been taken)

6. āctus eris   (you will have been driven, you had been driven)

7. datum erat   (it had been given, he had been given)

8. acceptae erātis   (you will have been received, you had been received)

9. mūnīta erunt   (they will have been fortified, they had been fortified)

10. petītus erās   (you had been sought, you will have been sought)

B. Write the pluperfect and future perfect passive of the following verbs in the form indicated:

	PLUPERFECT	FUTURE PERFECT
1. prōdūcere: third person plural		
2. vidēre: third person singular		
3. līberāre: first person plural		
4. facere: second person singular		
5. audīre: second person plural		

C. Change each verb to the plural.

1. iussus erat   _____
2. missus eris   _____
3. servātus eram   _____
4. iactum erit   _____
5. docta erō   _____

6. laudātus erās   _____
7. scītus eram   _____
8. cōnfectum erat   _____
9. exspectāta eris   _____
10. territus erit   _____

D. Translate into English.

1. remōtī erant _____
2. iussus eris _____
3. victus erās _____
4. remissae erāmus _____
5. mūnītum erit _____
6. relicta eram _____
7. līberātus erat _____
8. portātus erō _____
9. prohibitae erunt _____
10. pulsī erimus _____

E. Translate into Latin.

1. he had been defended _____
2. I shall have been saved _____
3. they had been seen _____
4. you (sing.) will have been taken _____
5. we had been led _____

63

Unit III—*Principal Parts of Verbs; Infinitives; Participles*

Lesson 27—PRINCIPAL PARTS OF VERBS

FIRST CONJUGATION

portō,	**portāre,**	**portāvī,**	**portātus,**
I carry	to carry	I carried	having been carried
	PRESENT STEM	PERFECT STEM	PARTICIPIAL STEM
	portā-	**portāv-**	**portāt-**

SECOND CONJUGATION

doceō,	**docēre,**	**docuī,**	**doctus,**
I teach	to teach	I taught	having been taught
	PRESENT STEM	PERFECT STEM	PARTICIPIAL STEM
	docē-	**docu-**	**doct-**

THIRD CONJUGATION

dūcō,	**dūcere,**	**dūxī,**	**ductus,**
I lead	to lead	I led	having been led
	PRESENT STEM	PERFECT STEM	PARTICIPIAL STEM
	dūce-	**dūx-**	**duct-**

-IŌ THIRD CONJUGATION

capiō,	**capere,**	**cēpī,**	**captus,**
I take	to take	I took	having been taken
	PRESENT STEM	PERFECT STEM	PARTICIPIAL STEM
	cape-	**cēp-**	**capt-**

FOURTH CONJUGATION

audiō,	**audīre,**	**audīvī,**	**audītus,**
I hear	to hear	I heard	having been heard
	PRESENT STEM	PERFECT STEM	PARTICIPIAL STEM
	audī-	**audīv-**	**audīt-**

Note

1. Most first conjugation verbs follow the pattern of **portāre**. An exception is:

| dō | dare | dedī | datus |

2. Most second conjugation verbs follow the pattern of **docēre**. Here are a few exceptions:

iubeō	iubēre	iussī	iussus
maneō	manēre	mānsī	mānsūrus
moveō	movēre	mōvī	mōtus
respondeō	respondēre	respondī	respōnsus
videō	vidēre	vīdī	vīsus

3. The principal parts of third conjugation verbs vary considerably. Like **dūcere** are **dīcere** and **īnstruere**. Other verbs are:

agō	agere	ēgī	āctus
cēdō	cēdere	cessī	cessus
cognōscō	cognōscere	cognōvī	cognitus
cōnstituō	cōnstituere	cōnstituī	cōnstitūtus
contendō	contendere	contendī	contentus
dēfendō	dēfendere	dēfendī	dēfēnsus
gerō	gerere	gessī	gestus
legō	legere	lēgī	lēctus
lūdō	lūdere	lūsī	lūsus
mittō	mittere	mīsī	missus
pellō	pellere	pepulī	pulsus
petō	petere	petīvī	petītus
pōnō	pōnere	posuī	positus
premō	premere	pressī	pressus
reddō	reddere	reddidī	redditus
relinquō	relinquere	relīquī	relictus
scrībō	scrībere	scrīpsī	scrīptus
vincō	vincere	vīcī	victus

4. **-iō** third conjugation verbs that follow the pattern of **capere** are **facere** and **iacere**. Compounds of these verbs, such as **accipere, cōnficere,** and **conicere,** follow this pattern:

| accipiō | accipere | accēpī | acceptus |

An exception to the above is the verb

| cupiō | cupere | cupīvī | cupītus |

5. Fourth conjugation verbs that follow the pattern of **audīre** are **mūnīre** and **scīre**. Exceptions to these are:

| sentiō | sentīre | sēnsī | sēnsus |
| veniō | venīre | vēnī | ventus |

EXERCISES

A. All the verbs on each line are in the same conjugation except one. Draw a line through the one that does *not* belong.

1. respondeō, maneō, dēficiō, pertineō
2. interficiō, inveniō, iaciō, cupiō
3. ēnūntiō, dō, pugnō, premō
4. perficiō, sentiō, mūniō, perveniō
5. cōgō, ostendō, relinquō, dubitō

6. accipiō, renūntiō, nūntiō, exīstimō
7. audiō, veniō, faciō, conveniō
8. addūcō, vincō, pōnō, temptō
9. dēbeō, incipiō, iubeō, terreō
10. coniciō, circumveniō, capiō, cōnficiō

B. Give the third principal part of each verb, and then translate it into English.

	THIRD PRINCIPAL PART	TRANSLATION
1. mittō	_____	_____
2. cupiō	_____	_____
3. vincō	_____	_____
4. videō	_____	_____
5. veniō	_____	_____
6. moveō	_____	_____
7. nūntiō	_____	_____
8. iubeō	_____	_____
9. sentiō	_____	_____
10. dō	_____	_____

C. Fill in the missing principal part.

	FIRST	SECOND	THIRD	FOURTH
1.	audiō	audīre	audīvī	_____
2.	faciō	facere	_____	factus
3.	nūntiō	_____	nūntiāvī	nūntiātus
4.	_____	prohibēre	prohibuī	prohibitus
5.	agō	agere	_____	āctus
6.	trādō	_____	trādidī	trāditus
7.	gerō	gerere	gessī	_____
8.	iubeō	_____	iussī	iussus
9.	pōnō	pōnere	posuī	_____
10.	pellō	pellere	_____	pulsus

D. Translate into English.

1. obtinēre _____

2. dēlēctus _____

3. sentiō _____

4. cupīvī _____

5. trādere _____

6. servātus _____

7. permōvī _____

8. iaciō _____

9. inventus _____

10. nāvigāvī _____

Lesson 28—INFINITIVES

portō

ACTIVE	PASSIVE
Present: portā*re,* to carry	portā*rī,* to be carried
Perfect: portā*visse,* to have carried	portā*tus, -a, -um esse,* to have been carried
Future: portā*tūrus, -a, -um esse,* to be about to carry	

dūcō

ACTIVE	PASSIVE
Present: dūce*re,* to lead	dūc*ī,* to be led
Perfect: dūx*isse,* to have led	duct*us, -a, -um esse,* to have been led
Future: duct*ūrus, -a, -um esse,* to be about to lead	

sum   possum

ACTIVE ONLY	
Present: es*se,* to be	pos*se,* to be able
Perfect: fu*isse,* to have been	potu*isse,* to have been able
Future: fut*ūrus, -a, -um esse,* to be about to be	

Note

1. The present active infinitive of all verbs is the second principal part.

2. The present passive infinitive is formed by changing the final **e** of the active infinitive to **ī**. This is true of all verbs except those in the third and **-iō** third conjugations, where the final **ere** is changed to **ī**.

ACTIVE	PASSIVE
portāre	portārī
docēre	docērī
audīre	audīrī

But

dūcere	dūcī
capere	capī

3. The perfect active infinitive of all verbs is found by adding the ending **-isse** to the perfect stem.

4. The perfect passive infinitive consists of the fourth principal part plus **esse**.

5. The future active infinitive is found by adding the endings **-ūrus, -a, -um** to the participial stem plus **esse**.

EXERCISES

A. Change to the passive voice.

1. superāre _____

2. vīcisse _____

3. cēpisse _____

4. agere _____

67

5. timēre _____   8. nūntiāvisse _____

6. mūnīvisse _____   9. iubēre _____

7. interficere _____   10. monuisse _____

B. Underline the correct Latin translation of the English infinitive.

1. to be heard   (audīre, audīrī, audīvisse)

2. to have drawn up   (īnstrūxisse, īnstrūctus esse, īnstrūctūrus esse)

3. to have been loved   (amāvisse, amātūrus esse, amātus esse)

4. to frighten   (terrēre, terrērī, terruisse)

5. to be about to seek   (petītus esse, petītūrus esse, petīvisse)

6. to have been   (esse, fuisse, futūrus esse)

7. to be thrown   (iacere, iēcisse, iacī)

8. to have been driven   (pulsūrus esse, pepulisse, pulsus esse)

9. to be about to prepare (parātūrus esse, parātus esse, parāvisse)

10. to have been able   (potuisse, posse, fuisse)

C. Change to the perfect tense, keeping the same voice.

1. vocārī _____   6. laudāre _____

2. relinquere _____   7. positūrus esse _____

3. sentīre _____   8. mittī _____

4. habitūrus esse _____ 9. respondēre _____

5. cōnficī _____   10. mānsūrus esse _____

D. In the space before each infinitive in column *A*, write the letter of the English translation in column *B*.

Column A	Column B
_____ **1.** dēfendī	*a.* to be fortified
_____ **2.** mūnīre	*b.* to have been able
_____ **3.** datūrus esse	*c.* to have been prevented
_____ **4.** prohibuisse	*d.* to be accomplished
_____ **5.** posse	*e.* to have been given
_____ **6.** perficī	*f.* to be defended
_____ **7.** dēfendisse	*g.* to have been
_____ **8.** scrīptūrus esse	*h.* to have accomplished
_____ **9.** datus esse	*i.* to fortify
_____ **10.** perfēcisse	*j.* to have been written
_____ **11.** mūnīrī	*k.* to have defended
_____ **12.** fuisse	*l.* to have prevented
_____ **13.** potuisse	*m.* to be able
_____ **14.** scrīptus esse	*n.* to be about to write
_____ **15.** prohibitus esse	*o.* to be about to give

68

Lesson 29—PARTICIPLES

portāre

ACTIVE	PASSIVE
Present: portā**ns**, carrying	——
Perfect: ——	portāt**us, -a, -um,** having been carried
Future: portāt**ūrus, -a, -um,** about to carry	porta**ndus, -a, -um,** must be carried

capere

ACTIVE	PASSIVE
Present: capi**ēns**, taking	——
Perfect: ——	capt**us, -a, -um,** having been taken
Future: capt**ūrus, -a, -um,** about to take	capi**endus, -a, -um,** must be taken

audīre

ACTIVE	PASSIVE
Present: audi**ēns,** hearing	——
Perfect: ——	audīt**us, -a, -um,** having been heard
Future: audit**ūrus, -a, -um,** about to hear	audi**endus, -a, -um,** must be heard

Note

1. The present active participle is formed by adding the ending **-ns** to the present stem. However, in **-iō** third conjugation verbs an **i** is inserted before the final **e** of the stem, and in fourth conjugation verbs an **e** is inserted before the **-ns** ending.

2. The future active participle is the same as the future active infinitive without the **esse.**

3. The perfect passive participle is the same as the perfect passive infinitive without the **esse.**

4. The future passive participle is formed by adding the endings **-ndus, -a, -um** to the present stem. However, in **-iō** third conjugation verbs an **i** is inserted before the final **e** of the stem, and in fourth conjugation verbs an **e** is inserted before the **-ndus** ending.

5. The verb **esse** has a future active participle, **futūrus, -a, -um,** and the verb **posse** has a present participle, **potēns.**

EXERCISES

A. Identify the following participles as to tense and voice:

	TENSE	VOICE
1. iactus		
2. spectāns		
3. mūnītūrus		
4. vīsus		
5. potēns		
6. accipiendus		
7. positūrus		

69

8. coāctus   ------------------------------   ------------------------------

9. movendus   ------------------------------   ------------------------------

10. futūrus   ------------------------------   ------------------------------

B. Draw a line through the form that does *not* belong with the others in each group.

1. temptāns, factūrus, scrīptus

2. gerendus, docēns, perfectus

3. īnstrūctus, habita, sēnsus

4. incipiēns, timēns, datus

5. līberātus, petītūrus, prohibendus

C. Underline the Latin participle that best translates the English verb form.

1. having been loved   (amāns, amātus, amandus)

2. sending   (mittēns, missūrus, mittendus)

3. must be read   (lēctūrus, legendus, lēctus)

4. about to advise   (monitūrus, monitus, monendus)

5. saving   (servātus, servandus, servāns)

6. having been taught   (docta, docenda, doctūra)

7. must be conquered   (victus, vincendus, vincēns)

8. about to yield   (cēdēns, cēdendus, cessūrus)

9. having been shown   (ostentūrum, ostentum, ostendendum)

10. knowing   (sciēns, sciendus, scītūrus)

D. Translate into English.

1. conveniēns   --

2. factūrus   --

3. dictus   --

4. nūntiandus   --

5. mānsūra   --

6. pulsum   --

7. laudanda   --

8. territus   --

9. nāvigāns   --

10. agenda   --

MASTERY VERB DRILL SHEET

This Verb Drill Sheet of twenty sentences can be used with any regular verb studied. Complete each Latin sentence with the correct form of the verb selected.

1. They are _____ -ing.   _____ .
2. Will you _____ ?   _____ tū?
3. Have you _____ ?   _____ vōs?
4. I shall _____ .   _____ .
5. He has been _____ .   _____ .
6. We were _____ -ing.   _____ .
7. Who _____ before?   Quis _____ anteā?
8. They had not _____ .   _____ .
9. He will have _____ .   _____ .
10. Were you being _____ ?   _____ tū?
11. We are not _____ .   _____ .
12. She has _____ .   _____ .
13. Who will _____ ?   Quī _____ ?
14. You had been _____ .   Vōs _____ .
15. I shall not be _____ .   _____ .
16. They will have been _____ .   _____ .
17. My friends were not _____ -ing.   Meī amīcī _____ .
18. Calpurnia used to _____ .   Calpurnia _____ .
19. Why have we been _____ ?   Cūr _____ ?
20. Does he _____ ?   _____ ?

The Olive

Because of the many uses of its oil, the olive was the most valuable fruit in ancient Rome. Olive oil took the place of butter in the diet and soap in the bath. It was also used for preparing food, for fuel in lamps, for cleaning purposes, for anointing the body, and for producing perfumes and cosmetics of every kind.

Unit IV—Nouns

Lesson 30—NOMINATIVE AND ACCUSATIVE CASE OF THE FIRST AND SECOND DECLENSIONS

	FIRST DECLENSION		SECOND DECLENSION	
	SINGULAR	PLURAL	SINGULAR	PLURAL
Nom.	port*a*	port*ae*	amīc*us*	amīc*ī*
Acc.	port*am*	port*ās*	amīc*um*	amīc*ōs*

Note

1. Nouns of the first and second declensions have the following endings:

	FIRST DECLENSION		SECOND DECLENSION	
Nom.	-a	-ae	-us	-ī
Acc.	-am	-ās	-um	-ōs

2. Nouns of the first declension are feminine unless they denote males. Thus, **puella** (girl) and **porta** (gate) are feminine, but **agricola** (farmer) is masculine.

3. Nouns of the second declension ending in **-us** are masculine.

4. The nominative case is used principally as *subject*, the accusative as *direct object* of a verb.

COMMON NOUNS OF THE FIRST DECLENSION

FEMININE

amīcitia, friendship
aqua, water
causa, reason
cōpia, supply
dīligentia, care, diligence
fēmina, woman
fīlia, daughter
fortūna, fortune
fuga, flight
grātia, gratitude, favor
hōra, hour
iniūria, wrong

inopia, lack
īnsula, island
lingua, tongue
lūna, moon
memoria, memory
nātūra, nature
patria, country
pecūnia, money
poena, punishment
porta, gate
prōvincia, province
puella, girl

pugna, battle
rēgīna, queen
rīpa, shore
sagitta, arrow
silva, forest
terra, land
toga, toga
tuba, trumpet
via, road
victōria, victory
vīlla, farmhouse
vīta, life

MASCULINE

agricola, farmer

nauta, sailor

poēta, poet

COMMON NOUNS OF THE SECOND DECLENSION

MASCULINE (-us)

amīcus, friend
animus, mind
annus, year
barbarus, foreigner, native
campus, plain
deus, god

dominus, master
equus, horse
fīlius, son
gladius, sword
līberī (*pl.*), children
locus, place

modus, manner
numerus, number
populus, people
servus, slave
socius, ally

Note

The word **populus** (people) is a collective noun and takes a singular verb. The plural form of **populus** is seldom used.

Populus **dēfenditur**.   The people *are* defended.

EXERCISES

A. Change the following singular forms to the plural:

1. numerus _____
2. pugnam _____
3. hōra _____
4. servum _____
5. fīlius _____

6. iniūriam _____
7. victōria _____
8. socium _____
9. deus _____
10. nautam _____

B. Draw a line through the form that does *not* belong with the others in each group.

1. gladium, fugam, barbarus, campus
2. tuba, locus, annum, fortūna
3. via, animum, poenam, populum
4. equōs, rīpae, dominus, īnsulās
5. vīta, poēta, prōvincia, puella

6. amīcī, linguae, vīllam, fīliōs
7. modī, silvae, locum, cōpia
8. fēminās, līberōs, gladium, vīta
9. equum, animōs, patria, lūna
10. socius, togās, portae, inopiam

C. Write the following specified forms:

1. nominative plural: *campus, causa, gladius*

_____

2. accusative singular: *agricola, annus, iniūria*

_____

3. accusative plural: *līberī, grātia*

_____

4. nominative singular: *poētās, barbarī*

_____

D. Identify the case and number of the following forms:

1. numerum _____
2. fuga _____
3. agricolās _____
4. locus _____
5. dominōs _____

6. tubae _____
7. prōvinciam _____
8. servī _____
9. populum _____
10. poenās _____

73

Lesson 31—GENITIVE, DATIVE, AND ABLATIVE OF THE FIRST AND SECOND DECLENSIONS

FIRST DECLENSION

	SINGULAR	PLURAL
Gen.	portae	portārum
Dat.	portae	portīs
Abl.	portā	portīs

SECOND DECLENSION

	SINGULAR	PLURAL
Gen.	amīcī	amīcōrum
Dat.	amīcō	amīcīs
Abl.	amīcō	amīcīs

Note

1. Nouns of the first declension have the following endings:

	SINGULAR	PLURAL
Gen.	-ae	-ārum
Dat.	-ae	-īs
Abl.	-ā	-īs

2. The ending **-ae** is the same for the genitive singular, the dative singular, and the nominative plural. The ending **-īs** is the same for the dative and ablative plural.

3. The ablative singular is distinguished from the nominative singular by a long mark, or *macron*, over the **ā**.

4. Nouns of the second declension have the following endings:

	SINGULAR	PLURAL
Gen.	-ī	-ōrum
Dat.	-ō	-īs
Abl.	-ō	-īs

5. The ending **-ī** is the same for the genitive singular and nominative plural. However, nouns ending in **-ius** generally have one i in the gentive singular. Thus, the genitive singular of **fīlius** is **fīlī**, and the nominative plural is **fīliī**.

6. The endings for the dative and ablative are the same: **-ō** in the singular and **-īs** in the plural.

7. The ending **-īs** in the dative and ablative plural is the same for both the first and second declensions.

8. The genitive is used principally to show possession (*of*, *'s*), the dative for the indirect object, and the ablative with the prepositions *from, by, with, at, in, on.*

EXERCISES

A. Identify the case and number of the following forms:

1. linguārum _____

2. populō _____

3. gladī _____

4. puellae _____

5. memoriā _____

6. deōrum _____

7. rīpīs _____

8. equī _____

9. dīligentiā _____

10. sociīs _____

74

B. Write the following specified forms:

1. dative plural: *rēgīna, socius* --

2. ablative singular: *locus, sagitta* --

3. genitive singular: *patria, annus* --

4. genitive plural: *aqua, equus* --

5. dative singular: *dominus, fēmina* --

C. Underline the correct form.

1. ablative singular: *puella, puellā, puellīs*

2. genitive plural: *deōrum, deīs, deī*

3. ablative plural: *servō, servōrum, servīs*

4. dative singular: *cōpiā, cōpiae, cōpiīs*

5. genitive singular: *socī, sociō, sociōrum*

D. Change the following singular forms to the plural:

1. īnsulā ------------------------------

2. locī ------------------------------

3. campō ------------------------------

4. fēminae ------------------------------

5. poenā ------------------------------

6. gladiō ------------------------------

7. poētae ------------------------------

8. fīlī ------------------------------

9. victōriā ------------------------------

10. modō ------------------------------

The Appian Way

Perhaps the most famous road in antiquity was the Appian Way, the "Rēgīna Viārum" (Queen of Roads). Begun in the fourth century B.C., it ultimately extended from Rome to Brundisium, 350 miles to the south. The road was constructed of immense blocks of stone laid with such perfect exactness that it is still used after 2,000 years of traffic.

Lesson 32—-ER, -IR, AND NEUTER NOUNS OF THE SECOND DECLENSION

	SINGULAR	PLURAL		SINGULAR	PLURAL
Nom.	puer	puerī		ager	agrī
Gen.	puerī	puerōrum		agrī	agrōrum
Dat.	puerō	puerīs		agrō	agrīs
Acc.	puerum	puerōs		agrum	agrōs
Abl.	puerō	puerīs		agrō	agrīs
Nom.	vir	virī		signum	signa
Gen.	virī	virōrum		signī	signōrum
Dat.	virō	virīs		signō	signīs
Acc.	virum	virōs		signum	signa
Abl.	virō	virīs		signō	signīs

Note

1. Nouns ending in **-er** or **-ir** should be regarded as if they originally had an ending **-us** in the nominative singular. Like nouns ending in **-us**, they are masculine.

2. The base of a noun is found by dropping the ending of the *genitive singular*. Thus, the base of **puer** is **puer-**, but the base of **ager** is **agr-**.

3. Nouns ending in **-um** are neuter and differ from masculine nouns in three cases only. In the nominative singular they end in **-um**, and in the nominative and accusative plural they end in **-a.**

4. Nouns ending in **-ium** generally have one i in the genitive singular.

COMMON NOUNS OF THE SECOND DECLENSION

MASCULINE (-er, -ir)

ager, agrī, field

liber, librī, book

magister (-trī), teacher

puer, boy

vir, man

NEUTER (-um)

arma (*pl.*), arms

auxilium, help

bellum, war

beneficium, kindness

castra (*pl.*), camp

cōnsilium, plan

factum, deed, act

forum, forum

frūmentum, grain

imperium, command

negōtium, task

oppidum, town

perīculum, danger

praemium, reward

praesidium, protection

proelium, battle

rēgnum, kingdom

signum, signal

spatium, space

verbum, word

Note

1. The word **castra** (camp) is used practically always in the plural and requires a plural verb. The singular form **castrum** (fort) is rarely used.

Castra **sunt** in Galliā.　　　　　　　There *is* a camp in Gaul.

2. The masculine noun **locus** is, by exception, neuter in the plural: **locus,** place; **loca,** places.

3. Distinguish between the following nouns: **līberī,** children; **librī,** books.

A. Change the following singular forms to the plural:

1. virī ....
2. rēgnum ....
3. librō ....
4. magister ....
5. proeliō ....

6. auxilium ....
7. perīculī ....
8. puer ....
9. verbum ....
10. praemiō ....

B. Underline the correct form.

1. ablative plural: *arma, armōrum, armīs*
2. accusative singular: *librum, librōs, liber*
3. dative singular: *agrīs, agrō, agrī*
4. nominative plural: *oppidī, oppidum, oppida*
5. genitive plural: *castrōrum, castrīs, castra*
6. ablative singular: *forī, forō, forīs*
7. accusative plural: *negōtia, negōtium, negōtiīs*
8. genitive singular: *virōrum, virō, virī*
9. dative plural: *bellīs, bellō, bella*
10. nominative singular: *magistrum, magistrī, magister*

C. Write the following specified forms:

1. accusative plural: *liber, spatium* ....
2. ablative singular: *ager, puer* ....
3. genitive singular: *vir, cōnsilium* ....
4. dative singular: *beneficium, magister* ....
5. nominative plural: *praemium, liber* ....

D. Identify the case and number of the following forms:

1. praesidium ....
2. virō ....
3. facta ....
4. signīs ....
5. magister ....

6. rēgnī ....
7. puerōrum ....
8. agrī ....
9. librōs ....
10. auxilia ....

Lesson 33—VOCATIVE CASE; ENDINGS OF THE FIRST AND SECOND DECLENSIONS

The *vocative* case, used to address a person, has the same form as the nominative, with the following exceptions: second declension nouns ending in **-us** form the vocative singular by changing **-us** to **-e**, while nouns ending in **-ius** change **-ius** to **-ī**.

NOMINATIVE	VOCATIVE
puella	puella
puellae	puellae
puer	puer
puerī	puerī

But

Mārcus	Mārce
fīlius	fīlī

Note

Unless used for special emphasis, the vocative never stands first in a sentence.

Scrībe, **Mārce**, cum dīligentiā.	Write carefully, Marcus.
Suntne equī parātī, **servī?**	Slaves, are the horses ready?

ENDINGS OF THE FIRST AND SECOND DECLENSIONS

	FIRST DECLENSION		SECOND DECLENSION			
			MASCULINE		NEUTER	
	SINGULAR	PLURAL	SINGULAR	PLURAL	SINGULAR	PLURAL
Nom.	-a	-ae	-us (-er, -ir)	-ī	-um	-a
Gen.	-ae	-ārum	-ī	-ōrum	-ī	-ōrum
Dat.	-ae	-īs	-ō	-īs	-ō	-īs
Acc.	-am	-ās	-um	-ōs	-um	-a
Abl.	-ā	-īs	-ō	-īs	-ō	-īs

Note

1. Observe the similarity in the endings of the two declensions:

	FIRST DECLENSION	SECOND DECLENSION
accusative singular:	**-am**	**-um**
accusative plural:	**-ās**	**-ōs**
genitive plural:	**-ārum**	**-ōrum**
dative and ablative plural:	**-īs**	**-īs**

2. Do not confuse a neuter plural noun in the nominative or accusative, such as **arma** or **oppida**, with a feminine singular noun in the nominative, such as **causa** or **vīta**.

EXERCISES

A. Translate the English noun to the Latin vocative.

1. Quid agis, *daughter?* ------------------------------

2. *Master*, līberā servōs. ------------------------------

3. Venī nunc, *boy*.

4. *Women*, petite pācem.

5. Mūnīte castra, *men*.

6. Pugnā bene, *ally*.

7. Cūr permovēminī, *friends?*

8. Portā aquam, *slave*.

9. Audīsne tubam, *teacher?*

10. Quis cēpit togam, *children?*

B. Draw a line through the case that does *not* belong with the others in each group.

1. poenam, sociōs, terrārum, praesidium

2. locīs, hōrās, fīliīs, poētīs

3. magistrī, puellae, arma, nautam

4. viam, silva, proelia, gladiōs

5. servī, deō, rēgīnae, rēgnō

6. vir, līberī, signa, agricolā

7. poenā, modō, puerōs, librīs

8. agrōrum, praesidium, fīliārum, vīllae

9. inopiae, campī, perīculī, annō

10. equīs, lūnae, castra, animō

C. In the space before each noun in column *A*, write the letter of its form in column *B*.

Column A	Column B
_____ 1. proelia	*a.* accusative singular
_____ 2. fīlī	*b.* nominative singular
_____ 3. agrīs	*c.* vocative singular
_____ 4. linguārum	*d.* ablative singular
_____ 5. iniūria	*e.* dative or ablative singular
_____ 6. numerum	*f.* nominative or accusative plural
_____ 7. domine	*g.* accusative plural
_____ 8. virō	*h.* dative or ablative plural
_____ 9. sagittā	*i.* genitive plural
_____ 10. aquās	*j.* genitive singular

D. Write the following specified forms:

1. ablative plural: *silva, negōtium*

2. accusative singular: *ager, poena*

3. dative singular: *nauta, equus*

4. nominative plural: *bellum, liber*

5. genitive plural: *fīlia, vir* ....

6. ablative singular: *magister, prōvincia* ....

7. vocative singular: *puer, servus* ....

8. genitive singular: *socius, cōpia* ....

9. accusative plural: *annus, forum* ....

10. dative plural: *poēta, fīlius* ....

E. Change the following singular forms to the plural:

1. spatium .... **6.** nautae ....

2. viam .... **7.** locus ....

3. socī .... **8.** lūnā ....

4. agrō .... **9.** liber ....

5. poena .... **10.** annum ....

F. Identify the case and number of the following forms:

1. dominō .... **11.** fīliārum ....

2. inopiā .... **12.** terrās ....

3. ager .... **13.** sociī ....

4. castra .... **14.** gladium ....

5. praemiīs .... **15.** silvae ....

6. serve .... **16.** līberōs ....

7. oppidōrum .... **17.** patriam ....

8. vīta .... **18.** amīcōrum ....

9. campus .... **19.** tubā ....

10. fīlī .... **20.** iniūriīs ....

Lesson 34—THIRD DECLENSION NOUNS, MASCULINE AND FEMININE

CONSONANT STEMS

	SINGULAR	PLURAL		SINGULAR	PLURAL
Nom.	cōnsul	cōnsul**ēs**		mīles	mīlit**ēs**
Gen.	cōnsul**is**	cōnsul**um**		mīlit**is**	mīlit**um**
Dat.	cōnsul**ī**	cōnsul**ibus**		mīlit**ī**	mīlit**ibus**
Acc.	cōnsul**em**	cōnsul**ēs**		mīlit**em**	mīlit**ēs**
Abl.	cōnsul**e**	cōnsul**ibus**		mīlit**e**	mīlit**ibus**

I-STEMS

	SINGULAR	PLURAL		SINGULAR	PLURAL
Nom.	host**is**	host**ēs**		mōns	mont**ēs**
Gen.	host**is**	host**ium**		mont**is**	mont**ium**
Dat.	host**ī**	host**ibus**		mont**ī**	mont**ibus**
Acc.	host**em**	host**ēs**		mont**em**	mont**ēs**
Abl.	host**e**	host**ibus**		mont**e**	mont**ibus**

Note

1. The endings of third declension nouns are:

	SINGULAR	PLURAL
Nom.	—	**-ēs**
Gen.	**-is**	**-um(-ium)**
Dat.	**-ī**	**-ibus**
Acc.	**-em**	**-ēs**
Abl.	**-e**	**-ibus**

2. **I-stem** nouns end in **-ium** in the genitive plural, whereas consonant-stem nouns end in **-um**.

3. Most **i-stem** nouns end in **-is** as **cīvis** and **nāvis**; **-ns** as **mōns** and **pōns** and **-rs** as **mors** and **pars**.

4. The following nouns of the third declension are masculine:

   a. Those denoting males: **mīles** (soldier), **cōnsul** (consul).
   b. Abstract nouns ending in **-or**: **timor** (fear).
   c. Other nouns such as **collis** (hill), **mōns** (mountain), **pēs** (foot).

5. The following nouns are feminine:

   a. Those denoting females: **māter** (mother), **soror** (sister).
   b. Those ending in **-tās, -tūs, -tūdō, -iō, -ns, -rs,** and **-x**: **aestās** (summer), **virtūs** (courage), **altitūdō** (height), **condiciō** (terms), **mēns** (mind), **mors** (death), **lūx** (light).
   c. Other nouns such as **arbor** (tree), **nāvis** (ship), **hiems** (winter).

6. The *genitive* singular of a noun, not the nominative, gives the clue to the rest of the declension. Thus, **lūx, lūcis**; **rēx, rēgis**; **mēns, mentis**; **pater, patris**; **mīles, mīlitis**, etc.

COMMON NOUNS OF THE THIRD DECLENSION

(Those ending in **-ium** in the genitive plural are so indicated.)

MASCULINE

cīvis, cīvis (-ium), citizen
collis, collis (-ium), hill
cōnsul, cōnsulis, consul
dux, ducis, leader
eques, equitis, horseman
fīnis, fīnis (-ium), boundary;
  (pl.), territory
frāter, frātris, brother

homō, hominis, man
hostis, hostis (-ium), enemy
imperātor, imperātōris, general
mēnsis, mēnsis (-ium), month
mīles, mīlitis, soldier
mōns, montis (-ium), mountain
ōrdō, ōrdinis, order
pater, patris, father

pēs, pedis, foot
pōns, pontis (-ium), bridge
prīnceps, prīncipis, chief
rēx, rēgis, king
sōl, sōlis, sun
timor, timōris, fear
victor, victōris, conqueror

FEMININE

aestās, aestātis, summer
altitūdō, altitūdinis, height, depth
arbor, arboris, tree
auctōritās, auctōritātis, influence
celeritās, celeritātis, speed
cīvitās, cīvitātis, state, citizenship
condiciō, condiciōnis, agreement,
  terms
cōnsuētūdō, cōnsuētūdinis, custom
cupiditās, cupiditātis, desire
difficultās, difficultātis, difficulty

facultās, facultātis, opportunity
hiems, hiemis, winter
lātitūdō, lātitūdinis, width
lēx, lēgis, law
lībertās, lībertātis, freedom
lūx, lūcis, light
magnitūdō, magnitūdinis, size
māter, mātris, mother
mēns, mentis (-ium), mind
mors, mortis (-ium), death
multitūdō, multitūdinis, crowd

nāvis, nāvis (-ium), ship
nox, noctis (-ium), night
ōrātiō, ōrātiōnis, speech
pars, partis (-ium), part
pāx, pācis, peace
potestās, potestātis, power
ratiō, ratiōnis, plan
soror, sorōris, sister
urbs, urbis (-ium), city
virtūs, virtūtis, courage
vōx, vōcis, voice

EXERCISES

A. Identify the case and number of the following forms:

1. urbem ------------------------
2. vōcis ------------------------
3. imperātōrī ------------------------
4. equitēs ------------------------
5. prīncipum ------------------------

6. homō ------------------------
7. montium ------------------------
8. lībertāte ------------------------
9. rēgibus ------------------------
10. cōnsulis ------------------------

B. Draw a line through the form that does *not* belong with the others in each group.

1. potestātem, nāvem, pedum, partem
2. victōre, frātrī, hieme, cōnsuētūdine
3. patrēs, ducēs, noctēs, difficultātis
4. timor, ōrdinis, lūcēs, ratiōne
5. facultātem, urbium, mīlitum, fīnium
6. rēgī, pācis, collibus, arboribus
7. ōrātiōnem, sōlem, sorōrem, virtūtem
8. mentēs, aestātum, cīvibus, hostis
9. cupiditās, mēnsis, homō, pēs
10. lātitūdō, vōcēs, prīnceps, equitibus

C. Write the following specified forms:

1. ablative singular and plural: *lēx* _____

2. genitive singular and plural: *frāter* _____

3. dative singular: *soror, prīnceps* _____

4. nominative plural: *ōrātiō, nox* _____

5. accusative singular: *ōrdō, auctōritās* _____

D. Change the following singular forms to the plural:

1. duce _____   6. hostī _____

2. urbs _____   7. mīles _____

3. lūcis _____   8. partem _____

4. hominī _____   9. cōnsulis _____

5. facultātem _____   10. condiciōne _____

E. Underline the correct form.

1. genitive singular: *cīvitātum, cīvitātis, cīvitās*

2. accusative plural: *lēgis, lēgem, lēgēs*

3. nominative plural: *nāvēs, nāvis, nāvibus*

4. ablative singular: *patrī, patribus, patre*

5. dative singular: *virtūtī, virtūte, virtūtem*

6. genitive plural: *partium, partem, partis*

7. ablative plural: *rēgēs, rēgibus, rēgis*

8. accusative singular: *eques, equitēs, equitem*

9. dative plural: *hostēs, hostium, hostibus*

10. nominative singular: *hiemēs, hiems, hiemis*

Lesson 35—THIRD DECLENSION NOUNS, NEUTER

CONSONANT STEMS

	SINGULAR	PLURAL		SINGULAR	PLURAL
Nom.	flūmen	flūmin*a*		iter	itiner*a*
Gen.	flūmin*is*	flūmin*um*		itiner*is*	itiner*um*
Dat.	flūmin*ī*	flūmin*ibus*		itiner*ī*	itiner*ibus*
Acc.	flūmen	flūmin*a*		iter	itiner*a*
Abl.	flūmin*e*	flūmin*ibus*		itiner*e*	itiner*ibus*

I-STEM

	SINGULAR	PLURAL
Nom.	mar*e*	mar*ia*
Gen.	mar*is*	mar*ium*
Dat.	mar*ī*	mar*ibus*
Acc.	mar*e*	mar*ia*
Abl.	mar*ī*	mar*ibus*

Note

1. Neuter nouns of the third declension have the same forms for the nominative and accusative. In the plural, these forms always end in **-a.**

2. Neuter **i**-stem nouns differ from neuter consonant stems in the ablative singular, which ends in **-ī**; in the genitive plural, which ends in **-ium**; and in the nominative and accusative plural, which end in **-ia.**

3. Neuter nouns of the third declension ending in **-us,** as **corpus** and **vulnus,** should not be confused with masculine nouns of the second declension ending in **-us,** as **servus** and **equus.** The genitive singular gives the clue to the declension.

	NOMINATIVE	GENITIVE
THIRD	corpus	corp**oris**
DECLENSION	vulnus	vuln**eris**

But

SECOND	equus	equ**ī**
DECLENSION	servus	serv**ī**

COMMON NEUTER NOUNS OF THE THIRD DECLENSION

caput, capitis, head
corpus, corporis, body
flūmen, flūminis, river
genus, generis, kind

iter, itineris, march
iūs, iūris, right
mare, maris (-ium), sea

nōmen, nōminis, name
tempus, temporis, time
vulnus, vulneris, wound

EXERCISES

A. Write the following specified forms:

1. ablative plural: *nōmen* ------------------------------

2. dative singular: *caput* ------------------------------

3. genitive plural: *genus* ....

4. accusative singular: *iter* ....

5. nominative plural: *iūs* ....

6. ablative singular: *tempus* ....

7. dative plural: *flūmen* ....

8. accusative plural: *vulnus* ....

9. genitive singular: *corpus* ....

10. ablative singular: *mare* ....

B. Identify the case and number of the following forms:

1. capitis .... 6. itinerum ....

2. vulnus .... 7. maria ....

3. nōmina .... 8. iūre ....

4. generibus .... 9. flūmen ....

5. corporī .... 10. temporibus ....

C. Change the following singular forms to the plural:

1. generis .... 6. corporis ....

2. iūs .... 7. vulnerī ....

3. capitī .... 8. mare ....

4. itinere .... 9. nōmine ....

5. tempus .... 10. flūmen ....

Masks

Masks served two very important purposes on the Roman stage. First, they enabled the actors to play many different characters in a single play. Secondly, the peculiar formation of the mask with its wide-open mouth amplified the actor's voice, which would otherwise hardly be heard in a large open-air theater. Occasionally, modern authors like Eugene O'Neill have employed the mask to indicate a dual personality in a character.

Lesson 36—REVIEW OF THIRD DECLENSION NOUNS

ENDINGS OF THE THIRD DECLENSION

	MASCULINE AND FEMININE		NEUTER	
	SINGULAR	PLURAL	SINGULAR	PLURAL
Nom.	—	-ēs	—	-a(-ia)
Gen.	-is	-um(-ium)	-is	-um(-ium)
Dat.	-ī	-ibus	-ī	-ibus
Acc.	-em	-ēs	—	-a(-ia)
Abl.	-e	-ibus	-e(-ī)	-ibus

Note

1. All nouns of the third declension have the same endings in the plural for the nominative and accusative (**-ēs, -a,** or **-ia**), and for the dative and ablative (**-ibus**).

2. Since the base of third declension nouns often differs in spelling from the nominative, the following hint in determining the base will be found useful. Think of an English derivative from the Latin noun. This will often give a clue to the base.

NOMINATIVE	ENGLISH DERIVATIVE	LATIN BASE
caput	*capit*al	**capit-**
corpus	*corpor*al	**corpor-**
genus	*gener*al	**gener-**
iter	*itiner*ary	**itiner-**
iūs	*iūr*y	**iūr-**
lēx	*lēg*al	**lēg-**
lūx	*lūc*id	**lūc-**
mēns	*ment*al	**ment-**
mīles	*mīlit*ary	**mīlit-**
mors	*mort*al	**mort-**
nōmen	*nōmin*ate	**nōmin-**
nox	*noct*urnal	**noct-**
ōrdō	*ōrdin*ary	**ōrdin-**
pāx	*pāc*ify	**pāc-**
pēs	*ped*al	**ped-**
prīnceps	*prīncip*al	**prīncip-**
rēx	*rēg*al	**rēg-**
tempus	*tempor*ary	**tempor-**
vōx	*vōc*al	**vōc-**
vulnus	*vulner*able	**vulner-**

EXERCISES

A. Write the following specified forms:

1. genitive singular: *eques, tempus* _____

2. accusative plural: *iūs, cīvitās* _____

3. ablative singular: *condiciō, mare* _____

4. dative plural: *genus, mēns* _____

5. nominative plural: *collis, iter* _____

6. ablative plural: *corpus, arbor* ....

7. genitive plural: *fīnis, caput* ....

8. accusative singular: *nōmen, ratiō* ....

9. dative singular: *imperātor, flūmen* ....

10. nominative singular: *vulnera, urbium* ....

B. In the space before each noun in column *A*, write the letter of its form in column *B*.

Column A	Column B
_____ **1.** sorōrem	*a.* dative or ablative plural
_____ **2.** itineris	*b.* nominative singular
_____ **3.** mātribus	*c.* genitive plural
_____ **4.** vulnere	*d.* nominative or accusative singular
_____ **5.** nāvium	*e.* dative singular
_____ **6.** prīnceps	*f.* accusative singular
_____ **7.** caput	*g.* dative or ablative singular
_____ **8.** multitūdinī	*h.* nominative or accusative plural
_____ **9.** genera	*i.* genitive singular
_____ **10.** marī	*j.* ablative singular

C. Identify the case and number of the following forms:

1. cupiditātem _____   **6.** flūmina _____

2. itinere _____   **7.** hominī _____

3. timōris _____   **8.** caput _____

4. frātrum _____   **9.** victōrēs _____

5. temporibus _____   **10.** montium _____

D. Underline the correct form.

1. accusative singular: *homō, hominem, hominum*   **6.** dative singular: *sorōribus, sorōre, sorōrī*

2. genitive plural: *hostium, hostis, hostem*   **7.** accusative plural: *tempus, tempora, temporum*

3. ablative plural: *vulnere, vulneris, vulneribus*   **8.** genitive singular: *potestātis, potestātum, potestātī*

4. nominative plural: *mentēs, mentium, mentibus*   **9.** dative plural: *fīnis, fīnī, fīnibus*

5. ablative singular: *itineribus, itinere, itinera*   **10.** nominative singular: *corpus, corpora, corporis*

E. Change the following singular forms to the plural:

1. arbore _____   **6.** vōcem _____

2. mare _____   **7.** pede _____

3. ōrdō _____   **8.** nōminis _____

4. equitī _____   **9.** caput _____

5. itineris _____   **10.** aestātem _____

Lesson 37—FOURTH DECLENSION NOUNS

	MASCULINE		NEUTER	
	SINGULAR	PLURAL	SINGULAR	PLURAL
Nom.	exercit*us*	exercit*ūs*	corn*ū*	corn*ua*
Gen.	exercit*ūs*	exercit*uum*	corn*ūs*	corn*uum*
Dat.	exercit*uī*	exercit*ibus*	corn*ū*	corn*ibus*
Acc.	exercit*um*	exercit*ūs*	corn*ū*	corn*ua*
Abl.	exercit*ū*	exercit*ibus*	corn*ū*	corn*ibus*

Note

1. Nouns of the fourth declension have the following endings:

	MASCULINE AND FEMININE		NEUTER	
	SINGULAR	PLURAL	SINGULAR	PLURAL
Nom.	-us	-ūs	-ū	-ua
Gen.	-ūs	-uum	-ūs	-uum
Dat.	-uī	-ibus	-ū	-ibus
Acc.	-um	-ūs	-ū	-ua
Abl.	-ū	-ibus	-ū	-ibus

2. The ending of the genitive singular determines to which declension a noun belongs.

NOMINATIVE	GENITIVE	DECLENSION
exercitus	exercit*ūs*	fourth
tempus	tempor*is*	third
dominus	domin*ī*	second

3. As in the second and third declensions, neuter nouns of the fourth declension have the same forms for the nominative and accusative. The plural of these forms ends in **-ua.**

4. Long marks are important in fourth declension endings. Thus, **-us** indicates nominative singular, but **-ūs** is either genitive singular or nominative or accusative plural.

5. With the exception of the genitive singular, which must end in **-ūs,** fourth declension neuter nouns have the same ending, **-ū,** in the rest of the singular.

6. Nouns of the fourth declension ending in **-us** are masculine. Feminine by exception are **domus** (home) and **manus** (hand). Neuters end in **-ū.**

COMMON NOUNS OF THE FOURTH DECLENSION

MASCULINE	FEMININE	NEUTER
adventus, arrival	**domus,** home	**cornū,** horn, wing
equitātus, cavalry	**manus,** hand	
exercitus, army		
passus, pace, step		
senātus, senate		

Note

Domus is sometimes declined as a second declension noun.

EXERCISES

A. Identify the case and number of the following forms:

1. equitātum   _____   6. domus   _____

2. cornūs   _____   7. adventū   _____

3. senātuī   _____   8. passūs   _____

4. manuum   _____   9. cornua   _____

5. exercitibus   _____   10. exercituī   _____

B. Underline the correct form.

1. accusative singular: *adventuum, adventum, adventūs*

2. genitive singular: *domūs, domus, domuum*

3. nominative plural: *cornū, cornuum, cornua*

4. ablative plural: *manū, manūs, manibus*

5. dative singular: *equitātūs, equitātuī, equitātibus*

C. Write the following specified forms:

1. accusative plural: *passus, cornū*   _____

2. ablative singular: *senātus, equitātus*   _____

3. dative plural: *exercitus, domus*   _____

4. accusative singular: *cornū, manus*   _____

5. genitive singular: *adventus, cornū*   _____

D. Change the following singular forms to the plural:

1. domum   _____

2. exercitus   _____

3. cornūs   _____

4. equitātū   _____

5. senātuī   _____

89

Lesson 38—FIFTH DECLENSION NOUNS

	SINGULAR	PLURAL	SINGULAR	PLURAL
Nom.	rēs	rēs	diēs	diēs
Gen.	reī	rērum	diēī	diērum
Dat.	reī	rēbus	diēī	diēbus
Acc.	rem	rēs	diem	diēs
Abl.	rē	rēbus	diē	diēbus

Note

1. Nouns of the fifth declension have the following endings:

	SINGULAR	PLURAL
Nom.	-ēs	-ēs
Gen.	-eī	-ērum
Dat.	-eī	-ēbus
Acc.	-em	-ēs
Abl.	-ē	-ēbus

2. An **e** appears in the ending of every case without exception.

3. The nominative singular, nominative plural, and accusative plural have the same ending: **-ēs.**

4. Nouns of the fifth declension are feminine. However, **diēs** (day) is masculine, except for the expression **cōnstitūtā diē** (on a set day).

COMMON NOUNS OF THE FIFTH DECLENSION

FEMININE	MASCULINE
aciēs, battle line	**diēs,** day
fidēs, faith	**merīdiēs,** noon
rēs, thing	
spēs, hope	

EXERCISES

A. Write the following specified forms:

1. dative singular and plural: *aciēs* _____

2. accusative singular and plural: *spēs* _____

3. genitive singular and plural: *rēs* _____

4. ablative singular: *merīdiēs, fidēs* _____

5. nominative plural: *diēs, aciēs* _____

B. Identify the case and number of the following forms:

1. rem _____   6. diē _____

2. merīdiēs _____   7. rēbus _____

3. spēbus _____   8. aciem _____

4. aciērum _____   9. spēs _____

5. fideī _____   10. diērum _____

C. Underline the correct form.

1. accusative singular: *spēs, spem, spērum*

2. ablative plural: *rēbus, rē, rēs*

3. genitive plural: *aciem, aciēī, aciērum*

4. ablative singular: *merīdiem, merīdiē, merīdiēī*

5. dative singular: *fideī, fidē, fidēs*

The Colosseum

Built in the first century A.D., the Colosseum is still one of the most impressive structures of the ancient world. It was used primarily for gladiatorial combats. Today in the United States, we witness football games in arenas modeled after the Colosseum, such as the Yale Bowl and the Rose Bowl.

Lesson 39—REVIEW OF THE FIVE DECLENSIONS

COMPARISON OF NOUN ENDINGS

SINGULAR							
	1st Decl.	*2nd Decl.*		*3rd Decl.*		*4th Decl.*	*5th Decl.*
	(f.)	(m.)	(n.)	(m. & f.)	(n.)	(m.) (n.)	(f.)
Nom.	a	us(er,ir)	um	—	—	us ū	ēs
Gen.	ae	ī	ī	is	is	ūs ūs	eī
Dat.	ae	ō	ō	ī	ī	uī ū	eī
Acc.	am	um	um	em	—	um ū	em
Abl.	ā	ō	ō	e	e(ī)	ū ū	ē

PLURAL							
	(f.)	(m.)	(n.)	(m. & f.)	(n.)	(m.) (n.)	(f.)
Nom.	ae	ī	a	ēs	a(ia)	ūs ua	ēs
Gen.	ārum	ōrum	ōrum	um(ium)	um(ium)	uum uum	ērum
Dat.	īs	īs	īs	ibus	ibus	ibus ibus	ēbus
Acc.	ās	ōs	a	ēs	a(ia)	ūs ua	ēs
Abl.	īs	īs	īs	ibus	ibus	ibus ibus	ēbus

Note

1. Observe the similarity in the endings of the five declensions.

	1ST	2ND	3RD	4TH	5TH
accusative singular:	-am	-um	-em	-um	-em
accusative plural:	-ās	-ōs	-ēs	-ūs	-ēs
genitive plural:	-ārum	-ōrum	-um(-ium)	-uum	-ērum

2. The endings of the dative and ablative plural in each declension are identical. Note also the similarity in the five declensions.

1ST	2ND	3RD	4TH	5TH
-īs	-īs	-ibus	-ibus	-ēbus

3. All neuter nouns, regardless of declension, have the same form for the accusative as the nominative. In the plural, these cases always end in **-a**.

4. Unless one knows the declension to which a particular noun belongs, errors can result. Note the following possibilities of error because of similarity of endings:

FORM	IDENTIFICATION
port*a*	nom. sing. fem. 1st declension
bell*a*	nom. or acc. pl. neuter 2nd declension
vulner*a*	nom. or acc. pl. neuter 3rd declension
serv*us*	nom. sing. masc. 2nd declension
corp*us*	nom. or acc. sing. neuter 3rd declension
man*us*	nom. sing. 4th declension
ag*er*	nom. sing. 2nd declension
pat*er*	nom. sing. 3rd declension

serv*ī*	gen. sing. or nom. pl. 2nd declension
cīv*ī*	dat. sing. 3rd declension
serv*um*	acc. sing. masc. 2nd declension
bell*um*	nom. or acc. sing. neuter 2nd declension
patr*um*	gen. pl. 3rd declension
exercit*um*	acc. sing. 4th declension
patr*em*	acc. sing. 3rd declension
di*em*	acc. sing. 5th declension
rēg*ēs*	nom. or acc. pl. 3rd declension
fid*ēs*	nom. sing. or pl. or acc. pl. 5th declension
aest*ās*	nom. sing. 3rd declension
puell*ās*	acc. pl. 1st declension
virt*ūs*	nom. sing. 3rd declension
pass*ūs*	gen. sing. or nom. or acc. pl. 4th declension
rati*ō*	nom. sing. 3rd declension
soci*ō*	dat. or abl. sing. 2nd declension

EXERCISES

A. Identify the case and number of the following forms:

1. cīvium _____
2. corpora _____
3. patris _____
4. morte _____
5. rēgem _____
6. mīlitibus _____
7. tempus _____
8. hominī _____
9. rēgēs _____
10. auctōritās _____

11. castra _____
12. cōpia _____
13. rērum _____
14. exercituum _____
15. virōs _____
16. aciē _____
17. equitātum _____
18. pugnā _____
19. capita _____
20. amīce _____

B. Change the following singular forms to the plural:

1. fīliam _____
2. oppidum _____
3. cōnsuētūdō _____
4. equitī _____
5. iter _____

6. ducis _____
7. manū _____
8. rē _____
9. gladiō _____
10. vulnus _____

C. Change the following plural forms to the singular:

1. victōriās _____
2. praemia _____
3. diērum _____
4. prīncipibus _____
5. fīliōs _____

6. noctēs _____
7. nāvibus _____
8. itinera _____
9. hominēs _____
10. manuum _____

93

D. Draw a line through the one noun in each group that is *not* in the same *case* as the others.

1. puellārum, mīlitis, passuum, oppidō, speī

2. diem, ducum, arma, partēs, cornū

3. cīvitās, corpus, itinera, senātum, altitūdō

4. lēgibus, servīs, exercituī, rēbus, prīncipis

5. mare, tempore, sociīs, terrā, aciēbus

E. Draw a line through the one noun in each group that is *not* in the same *number* as the others.

1. agricolae, equī, vōcum, mortis, iūra

2. spēs, genera, equitātum, flūmine, librō

3. cupiditās, cōpia, locī, capitis, castra

4. cornua, manūs, pedēs, vulnus, cīvium

5. pecūniā, puerīs, perīcula, rēgum, rēs

F. Write the following specified forms:

1. ablative singular: *iter* ------------------------------

2. ablative plural: *iniūria* ------------------------------

3. genitive plural: *vir* ------------------------------

4. accusative plural: *oppidum* ------------------------------

5. accusative singular: *aciēs* ------------------------------

6. ablative singular: *adventus* ------------------------------

7. dative plural: *hostis* ------------------------------

8. dative singular: *imperātor* ------------------------------

9. nominative plural: *corpus* ------------------------------

10. genitive singular: *virtūs* ------------------------------

11. accusative singular: *flūmen* ------------------------------

12. accusative singular: *liber* ------------------------------

13. nominative plural: *cīvitās* ------------------------------

14. dative plural: *mīles* ------------------------------

15. genitive plural: *passus* ------------------------------

16. accusative plural: *pēs* ------------------------------

17. ablative singular: *prōvincia* ------------------------------

18. ablative plural: *rēs* ------------------------------

19. nominative plural: *vulnus* ------------------------------

20. genitive singular: *homō* ------------------------------

G. Underline the correct form.

1. genitive plural: *speī, exercitūs, cīvium*

2. accusative singular: *corpus, fortūnās, lēgum*

3. ablative singular: *adventū, ōrātiō, mare*

94

4. nominative plural: *fuga, rēgna, imperātōrī*

5. dative singular: *imperī, manūs, multitūdinī*

6. ablative plural: *vulneris, cōpiīs, diēs*

7. genitive singular: *exercitūs, virtūs, barbarus*

8. accusative plural: *cīvitās, eques, prōvinciās*

9. dative plural: *prīncipis, partibus, equitātus*

10. nominative singular: *cōnsuētūdō, cōnsiliō, passūs*

H. In the space before each noun in column *A*, write the letter of its form in column *B*.

	Column A		*Column B*
-------	**1.** aciē	*a.*	genitive singular
-------	**2.** exercituum	*b.*	dative or ablative plural
-------	**3.** togam	*c.*	nominative singular
-------	**4.** perīculī	*d.*	genitive plural
-------	**5.** deōs	*e.*	nominative or accusative plural
-------	**6.** auctōritātī	*f.*	ablative singular
-------	**7.** rēbus	*g.*	vocative singular
-------	**8.** itinera	*h.*	dative singular
-------	**9.** amīce	*i.*	accusative plural
-------	**10.** lātitūdō	*j.*	accusative singular

95

Unit V—Adjectives, Numerals, and Adverbs

Lesson 40—FIRST AND SECOND DECLENSION ADJECTIVES

		SINGULAR			PLURAL	
	(m.)	(f.)	(n.)	(m.)	(f.)	(n.)
Nom.	altus	alta	altum	altī	altae	alta
Gen.	altī	altae	altī	altōrum	altārum	altōrum
Dat.	altō	altae	altō	altīs	altīs	altīs
Acc.	altum	altam	altum	altōs	altās	alta
Abl.	altō	altā	altō	altīs	altīs	altīs

Note

1. The masculine and neuter forms of the adjective are declined like second declension nouns; the feminine forms are declined like first declension nouns.

2. Some adjectives end in **-er** in the masculine nominative singular. Otherwise they are declined like **altus, -a, -um.** For example:

> **līber, lībera, līberum**
> **miser, misera, miserum**

3. Some adjectives ending in **-er** in the masculine nominative singular drop the **e** in all other forms. For example:

> **dexter, dextra, dextrum**
> **noster, nostra, nostrum**

4. An adjective agrees with its noun in gender, number, and case.

> **servus bonus**   **parvam puellam**   **hostibus malīs**

5. In agreeing with its noun, an adjective need not have the same ending as the noun, nor be in the same declension as the noun.

> **puer ēgregius**   **agricolās novōs**
> **multīs rēbus**   **flūmen altum**

6. An adjective usually follows its noun, but it may precede it for emphasis.

> **servus miser,** a wretched slave — gen. state
> **miser servus,** a *wretched* slave — his particular...

7. An adjective may be used alone when the noun it modifies is understood. If the adjective is in the masculine form, then supply a person or persons; if neuter, supply a thing or things.

Omnēs discessērunt.	Everybody left. (all men left)
Omnia scit.	He knows everything. (all things)
Multī aderant.	Many men were present.
Multa perfēcit.	He accomplished many things.

8. An adjective can often furnish a clue to the identification of a noun whose form is uncertain. Take, for example, the combination **mīlitēs multōs. Mīlitēs** in form may be either nominative or accusative plural. However, since **multōs,** which modifies **mīlitēs,** can be only accusative plural, **mīlitēs** must therefore also be accusative plural.

9. The formation of the vocative case of adjectives follows the same rule as for nouns. The vocative singular of **bonus,** for example, is **bone. Meus** has a special form, **mī.**

COMMON ADJECTIVES OF THE FIRST AND SECOND DECLENSIONS

(-us, -a, -um)

aequus, equal
altus, high, deep
amīcus, friendly
barbarus, foreign
bonus, good
certus, certain
cupidus, desirous
ēgregius, outstanding
fīnitimus, neighboring
idōneus, suitable
inimīcus, unfriendly

inīquus, unequal, unfavorable
lātus, wide
longus, long
magnus, great, large
malus, bad
maritimus, of the sea
meus, my
multus, much
necessārius, necessary
nōtus, known, famous

novus, new
parātus, ready
parvus, small
paucī (pl.), few
propinquus, near
pūblicus, public
reliquus, remaining
suus, his (her, their) own
timidus, fearful, timid
tuus, your (addressing one person)
vērus, true

(-er, -era, -erum)

līber, free
miser, wretched, poor

(-er, -ra, -rum)

dexter, right
noster, our
sinister, left
vester, your (addressing more than one person)

EXERCISES

A. In the space before each noun in column A, write the letter of its modifying adjective in column B.

Column A	Column B
------- 1. rīpam	a. paucīs
------- 2. caput	b. cupidōs
------- 3. cornū	c. aequōrum
------- 4. diēbus	d. parvum
------- 5. rēgēs	e. meus
------- 6. magister	f. novam
------- 7. domūs	g. multārum
------- 8. mēnsium	h. bone
------- 9. amīce	i. sinistrō
------- 10. rērum	j. tuae

B. Identify the case and number of the following forms:

1. multō _____
2. longārum _____
3. sinister _____
4. lātīs _____
5. vērōs _____

6. miserā _____
7. nōtī _____
8. altōrum _____
9. parvās _____
10. barbaram _____

C. Underline the correct form of the adjective.

1. genitive plural masculine: *altī, altōrum, altārum*

2. accusative singular feminine: *dextra, dextrum, dextram*

3. dative plural masculine: *līberīs, līberō, līberōs*

97

4. nominative plural neuter: *longī, longae, longa*

5. ablative singular feminine: *misera, miserā, miserō*

6. vocative singular masculine: *magnus, magne, magnī*

7. accusative plural masculine: *līberōs, līberās, līberī*

8. genitive singular feminine: *vērī, vērārum, vērae*

9. dative singular neuter: *pūblicīs, pūblicō, pūblicae*

10. ablative plural neuter: *vestrīs, vestrō, vestrōrum*

D. Make each adjective agree with its noun.

1. cōpiā—magnus   -

2. praemiīs—idōneus   -

3. mēns—ēgregius   -

4. lēgēs—bonus   -

5. virōrum—līber   -

6. equitī—miser   -

7. fidem—tuus   -

8. generis—noster   -

9. amīce—meus   -

10. exercitū—timidus   -

E. Underline the noun in parentheses with which the adjective agrees.

1. certum   (tempus, flūminum, puerōrum)

2. inimīcus   (locīs, homō, corpus)

3. necessāriīs (mīlitis, nautās, rēbus)

4. sinistrō   (cornū, ōrdō, aciem)

5. novā   (terra, potestāte, togae)

6. paucārum   (manuum, servōrum, mīlitum)

7. reliqua   (horā, vulnera, fortūnae)

8. ēgregī   (fīliī, cōnsulēs, hominis)

9. vestrās   (facultās, vōcēs, prōvinciae)

10. amīcae   (sorōrēs, tempora, līberī)

Lesson 41—THIRD DECLENSION ADJECTIVES

THREE ENDINGS

	SINGULAR			PLURAL		
	(m.)	*(f.)*	*(n.)*	*(m.)*	*(f.)*	*(n.)*
Nom.	celer	celer*is*	celer*e*	celer*ēs*	celer*ēs*	celer*ia*
Gen.	celer*is*	celer*is*	celer*is*	celer*ium*	celer*ium*	celer*ium*
Dat.	celer*ī*	celer*ī*	celer*ī*	celer*ibus*	celer*ibus*	celer*ibus*
Acc.	celer*em*	celer*em*	celer*e*	celer*ēs*	celer*ēs*	celer*ia*
Abl.	celer*ī*	celer*ī*	celer*ī*	celer*ibus*	celer*ibus*	celer*ibus*

TWO ENDINGS

	SINGULAR		PLURAL	
	(m. & f.)	*(n.)*	*(m. & f.)*	*(n.)*
Nom.	fort*is*	fort*e*	fort*ēs*	fort*ia*
Gen.	fort*is*	fort*is*	fort*ium*	fort*ium*
Dat.	fort*ī*	fort*ī*	fort*ibus*	fort*ibus*
Acc.	fort*em*	fort*e*	fort*ēs*	fort*ia*
Abl.	fort*ī*	fort*ī*	fort*ibus*	fort*ibus*

ONE ENDING

	SINGULAR		PLURAL	
	(m. & f.)	*(n.)*	*(m. & f.)*	*(n.)*
Nom.	pār	pār	par*ēs*	par*ia*
Gen.	par*is*	par*is*	par*ium*	par*ium*
Dat.	par*ī*	par*ī*	par*ibus*	par*ibus*
Acc.	par*em*	pār	par*ēs*	par*ia*
Abl.	par*ī*	par*ī*	par*ibus*	par*ibus*

Note

1. Third declension adjectives follow the general pattern of third declension i-stem nouns. Note particularly that the ablative singular ends in **-ī** and the genitive plural in **-ium**.

2. Some adjectives ending in **-er** in the masculine nominative singular drop the **-e** in all other forms.

ācer, ācris, ācre

3. Like neuter nouns, the accusative forms of neuter adjectives are always the same as the nominative. In the plural, these forms end in **-ia**.

COMMON ADJECTIVES OF THE THIRD DECLENSION

THREE ENDINGS

(-er, -ris, -re)	(-er, -eris, -ere)
ācer, sharp	**celer,** swift

TWO ENDINGS

brevis, short	**gravis,** heavy
commūnis, common	**levis,** light
difficilis, difficult	**nōbilis,** noble
facilis, easy	**omnis,** all
fortis, brave	**similis,** similar

ONE ENDING

pār, equal	***prūdēns,** wise
***potēns,** powerful	***recēns,** recent

*Base ends in **-ent.** For example: **potēns, potentis, potentī,** etc.

99

4. The present participle in Latin is declined like **potēns**. However, the ablative singular usually ends in **-e**. The plural is regular. For example:

SINGULAR

	(m. & f.)	(n.)
Nom.	portā**ns**	portā**ns**
Gen.	porta**ntis**	porta**ntis**
Dat.	porta**ntī**	porta**ntī**
Acc.	porta**ntem**	portā**ns**
Abl.	porta**nte**	porta**nte**

EXERCISES

A. Identify the case and number of the following forms:

1. ācrium   ----------------------------

2. celere   ----------------------------

3. similibus   ----------------------------

4. levia   ----------------------------

5. difficilem   ----------------------------

6. fortēs   ----------------------------

7. recentis   ----------------------------

8. omnī   ----------------------------

9. nōbilium   ----------------------------

10. grave   ----------------------------

B. Make each adjective agree with its noun.

1. fēminam—nōbilis   ----------------------------

2. imperiō—pār   ----------------------------

3. tempus—brevis   ----------------------------

4. ducum—fortis   ----------------------------

5. equīs—difficilis   ----------------------------

6. frātribus—prūdēns   ----------------------------

7. causīs—omnis   ----------------------------

8. equitēs—potēns   ----------------------------

9. pedibus—celer   ----------------------------

10. perīcula—commūnis   ----------------------------

C. Underline the correct form of the adjective.

1. accusative plural feminine: *gravis, gravēs, gravia*

2. ablative singular neuter: *omnī, omne, omnis*

3. nominative plural masculine: *levium, levis, levēs*

4. accusative singular neuter: *parem, pār, paria*

5. genitive plural feminine: *ācrium, ācris, ācrem*

6. dative singular masculine: *facilī, facilibus, facilis*

7. ablative plural neuter: *celerēs, celerī, celeribus*

8. genitive singular feminine: *recēns, recentis, recentium*

9. dative plural neuter: *fortibus, fortī, fortium*

10. nominative singular masculine: *potentis, potentēs, potēns*

D. Underline the noun in parentheses with which the adjective agrees.

1. celere   (flūmine, flūmen, flūminī)

2. nōbilium   (poētārum, magistrum, praesidium)

3. prūdentia   (fēmina, multitūdō, nōmina)

4. difficilibus   (viīs, equitātus, tempus)

5. brevem   (mēnsium, mēnsem, mēnsis)

6. omnēs   (pēs, cīvis, servī)

7. levī   (poenā, modī, manūs)

8. commūnis   (fortūnīs, fortūnae, fortūnās)

9. pār   (arborem, negōtium, rem)

10. potentibus   (exercitus, exercitūs, exercitibus)

E. Translate each English adjective into Latin, making it agree with its noun.

1. *easy*   negōtium   ------------------------

2. *swift*   equīs   ------------------------

3. *powerful*   sociōrum   ------------------------

4. *noble*   rēgī   ------------------------

5. *short*   tempore   ------------------------

6. *all*   diem   ------------------------

7. *equal*   cornua   ------------------------

8. *common*   inopiā   ------------------------

9. *sharp*   vulneris   ------------------------

10. *similar*   montēs   ------------------------

Wrestling

In the games of ancient Greece and Rome, wrestling occupied a very important place. Today, with the advent of television, wrestling has become popular as an exhibition rather than a sport.

Lesson 42—NUMERALS

	SINGULAR ONLY		
	(m.)	(f.)	(n.)
Nom.	ūnus	ūna	ūnum
Gen.	ūnīus	ūnīus	ūnīus
Dat.	ūnī	ūnī	ūnī
Acc.	ūnum	ūnam	ūnum
Abl.	ūnō	ūnā	ūnō

	PLURAL ONLY		
	(m.)	(f.)	(n.)
Nom.	duo	duae	duo
Gen.	duōrum	duārum	duōrum
Dat.	duōbus	duābus	duōbus
Acc.	duōs	duās	duo
Abl.	duōbus	duābus	duōbus

	PLURAL ONLY	
	(m. & f.)	(n.)
Nom.	trēs	tria
Gen.	trium	trium
Dat.	tribus	tribus
Acc.	trēs	tria
Abl.	tribus	tribus

	SINGULAR	PLURAL
Nom.	mīlle	mīlia
Gen.	mīlle	mīlium
Dat.	mīlle	mīlibus
Acc.	mīlle	mīlia
Abl.	mīlle	mīlibus

Note

1. **Ūnus, -a, -um** is declined like adjectives of the first and second declensions, except in the genitive singular where it ends in **-īus,** and in the dative singular where it ends in **-ī.**

2. All cardinal numbers from *four* to *one hundred* are indeclinable.

102

3. Numerals are really adjectives and as such agree with their nouns. However, **mīlia**, the plural of **mīlle**, is a neuter noun and is followed by a genitive.

> **mīlle servī**, a thousand slaves
> **tria mīlia servōrum**, three thousand slaves

4. Ordinal numbers are declined like **altus, -a, -um.**

CARDINAL NUMBERS

ūnus, one	**quīnque**, five	**decem**, ten
duo, two	**sex**, six	**vīgintī**, twenty
trēs, three	**septem**, seven	**centum**, one hundred
quattuor, four	**octō**, eight	**mīlle**, one thousand
	novem, nine	

ORDINAL NUMBERS

prīmus, first	**quārtus**, fourth	**octāvus**, eighth
secundus, second	**quīntus**, fifth	**nōnus**, ninth
tertius, third	**sextus**, sixth	**decimus**, tenth
	septimus, seventh	

EXERCISES

A. Identify the case and number of the following forms:

1. tribus _____
2. mīlia _____
3. decimō _____
4. ūnīus _____
5. duōrum _____

6. prīmī _____
7. trium _____
8. duās _____
9. ūnī _____
10. mīlibus _____

B. Make each numeral agree with its noun.

1. annō—quārtus _____
2. virī—mīlle _____
3. itineribus—trēs _____
4. mīlitum—duo _____
5. tempore—ūnus _____

6. victōriae—centum _____
7. aciem—tertius _____
8. hōrīs—quīnque _____
9. passūs—vīgintī _____
10. mēnse—secundus _____

C. Translate each English numeral into Latin, making it agree with its noun.

1. *ten*   mīlitēs   _____
2. *fifth*   diē   _____
3. *six*   pedum   _____
4. *three*   flūmina   _____
5. *first*   pugnam   _____
6. *one*   oppidī   _____
7. *two*   viīs   _____
8. *tenth*   partem   _____
9. *one thousand* hominibus   _____
10. *fourth*   tempus   _____

D. Underline the form of the numeral that agrees with its noun.

1. ōrātiōnem   (trēs, tertiam, tertia)
2. puerī   (mīlle, mīlia, mīlium)
3. diē   (decem, decimus, decimō)
4. fīliō   (ūnus, ūnīus, ūnī)
5. līberōs   (sextus, sextum, sex)
6. rēbus   (novem, nōnus, nōnī)
7. agricolās   (duōs, duās, duo)
8. signa   (trēs, tria, trium)
9. amīcōrum   (quārtum, quārtam, quattuor)
10. hōrā   (septima, septem, septimā)

Pont du Gard

This is the greatest of the Roman aqueducts, built in the first century A.D. near Nîmes, France. It is a tribute to the engineering genius of Rome that some of its highly developed water systems with their characteristic aqueducts are still in use today.

Lesson 43—REVIEW OF DECLENSION OF ADJECTIVES AND NUMERALS

A. Identify the case and number of the following forms:

1. equōs celerēs _____   11. cornū dextrō _____
2. mare nostrum _____   12. reliquīs diēbus _____
3. duābus viīs _____   13. vulnera gravia _____
4. rēgī potentī _____   14. tertius mēnsis _____
5. nautae omnēs _____   15. proeliīs ācribus _____
6. ratiō similis _____   16. tribus fīliīs _____
7. pācis longae _____   17. magnā celeritāte _____
8. nostram domum _____   18. mīles ēgregius _____
9. tempore idōneō _____   19. paucōs hominēs _____
10. decem urbium _____   20. nāvem longam _____

B. For each noun, write the proper form of **bonus.**

1. ōrātiō _____   6. tempora _____
2. itinere _____   7. condiciōnibus _____
3. exercituī _____   8. agricolam _____
4. diērum _____   9. līberōs _____
5. lēgis _____   10. nōmen _____

C. For each noun, write the proper form of **ācer.**

1. equīs _____   6. vulnus _____
2. vōx _____   7. ducem _____
3. proelium _____   8. magistrōs _____
4. equitātū _____   9. poenā _____
5. rērum _____   10. cōnsiliīs _____

D. In the space before each noun in column *A*, write the letter of its modifying adjective in column *B*.

	Column A	Column B
_____	1. bellum	*a.* nostrae
_____	2. itineribus	*b.* ācer
_____	3. cōnsuētūdinēs	*c.* sinistrā
_____	4. manū	*d.* parvī
_____	5. aciem	*e.* fortium
_____	6. capitis	*f.* breve
_____	7. equitī	*g.* reliquōs
_____	8. sociōrum	*h.* tertiam
_____	9. hostēs	*i.* miserō
_____	10. poēta	*j.* magnīs

E. Next to each of the following nouns are three adjectives. All of them agree with the noun except one. Make it agree.

1. *corpore:*   magnō, similī, tuī   ------------------------------

2. *fidem:*   multum, suam, commūnem   ------------------------------

3. *cōnsulum:*   duōrum, idōneum, nōbilium   ------------------------------

4. *diēbus:*   longus, multīs, vīgintī   ------------------------------

5. *cīvēs:*   octō, vērī, gravis   ------------------------------

F. Write the following specified forms:

nominative plural of:

1. novus homō ------------------------------

2. urbs nostra ------------------------------

3. magnus passus ------------------------------

4. terra omnis ------------------------------

5. meum perīculum ------------------------------

6. rēs pūblica ------------------------------

genitive singular and plural of:

7. vester dux ------------------------------

8. bonus prīnceps ------------------------------

9. iter difficile ------------------------------

10. toga lāta ------------------------------

11. senātus aequus ------------------------------

12. proelium omne ------------------------------

dative singular and plural of:

13. victor ēgregius ------------------------------

14. nauta barbarus ------------------------------

15. puer fortis ------------------------------

16. equitātus celer ------------------------------

17. nostra māter ------------------------------

18. mīles malus ------------------------------

accusative singular and plural of:

19. flūmen fīnitimum ------------------------------

20. omnis diēs ------------------------------

21. nox longa ------------------------------

22. deus prūdēns ------------------------------

23. poena levis ------------------------------

24. reliqua pars ------------------------------

ablative singular and plural of:

25. tua manus --

26. aciēs nova --

27. genus simile --

28. suus pēs --

29. cīvitās maritima --

30. cōnsilium facile --

G. Underline the correct answer in each of the following combinations:

1. exercitūs fortis   (genitive singular, nominative plural)

2. hominēs paucōs   (nominative plural, accusative plural)

3. barbarī celeris   (genitive singular, nominative plural)

4. diēs longī   (nominative plural, nominative singular)

5. fēminae nōbilī   (dative singular, genitive singular)

6. reī difficilis   (genitive singular, dative singular)

7. vītae ūnīus   (genitive singular, dative singular)

8. lēgēs certae   (accusative plural, nominative plural)

9. manūs multās   (genitive singular, accusative plural)

10. deī prūdentēs   (genitive singular, nominative plural)

H. Underline the adjective in parentheses that agrees with the noun.

1. poenae   (gravis, idōneīs, celere)

2. oppidum   (potentium, ūnum, lātōrum)

3. itineris   (longīs, brevēs, bonī)

4. aciem   (tertiam, dextrum, pār)

5. terrīs   (omnis, omnibus, omnēs)

6. exercitūs   (magnōs, magnus, magnīs)

7. equitēs   (nōbilis, tribus, paucī)

8. poētā   (ēgregiō, ēgregius, ēgregiā)

9. iūs   (similibus, commūnis, pūblicum)

10. sociō   (fortis, fortī, fortēs)

107

Lesson 44—COMPARISON OF ADJECTIVES

REGULAR COMPARISON OF ADJECTIVES

POSITIVE	COMPARATIVE	SUPERLATIVE
	(m. & f.) (n.)	(m.) (f.) (n.)
longus, -a, -um	longior, -ius	longissimus, -a, -um
brevis, -e	brevior, -ius	brevissimus, -a, -um
potēns	potentior, -ius	potentissimus, -a, -um
miser, -era, -erum	miserior, -ius	miserrimus, -a, -um
ācer, -cris, -cre	ācrior, -ius	ācerrimus, -a, -um
facilis, -e	facilior, -ius	facillimus, -a, -um

IRREGULAR COMPARISON OF ADJECTIVES

POSITIVE	COMPARATIVE	SUPERLATIVE
	(m. & f.) (n.)	(m.) (f.) (n.)
bonus, -a, -um	melior, melius	optimus, -a, -um
malus, -a, -um	peior, peius	pessimus, -a, -um
magnus, -a, -um	maior, maius	maximus, -a, -um
parvus, -a, -um	minor, minus	minimus, -a, -um
multus, -a, -um	———, plūs	plūrimus, -a, -um

Note

1. The comparative degree is formed by adding **-ior** to the base of the positive for the masculine and feminine, and **-ius** for the neuter.

2. The superlative is formed by adding **-issimus, -a, -um** to the base of the positive.

3. Adjectives ending in **-er** form the superlative by adding **-rimus, -a, -um** to the nominative.

4. Four adjectives ending in **-lis (facilis, difficilis, similis, dissimilis)** form the superlative by adding **-limus, -a, -um** to the base.

5. All superlative degree adjectives are declined like **altus, -a, -um.** The declension of comparatives will be discussed in the next lesson.

6. The comparative degree is translated as follows:

> **altior, -ius,** higher, rather high, too high
> **potentior, -ius,** more powerful

7. The superlative degree is translated as follows:

> **altissimus, -a, -um,** highest, very high
> **potentissimus, -a, -um,** most or very powerful

EXERCISES

A. Identify the degree of each adjective by putting a check in the appropriate column.

	POSITIVE	COMPARATIVE	SUPERLATIVE
1. recentior	-------	-------	-------
2. ācerrimus	-------	-------	-------

3. nōbilis   -------   -------   -------

4. peior   -------   -------   -------

5. certius   -------   -------   -------

6. novissima   -------   -------   -------

7. inimīcus   -------   -------   -------

8. simillimum   -------   -------   -------

9. plūrimus   -------   -------   -------

10. minus   -------   -------   -------

B. Underline the correct translation of the Latin adjective.

1. fortior   (brave, braver, bravest)

2. maximus   (great, greater, greatest)

3. prūdēns   (wise, very wise, rather wise)

4. facillimus   (easy, too easy, easiest)

5. levius   (light, lighter, lightest)

6. līberrima   (free, rather free, most free)

7. melior   (good, better, best)

8. commūnis   (common, more common, most common)

9. gravissimus   (heavy, heavier, heaviest)

10. multum   (much, more, most)

C. Write the comparative and superlative of the following adjectives:

POSITIVE	COMPARATIVE	SUPERLATIVE
1. brevis		
2. longus		
3. malus		
4. celer		
5. difficilis		
6. prūdēns		
7. miser		
8. multus		
9. ācer		
10. parvus		

D. Make each adjective agree with its noun.

1. auxilium—melior   ---------------

2. causam—gravissimus   ---------------

3. arbor—altior   ---------------

4. rēbus—maximus   ---------------

5. senātū—gravis   ---------------

6. gladiōs—ācerrimus   ---------------

7. nōmen—facilior   ---------------

8. rēgī—optimus   ---------------

9. terrārum—novissimus   ---------------

10. deō—amīcissimus   ---------------

Lesson 45—DECLENSION OF COMPARATIVES

	SINGULAR		PLURAL	
	(m. & f.)	(n.)	(m. & f.)	(n.)
Nom.	longior	longius	longiōrēs	longiōra
Gen.	longiōris	longiōris	longiōrum	longiōrum
Dat.	longiōrī	longiōrī	longiōribus	longiōribus
Acc.	longiōrem	longius	longiōrēs	longiōra
Abl.	longiōre	longiōre	longiōribus	longiōribus

Note

1. All comparatives, whether they come from first and second or third declension adjectives, are declined like third declension consonant-stem nouns.

2. Observe the differences in declining a third declension positive adjective and a comparative.

	POSITIVE	COMPARATIVE
ablative singular:	fortī	fortiōre
genitive plural:	fortium	fortiōrum
nominative or accusative plural neuter:	fortia	fortiōra

EXERCISES

A. Make each comparative agree with its noun.

1. victōrem—nōbilior _____
2. praemia—melior _____
3. vītā—līberior _____
4. hostium—fortior _____
5. iter—longior _____

6. adventuī—celerior _____
7. fidem—potentior _____
8. virīs—peior _____
9. beneficī—minor _____
10. agrōs—brevior _____

B. Underline the correct form of the comparative.

1. accusative singular masculine: *lātius, lātiōrem, lātum*
2. genitive plural neuter: *ācrium, ācriōrem, ācriōrum*
3. ablative singular feminine: *celeriōre, celerī, celere*
4. nominative plural neuter: *recentēs, recentia, recentiōra*
5. ablative plural masculine: *levibus, leviōribus, leviōre*
6. nominative singular neuter: *certius, certum, certissimum*
7. dative singular feminine: *miserae, miseriōrī, miseriōre*
8. accusative plural masculine: *cupidōs, cupidiōrem, cupidiōrēs*
9. dative plural feminine: *prūdentiōribus, prūdentibus, prūdentiōrī*
10. genitive singular neuter: *parvī, minōris, minimī*

C. Translate into Latin the English comparative in each group.

1. fīlium *taller* _____
2. flūmen *swifter* _____
3. exercitū *braver* _____
4. diēbus *longer* _____
5. togārum *better* _____

6. equōs *smaller* _____
7. forī *greater* _____
8. mīlitēs *worse* _____
9. portā *newer* _____
10. maris *more difficult* _____

Lesson 46—FORMATION AND COMPARISON OF ADVERBS

FORMATION OF ADVERBS FROM ADJECTIVES

ADJECTIVE	ADVERB	ADJECTIVE	ADVERB
alt*us*	alt*ē*	fort*is*	fort*iter*
līber	līber*ē*	ācer	ācr*iter*

Note

1. Adverbs are formed from adjectives of the first and second declensions by adding **-ē** to the base, and from adjectives of the third declension by adding **-iter.**

2. A few irregular formations are:

ADJECTIVE	ADVERB	ADJECTIVE	ADVERB
bonus	bene	multus	multum
magnus	magnopere	facilis	facile

COMPARISON OF ADVERBS

POSITIVE	COMPARATIVE	SUPERLATIVE
alt*ē*	alt*ius*	alt*issimē*
brev*iter*	brev*ius*	brev*issimē*
līber*ē*	līber*ius*	līber*rimē*
ācr*iter*	ācr*ius*	ācer*rimē*
facil*e*	facil*ius*	facil*limē*
ben*e*	mel*ius*	opt*imē*
mal*e*	pe*ius*	pess*imē*
magnopere	magis	max*imē*
multum	plūs	plūr*imum*

Note

1. With the exception of **magis,** the comparative form of the adverb is the same as the neuter comparative form of the adjective.

2. With the exception of **plūrimum,** the superlative of the adverb is formed from the superlative of the adjective by changing **-us** to **-ē.** A few examples are:

ADJECTIVE	ADVERB
longissimus	longissimē
ācerrimus	ācerrimē
facillimus	facillimē
optimus	optimē

111

3. The three degrees are translated as follows:

POSITIVE	COMPARATIVE	SUPERLATIVE
lātē, widely	**lātius,** more widely	**lātissimē,** most or very widely
bene, well	**melius,** better	**optimē,** best

4. The adverb **diū** has a special comparison.

POSITIVE	COMPARATIVE	SUPERLATIVE
diū, a long time	**diūtius,** a longer time	**diūtissimē,** a very long time

5. The adverbs **magis** (more) and **maximē** (most) are used to compare adjectives ending in **-us** preceded by **e** or **i.**

POSITIVE	COMPARATIVE	SUPERLATIVE
idōneus, suitable	*magis* **idōneus,** more suitable	*maximē* **idōneus,** most or very suitable
necessārius, necessary	*magis* **necessārius,** more necessary	*maximē* **necessārius,** most or very necessary

EXERCISES

A. Form the adverb from each of the following adjectives:

1. aequus _____
2. fortis _____
3. miser _____
4. bonus _____
5. ācer _____

6. magnus _____
7. brevis _____
8. multus _____
9. celer _____
10. facilis _____

B. Identify the degree of each adverb by putting a check in the appropriate column.

ADVERB	POSITIVE	COMPARATIVE	SUPERLATIVE
1. simillimē	-------	-------	-------
2. commūniter	-------	-------	-------
3. diūtius	-------	-------	-------
4. barbarē	-------	-------	-------
5. longissimē	-------	-------	-------
6. certius	-------	-------	-------
7. ācerrimē	-------	-------	-------
8. optimē	-------	-------	-------
9. facile	-------	-------	-------
10. melius	-------	-------	-------

C. Write the comparative and superlative of the following:

POSITIVE	COMPARATIVE	SUPERLATIVE
1. certē	_____	_____
2. male	_____	_____
3. celeriter	_____	_____
4. facile	_____	_____
5. ēgregius	_____	_____

112

D. Translate into English the following adverbs:

1. diū ....
2. peius ....
3. līberrimē ....
4. maximē ....
5. recentius ....

6. nōbilissimē ....
7. ācriter ....
8. fortius ....
9. facillimē ....
10. pūblicē ....

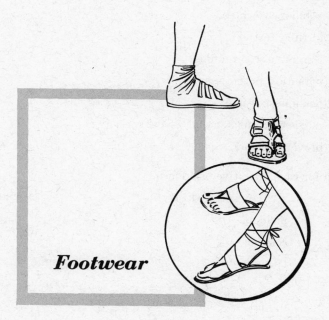

Footwear

The Romans wore sandals indoors and high shoes outdoors. Footwear was usually made of leather or cork. Modern shoe stylists have often adapted the Roman sandal in footwear for both men and women.

Lesson 47—REVIEW OF COMPARISON OF ADJECTIVES AND ADVERBS

A. Underline the correct translation of the italicized words.

1. he ran *very swiftly*   (celerrimus, celerrimē)
2. *a truer* friend   (vērior, vērius)
3. *the greatest* town   (maximum, maximē)
4. he acted *more nobly*   (nōbilior, nōbilius)
5. they fought *bravely*   (fortiter, fortius)
6. *a common* danger   (commūne, commūnius)
7. *a most powerful* king   (potentior, potentissimus)
8. she sang *very poorly*   (pessima, pessimē)
9. he was *more outstanding*   (magis ēgregius, maximē ēgregius)
10. it is *rather short*   (brevis, brevior)

B. Supply the missing form for each adjective or adverb.

POSITIVE	COMPARATIVE	SUPERLATIVE
1. bene	melius	------------------
2. celer	celerior	------------------
3. ------------------	lātius	lātissimē
4. ācer	------------------	ācerrimus
5. parvus	minor	------------------
6. ------------------	plūs	plūrimus
7. ------------------	levius	levissimē
8. idōneus	------------------	maximē idōneus
9. prūdēns	------------------	prūdentissimus
10. facilis	facilior	------------------

C. Identify the degree of each adjective or adverb by putting a check in the appropriate column.

ADJECTIVE OR ADVERB	POSITIVE	COMPARATIVE	SUPERLATIVE
1. graviter	-------	-------	-------
2. maximē	-------	-------	-------
3. minus	-------	-------	-------
4. simillimus	-------	-------	-------
5. miserrimē	-------	-------	-------
6. parātior	-------	-------	-------
7. recēns	-------	-------	-------
8. fortissimus	-------	-------	-------
9. nōbilius	-------	-------	-------
10. diū	-------	-------	-------

114

D. Underline the correct translation of the Latin form.

1. lībere   (free, freely, more freely)

2. facillimē   (easiest, easily, very easily)

3. potentior   (powerful, more powerful, most powerful)

4. commūnis   (common, commonly, more common)

5. altius   (high, highly, more highly)

6. celeriter   (swift, swiftly, more swiftly)

7. levissimus   (light, lighter, lightest)

8. ācerrimē   (very sharp, very sharply, more sharply)

9. plūs   (much, more, most)

10. propinquus   (near, nearer, nearest)

E. In the space before each noun in column *A*, write the letter of its modifying adjective in column *B*.

	Column A	Column B
- - - - - - -	1. temporibus	*a.* maiōra
- - - - - - -	2. adventū	*b.* altior
- - - - - - -	3. noctēs	*c.* fortissimī
- - - - - - -	4. negōtium	*d.* miseriōrum
- - - - - - -	5. rem	*e.* pessimīs
- - - - - - -	6. hostium	*f.* meliōrī
- - - - - - -	7. homō	*g.* peius
- - - - - - -	8. rēgis	*h.* brevissimae
- - - - - - -	9. castra	*i.* celeriōre
- - - - - - -	10. exercituī	*j.* facillimam

F. Write the following specified forms:

1. nominative singular and plural: *diem breviōrem*

----

2. accusative singular and plural: *iter facilius*

----

3. ablative singular and plural: *exercitus fortissimus*

----

4. dative singular and plural: *socius potentior*

----

5. genitive singular and plural: *cīvitās barbarissima*

G. For each of the following nouns, write the correct form of the adjective:

1. rērum   (comparative of *bonus*)   --
2. pācem   (superlative of *certus*)   --
3. vulnera   (comparative of *gravis*)   --
4. pede   (comparative of *parvus*)   --
5. tempus   (superlative of *difficilis*)   --
6. memoriam   (superlative of *malus*)   --
7. proeliīs   (comparative of *magnus*)   --
8. vōce   (superlative of *miser*)   --
9. passibus   (superlative of *multus*)   --
10. librum   (comparative of *recēns*)   --

Hadrian's Tomb

Erected in the second century A.D. by the emperor Hadrian as a mausoleum for himself and his successors, Hadrian's Tomb remains today a symbol in stone of Rome, the Eternal City. Now the tomb, called Castel Sant'Angelo, is a museum that attracts many tourists.

Unit VI—Pronouns

Lesson 48—DEMONSTRATIVE PRONOUNS

IS

	SINGULAR			PLURAL		
	(m.)	*(f.)*	*(n.)*	*(m.)*	*(f.)*	*(n.)*
Nom.	is	ea	id	eī	eae	ea
Gen.	eius	eius	eius	eōrum	eārum	eōrum
Dat.	eī	eī	eī	eīs	eīs	eīs
Acc.	eum	eam	id	eōs	eās	ea
Abl.	eō	eā	eō	eīs	eīs	eīs

HIC

	SINGULAR			PLURAL		
	(m.)	*(f.)*	*(n.)*	*(m.)*	*(f.)*	*(n.)*
Nom.	hic	haec	hoc	hī	hae	haec
Gen.	huius	huius	huius	hōrum	hārum	hōrum
Dat.	huic	huic	huic	hīs	hīs	hīs
Acc.	hunc	hanc	hoc	hōs	hās	haec
Abl.	hōc	hāc	hōc	hīs	hīs	hīs

ILLE

	SINGULAR			PLURAL		
	(m.)	*(f.)*	*(n.)*	*(m.)*	*(f.)*	*(n.)*
Nom.	ille	illa	illud	illī	illae	illa
Gen.	illīus	illīus	illīus	illōrum	illārum	illōrum
Dat.	illī	illī	illī	illīs	illīs	illīs
Acc.	illum	illam	illud	illōs	illās	illa
Abl.	illō	illā	illō	illīs	illīs	illīs

ĪDEM

	SINGULAR			PLURAL		
	(m.)	*(f.)*	*(n.)*	*(m.)*	*(f.)*	*(n.)*
Nom.	īdem	eadem	idem	eīdem	eaedem	eadem
Gen.	eiusdem	eiusdem	eiusdem	eōrundem	eārundem	eōrundem
Dat.	eīdem	eīdem	eīdem	eīsdem	eīsdem	eīsdem
Acc.	eundem	eandem	idem	eōsdem	eāsdem	eadem
Abl.	eōdem	eādem	eōdem	eīsdem	eīsdem	eīsdem

117

Note

1. **Is, hic,** and **ille** may be used both as pronouns and as adjectives. As pronouns, the masculine form means *he*, the feminine *she*, and the neuter *it*. As adjectives, they are translated as follows:

is = *this, that* (plural *these, those*)
hic = *this* (plural *these*)
ille = *that* (plural *those*)

2. **Īdem,** meaning *the same*, is a compound of **is** plus the suffix **-dem.** It follows the declension of **is** with a few changes in spelling.

3. Demonstrative adjectives are generally placed before the nouns they modify.

EXERCISES

A. Identify the case, number, and gender of the following forms:

1. eārum ....
2. illōs ....
3. idem ....
4. hāc ....
5. illīs ....
6. huius ....
7. eum ....
8. eandem ....
9. id ....
10. illōrum ....

B. Each group contains one incorrect form. Correct it.

1. ablative singular feminine   (eā, eādem, hōc)   ....
2. accusative plural neuter   (illud, haec, ea)   ....
3. genitive singular masculine   (eius, illī, huius)   ....
4. nominative plural feminine   (haec, illae, eaedem)   ....
5. dative singular neuter   (eī, hī, illī)   ....
6. accusative singular masculine   (īdem, eum, hunc)   ....
7. genitive plural feminine   (eārum, eiusdem, illārum)   ....
8. nominative singular neuter   (hoc, īdem, illud)   ....
9. ablative plural masculine   (illīs, hīs, eōsdem)   ....
10. ablative singular neuter   (hoc, eō, illō)   ....

C. Make each demonstrative agree with its noun.

1. verba—īdem ....
2. imperātōrī—hic ....
3. aciem—ille ....
4. prōvinciā—is ....
5. gladiī—hic ....
6. passuum—īdem ....
7. vulneris—is ....
8. cornibus—hic ....
9. homine—ille ....
10. līberōs—is ....

D. In the space before each noun in column *A*, write the letter of the modifying demonstrative in column *B*.

	Column A	Column B
-------	**1.** agrōs	*a.* illārum
-------	**2.** iūra	*b.* eius
-------	**3.** exercitum	*c.* eīdem
-------	**4.** viārum	*d.* haec
-------	**5.** spē	*e.* illam
-------	**6.** corporis	*f.* eōsdem
-------	**7.** virtūtī	*g.* id
-------	**8.** grātiam	*h.* hāc
-------	**9.** praesidium	*i.* eīsdem
-------	**10.** prīncipibus	*j.* eum

E. Underline the demonstrative in parentheses that agrees with its noun.

1. spem   (eadem, eandem, eādem)

2. caput   (ille, illa, illud)

3. frātribus   (is, eius, eīs)

4. natūrā   (hāc, haec, hōc)

5. perīcula   (eadem, eae, hae)

6. senātuī   (illīus, eīs, huic)

7. sociōs   (eāsdem, illōs, hunc)

8. nāvium   (illārum, eōrum, eandem)

9. bellī   (illī, huic, eius)

10. agricolās (eōsdem, illās, hās)

Lesson 49—PERSONAL, REFLEXIVE, AND INTENSIVE PRONOUNS

PERSONAL PRONOUNS

	FIRST PERSON		SECOND PERSON	
	SINGULAR	PLURAL	SINGULAR	PLURAL
Nom.	ego (*I*)	nōs (*we*)	tū (*you*)	vōs (*you*)
Gen.	meī	nostrum	tuī	vestrum
Dat.	mihi	nōbīs	tibi	vōbīs
Acc.	mē	nōs	tē	vōs
Abl.	mē	nōbīs	tē	vōbīs

Note

1. For the third person, the demonstrative pronouns **is, hic,** and **ille,** all meaning *he,* are used.

2. Personal pronouns as subject are not needed except for emphasis.

REFLEXIVE PRONOUN

	SINGULAR	PLURAL
Nom.	—	—
Gen.	suī	suī
Dat.	sibi	sibi
Acc.	sē (sēsē)	sē (sēsē)
Abl.	sē (sēsē)	sē (sēsē)

Note

1. The reflexive pronoun **suī** is a third person pronoun. For the first and second persons, the personal pronouns are used.

Sē interfēcit.	He killed himself.
Mē vīdī.	I saw myself.
Vōs dēfenditis.	You are defending yourselves.

2. The meaning of **suī** is determined by the subject.

Puer sē videt.	The boy sees *himself.*
Puella sē videt.	The girl sees *herself.*
Hominēs sē vident.	The men see *themselves.*

INTENSIVE PRONOUN
IPSE (SELF)

	SINGULAR			PLURAL		
	(*m.*)	(*f.*)	(*n.*)	(*m.*)	(*f.*)	(*n.*)
Nom.	ipse	ipsa	ipsum	ipsī	ipsae	ipsa
Gen.	ipsīus	ipsīus	ipsīus	ipsōrum	ipsārum	ipsōrum
Dat.	ipsī	ipsī	ipsī	ipsīs	ipsīs	ipsīs
Acc.	ipsum	ipsam	ipsum	ipsōs	ipsās	ipsa
Abl.	ipsō	ipsā	ipsō	ipsīs	ipsīs	ipsīs

120

Note

1. The intensive pronoun **ipse** is used to emphasize a particular noun or pronoun. The reflexive pronoun **suī** is used to refer to the subject of a sentence or clause.

2. **Ipse** may be used in any case, **suī** in all cases but the nominative.

Caesar **ipse** hostēs vīcit.   Caesar himself defeated the enemy.
Caesar **sē** vulnerāvit.   Caesar wounded himself.

EXERCISES

A. Draw a line through the incorrect form.

1. ablative plural   (nōbīs, sē, ipsōs)   6. ablative singular   (sē, ipsīs, tē)
2. dative singular   (ipsō, sibi, tibi)   7. accusative singular (mē, tē, ipsa)
3. accusative plural   (ipsās, tē, sē)   8. dative plural   (ipsī, sibi, vōbīs)
4. genitive plural   (ipsōrum, ipsārum, sibi) 9. genitive singular   (meī, sibi, ipsīus)
5. nominative singular (mē, tū, ipsum)   10. nominative plural   (vōs, nōs, suī)

B. Place a check in the proper column to indicate whether a form of **suī** or of **ipse** is to be used.

	SUĪ	IPSE
1. Cicero *himself* delivered the speech.	-------	-------
2. We saw the poet *himself*.	-------	-------
3. They freed *themselves* from slavery.	-------	-------
4. He was speaking *to himself*.	-------	-------
5. Cornelia *herself* swam to shore.	-------	-------
6. The gods *themselves* were angry.	-------	-------
7. He called *himself* consul.	-------	-------
8. Marcus built the boat *himself*.	-------	-------
9. She was angry *with herself*.	-------	-------
10. The citizens were mindful *of themselves*.	-------	-------

C. Identify the case and number of the following forms:

1. tibi _____   6. vōs _____
2. suī _____   7. meī _____
3. ipsōrum _____   8. ipsīus _____
4. nostrum _____   9. tē _____
5. ipsae _____   10. nōbīs _____

D. Write the following specified forms:

1. ablative singular: *ego, suī* _____
2. dative plural: *tū, ipse* _____
3. genitive singular: *ipsa, ego* _____
4. accusative plural: *suī, tū* _____
5. nominative plural: *ipsum, ego* _____

121

Lesson 50—RELATIVE AND INTERROGATIVE PRONOUNS

RELATIVE PRONOUN
QUĪ (WHO, WHICH)

	SINGULAR			PLURAL		
	(m.)	*(f.)*	*(n.)*	*(m.)*	*(f.)*	*(n.)*
Nom.	quī	quae	quod	quī	quae	quae
Gen.	cuius	cuius	cuius	quōrum	quārum	quōrum
Dat.	cui	cui	cui	quibus	quibus	quibus
Acc.	quem	quam	quod	quōs	quās	quae
Abl.	quō	quā	quō	quibus	quibus	quibus

INTERROGATIVE PRONOUN
QUIS (WHO?), *QUID* (WHAT?)

	SINGULAR		PLURAL		
	(m. & f.)	*(n.)*	*(m.)*	*(f.)*	*(n.)*
Nom.	quis	quid	quī	quae	quae
Gen.	cuius	cuius	quōrum	quārum	quōrum
Dat.	cui	cui	quibus	quibus	quibus
Acc.	quem	quid	quōs	quās	quae
Abl.	quō	quō	quibus	quibus	quibus

Note

1. The relative pronoun refers to an antecedent; the interrogative pronoun asks a question.

    Puer **quem** docuī erat Mārcus.   The boy *whom* I taught was Marcus. (*relative*)
    Quis habet meum librum?   *Who* has my book? (*interrogative*)

2. The interrogative pronoun may also be used as an adjective. As such, it is declined like the relative pronoun **quī, quae, quod.**

    quī gladius?   what sword?
    quae causa?   what reason?
    quod proelium?   what battle?

EXERCISES

A. Identify the case and number of the following forms.

1. quem -----------------------------   **6.** cuius -----------------------------

2. quibus -----------------------------   **7.** quā -----------------------------

3. quid -----------------------------   **8.** cui -----------------------------

4. quārum -----------------------------   **9.** quod -----------------------------

5. quōs -----------------------------   **10.** quōrum -----------------------------

B. Make the interrogative adjective **quī, quae, quod** agree with its noun.

1. vīllās   ....
2. itinera   ....
3. auctōritās   ....
4. nautam   ....
5. castrōrum   ....

6. exercituī   ....
7. negōtī   ....
8. potestātis   ....
9. annōs   ....
10. genus   ....

C. Write the following specified forms:

1. genitive plural: *quī, quae*   ....
2. accusative singular: *quis, quid*   ....
3. ablative singular and plural: *quae*   ....
4. dative singular and plural: *quid*   ....
5. nominative plural: *quī, quod*   ....

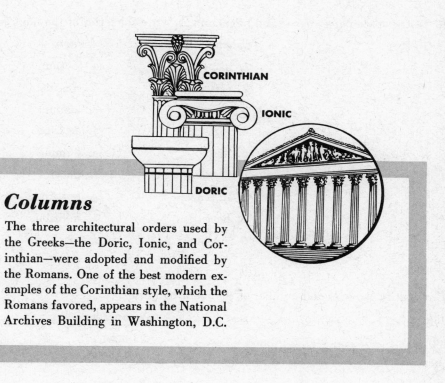

Columns

The three architectural orders used by the Greeks—the Doric, Ionic, and Corinthian—were adopted and modified by the Romans. One of the best modern examples of the Corinthian style, which the Romans favored, appears in the National Archives Building in Washington, D.C.

Lesson 51—REVIEW OF PRONOUNS

A. Next to each of the following nouns are four demonstrative or intensive adjectives. All of them agree with the noun except one. Write that one correctly to make it agree.

1. *tempore:* eō, eōdem, ipse, hōc   ------------------------
2. *urbem:* eadem, hanc, eam, illam   ------------------------
3. *cōnsuētūdō:* haec, illa, eadem, ipsā ------------------------
4. *puerīs:* illīs, eīdem, ipsīs, eīs   ------------------------
5. *rērum:* hōrum, eārundem, eārum, ipsārum ------------------------
6. *perīculī:* huius, eiusdem, ipsīus, eī ------------------------
7. *līberī:* illī, idem, ipsī, hī   ------------------------
8. *hominī:* huic, eīdem, ipse, eī   ------------------------
9. *nautās:* eās, eōsdem, ipsōs, illōs   ------------------------
10. *vulnus:* eius, hoc, illud, ipsum   ------------------------

B. In the space before each form in column *A*, write the letter of the noun it modifies in column *B*.

	Column A	Column B
--------	1. hāc	*a.* factum
--------	2. eārundem	*b.* cōnsulī
--------	3. ille	*c.* manum
--------	4. eius	*d.* aciērum
--------	5. illud	*e.* flūmina
--------	6. eaedem	*f.* ducis
--------	7. ipsam	*g.* portā
--------	8. haec	*h.* mīlitibus
--------	9. eīdem	*i.* vir
--------	10. eīs	*j.* partēs

C. Identify the case and number of the following forms:

1. mihi ------------------------------   6. quōrum ------------------------------
2. suī   ------------------------------   7. nōs   ------------------------------
3. quem ------------------------------   8. tibi   ------------------------------
4. tē   ------------------------------   9. sē   ------------------------------
5. vōbīs ------------------------------   10. ego   ------------------------------

D. Write the following specified forms:

nominative plural of:

1. hoc tempus --
2. illa vōx --
3. ego, quis --
4. rēs ipsa --

5. idem cōnsilium _____

6. is poēta _____

genitive singular and plural of:

7. quis, tū _____

8. is diēs _____

9. illud cornū _____

10. haec prōvincia _____

11. homō ipse _____

12. eadem lēx _____

ablative singular and plural of: _____

13. hic cōnsul _____

14. illud flūmen _____

15. suī, ego _____

16. eadem aciēs _____

17. is gladius _____

18. manus ipsa _____

accusative singular and plural of:

19. eadem nox _____

20. quid, suī _____

21. illa silva _____

22. hic vir _____

23. ego, tū _____

24. prīnceps ipse _____

dative singular and plural of:

25. suī, quis _____

26. ille hostis _____

27. hoc oppidum _____

28. eadem puella _____

29. tū, ego _____

30. ea multitūdō _____

E. Underline the correct form in parentheses.

1. Puer *himself* id fēcit.   (ipse, sē)

2. *What* oppidum est?   (quid, quod)

3. Habeō *the same* togam.   (idem, eandem)

4. Ēnūntiāvit *himself* rēgem.   (sē, ipse)

5. Vidēmus *them* in agrīs.   (eum, hōs)

6. Amō *that* ōrātiōnem.   (illam, hanc)

7. Laudāvērunt *us*.   (vōs, nōs)

8. Invēnī gladium *that* āmīsistī.   (quem, illum)

9. Dedit librum *to me*.   (tibi, mihi)

10. Equus perterruit *her*.   (hanc, quam)

F. Underline the correct form.

1. nominative plural: *suī, ego, ipsae*

2. accusative singular: *īdem, eundem, eōsdem*

3. genitive plural: *quōrum, eiusdem, ipsīus*

4. dative singular: *eōdem, ipsī, suī*

5. ablative plural: *vestrum, eīsdem, hās*

6. accusative plural: *hae, quem, ea*

7. genitive singular: *illīus, illī, illō*

8. dative plural: *sibi, ipsī, eiusdem*

9. nominative singular: *sē, eīdem, hoc*

10. ablative singular: *eīsdem, tē, eī*

Unit VII—Prepositions

Lesson 52

PREPOSITIONS WITH THE ACCUSATIVE

ad, to, toward
ante, before, in front of
apud, among, in the presence of
in, into, against

inter, between, among
ob, on account of
per, through
post, after, behind

propter, on account of
sub, under (with verbs of motion)
trāns, across

PREPOSITIONS WITH THE ABLATIVE

ā (ab), from, by
cum, with
dē, down from, concerning

ē (ex), out of, from
in, in, on
prō, in front of, in behalf of

sine, without
sub, under (with verbs of rest)

Note

1. The prepositions **ā** and **ē** are used before words beginning with a consonant, **ab** and **ex** before vowels or consonants.

> **Ā** (or **Ab**) terrā nāvigat.

>> *But*

> **Ab** aquā discēdit.

> Hostēs **ē** (or **ex**) patriā pellit.

>> *But*

> Hostēs **ex** omnibus partibus pellit.

2. Distinguish between the Latin preposition **in** meaning *in* or *on* used with a verb of rest, and the preposition **in** meaning *into* or *against* used with a verb of motion.

> Equī **in agrīs** erant.
> Equī **in agrōs** contendēbant.

> The horses were in the fields.
> The horses were hurrying into the fields.

EXERCISES

A. Underline the correct form in parentheses.

1. inter (sociīs, sociōs)

2. cum (patre, patrem)

3. sine (vulnus, vulnere)

4. ad (montem, monte)

5. ex (librōs, librīs)

6. post (flūmen, flūmine)

7. dē (illōs, illīs)

8. per (mīlitem, mīlite)

9. ob (eā rē, eam rem)

10. ā (puerōs, puerīs)

B. Translate into English.

1. propter hoc --

2. sine amīcīs --

3. in aquam --

4. ob perīculum --

5. ad silvās --

6. in viā --

127

7. dē monte --

8. per oppidum --

9. sub arboribus --

10. ab urbe --

    C. Translate into Latin.

1. in the presence of the consul --

2. in behalf of the king --

3. out of danger --

4. across the river --

5. behind the camp --

6. before noon --

7. against the enemy --

8. by the citizens --

9. without help --

10. with speed --

    D. Underline the correct translation.

1. Pugnāvērunt *with* mīlitibus.   (cum, sine)

2. Ōrātiōnem scrīpsit *concerning* amīcitiā.   (ob, dē)

3. Contendunt *into* mare.   (in, ad)

4. Excēdimus *through* silvās.   (per, post)

5. *Toward* īnsulam appropinquant.   (Ab, Ad)

6. Sē dēfendunt *in front of* castra.   (post, ante)

7. Ēgit nāvem *under* pontem.   (trāns, sub)

8. Equōs *out of* aquā agit.   (ē, ex)

9. Discēdent *on account of* perīculum.   (ob, ab)

10. Auxilium obtinet *in behalf of* patriā.   (per, prō)

Unit VIII—*Idioms*

Lesson 53

An idiom is a form of expression peculiar to a particular language. For example:

The Latin word **pōnere** normally means *to put* or *place*. Used with **castra,** it means *to pitch* or *set up.*

Nāvem in aquam **pōnunt.**	They *put* the boat in the water.
Castra celeriter **pōnunt.**	They quickly *pitch* camp.

Another example: **Capere** normally means *to take* or *seize*. Used with **cōnsilium,** it means *to form.*

Servum **cēpit.**	He *seized* the slave.
Cōnsilium **cēpit.**	He *formed* a plan.

VERBAL IDIOMS

agere

> **grātiās agere,** to thank
> > Mihi **grātiās agent.**

They will thank me.

> **vītam agere,** to live a life
> > Dūram **vītam agit.**

He lives a hard life.

capere

> **cōnsilium capere,** to form a plan
> > Caesar novum **cōnsilium cēpit.**

Caesar formed a new plan.

committere

> **proelium committere,** to begin battle
> > Hostēs **proelium** hodiē **committent.**

The enemy will begin battle today.

dare

> **in fugam dare,** to put to flight
> > Gallōs **in fugam dedit.**

He put the Gauls to flight.

> **in fugam sēsē dare,** to flee
> > Fēminae **in fugam sēsē dant.**

The women are fleeing.

> **iter dare,** to give the right of way
> > Caesar eīs **iter** nōn **dat.**

Caesar does not give them the right of way.

> **poenam dare,** to suffer punishment
> > Dabitne **poenam?**

Will he suffer punishment?

facere

> **certiōrem facere,** to inform
> > Nūntius Caesarem **certiōrem fēcit.**

The messenger informed Caesar.

> **iter facere,** to march
> > Exercitus ad Galliam **iter faciet.**

The army will march toward Gaul.

> **proelium facere,** to engage in battle
> > Equitēs **proelium fēcērunt.**

The cavalry engaged in battle.

> **verba facere,** to make a speech
> > Cicerō **verba fēcerat.**

Cicero had made a speech.

habēre

> **grātiam habēre,** to feel grateful
> > Omnēs **grātiam habēbant.**

All felt grateful.

> **ōrātiōnem habēre,** to make a speech
> > In senātū **ōrātiōnem habuit.**

He made a speech in the senate.

129

movēre

    castra movēre, to break camp
        Dux suōs **castra movēre** iussit.   The leader ordered his men to break camp.

mūnīre

    viam mūnīre, to build a road
        Captīvī **viam mūniēbant.**   The prisoners were building a road.

pōnere

    castra pōnere, to pitch camp
        Mīlitēs ad flūmen **castra posuērunt.**   The soldiers pitched camp near a river.

posse

    plūrimum posse, to be very powerful
        Dux Helvetiōrum **plūrimum poterat.**   The leader of the Helvetians was very powerful.

tenēre

    memoriā tenēre, to remember
        Galba omnia **memoriā tenēbat.**   Galba remembered everything.

OTHER IDIOMS

ā dextrō cornū, on the right wing
ā sinistrō cornū, on the left wing

        Signum **ā dextrō (sinistrō) cornū** datum   The signal was given on the right (left) wing.
        est.

quā dē causā, for this reason, for what reason

        Quā dē causā diū manēbant.   For this reason they remained a long time.

quam celerrimē, as quickly as possible

        Servī **quam celerrimē** contendērunt.   The slaves hurried as quickly as possible.

mīlle passūs, a mile
mīlia passuum, miles

        Castra **mīlle passūs** (tria **mīlia passuum)**   The camp extended a mile (three miles).
        pertinēbant.

nē . . . quidem, not even

        Nē Caesar **quidem** bellum cōnficere   Not even Caesar was able to finish the war.
        potuit.

prīmā lūce, at dawn
    Prīmā lūce excessērunt.   They left at dawn.

EXERCISES

    A. Complete the Latin translation.

1. He lives an easy life.   Vītam facilem _____.

2. They marched quickly.   Celeriter iter _____.

3. Cicero will make a speech.   Cicerō verba _____.

4. He collected his troops on the right wing.   Cōpiās coēgit _____.

5. The general decided to build a road.   Dux cōnstituit _____.

6. The camp extends a mile.   Castra pertinent _____.

7. Caesar did not give the right of way.   Caesar iter nōn _____.

8. Who will suffer punishment?   Quis poenam _____?

9. She replied as quickly as possible.   Respondit _____.

10. Sextus remembers everything.   Sextus omnia _____ tenet.

B. Underline the correct answer in parentheses.

1. in fugam   (pōnit, agit, dat)   6. proelium   (committunt, dant, habent)

2. plūrimum   (possunt, pōnunt, tenent)   7. castra   (potest, pōnit, agit)

3. grātiās   (fēcit, ēgit, dedit)   8. nē . . .   (īdem, quidem, quem)

4. viam   (dant, mūniunt, agunt)   9. certiōrem   (agit, capit, facit)

5. quam   (celeriter, celerius, celerrimē)   10. cōnsilium   (capiunt, movent, mūniunt)

C. Translate into idiomatic English.

1. Iter exercituī dedit. _____

2. Plūrimum potest. _____

3. Castra pōnere poterat. _____

4. Populum certiōrem faciō. _____

5. Memoriā victōriam tenēmus. _____

6. Puerō grātiās ēgērunt. _____

7. Cōnsilium cēpit. _____

8. In fugam sēsē dedērunt. _____

9. Proelium committunt. _____

10. Castra movēbit. _____

11. Poenam dabis. _____

12. Rōmānī proelium fēcērunt. _____

13. Ōrātiōnem habuerat. _____

14. Tibi grātiam habēmus. _____

15. Hostēs in fugam dedimus. _____

16. Quam celerrimē perveniam. _____

17. Tria mīlia passuum iter fēcērunt. _____

18. Quā dē causā dux viam mūnīvit. _____

19. Nē imperātor quidem populum addūcere poterat. _____

20. Prīmā lūce aciem ā dextrō cornū īnstrūxit. _____

131

Unit IX—Grammar

Lesson 54—THE NOMINATIVE CASE

1. The *subject* of a verb is in the nominative.

Vir contendit.
Illī convēnērunt.

The man is hastening.
They came together.

2. A *predicate noun* or *predicate adjective* (one used with the verb **sum**) is in the nominative.

Mārcus est **agricola.**
Erant **miserī.**

Marcus is a farmer.
They were unhappy.

EXERCISES

A. In each sentence, underline the word or words that go in the nominative, and then translate them into Latin.

1. The slave carried the grain. ------------------------------

2. The citizens heard the oration. ------------------------------

3. Did the army march to Gaul? ------------------------------

4. The general will summon his troops. ------------------------------

5. The women were brave. ------------------------------

6. Why was the consul absent? ------------------------------

7. Marcus is a teacher. ------------------------------

8. Were the soldiers friendly? ------------------------------

9. All the farmers have horses. ------------------------------

10. The king and queen ruled a long time. ------------------------------

B. In each sentence, underline the nominative case and indicate whether it is a subject, a predicate noun, or a predicate adjective.

1. Lesbia patriam amat. ------------------------------

2. Erant hostēs. ------------------------------

3. Discēduntne prīncipēs? ------------------------------

4. Nōn est prūdēns. ------------------------------

5. Erāsne cupidus pecūniae? ------------------------------

6. Signa ā duce dabantur. ------------------------------

7. Ad agrōs contendērunt virī. ------------------------------

8. Eques bene pugnāvit. ------------------------------

9. Fuitne poēta? ------------------------------

10. Cūr perterritus est puer? ------------------------------

C. Translate the English words into Latin.

1. *The mother* līberōs monuit. ------------------------------

2. Equī erant *swift.* ------------------------------

3. Estne Sextus *your brother?*

4. *The gods* bellum prohibēbant.

5. Manēbatne *the crowd* in agrīs?

6. Arbor nōn erat *high.*

7. *The senate* convocātus est.

8. Dūxitne *the leader* cōpiās in pugnam?

9. Tū nōn erās *first.*

10. *The brave allies* hostēs vīcērunt.

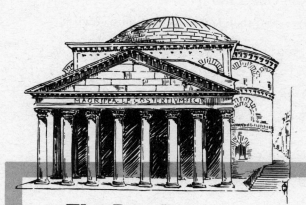

The Pantheon

The Pantheon represents the supreme triumph of Roman engineering, and remains one of the architectural wonders of the world. This well-preserved temple with its famous dome has served as the model of some of the most noted buildings in the world. Among them are St. Peter's in Rome, the Capitol in Washington, and the National Gallery of Art in Washington.

Lesson 55—THE GENITIVE CASE

1. The genitive is used to show *possession*. In English, possession is expressed by an apostrophe or the word *of*.

Gladius **mīlitis** gravis erat.

The soldier's sword (sword of the soldier) was heavy.

Fīliī **rēgīnae** laudātī sunt.

The sons of the queen (queen's sons) were praised.

2. The genitive is also used to *describe* or *limit* another noun.

Erat vir **magnae virtūtis.**
Magnam partem **hostium** interfēcit.

He was a man of great courage.
He killed a large part of the enemy.

EXERCISES

A. Underline all the words in the genitive, and then translate them into English.

1. Vīs hostium erat gravissima. ----------------------------------

2. Hominis virtūs omnēs servāvit. ----------------------------------

3. Est vir magnae potestātis. ----------------------------------

4. Celeritās flūminis mīlitēs perterruit. ----------------------------------

5. Pars cōpiārum victa est. ----------------------------------

6. Caesar erat cōnsul maximae auctōritātis. ----------------------------------

7. Omnium ratiō cīvitātum ēnūntiāta erat. ----------------------------------

8. Erat amīcus barbarōrum. ----------------------------------

9. Petiturne equitātūs cōnsilium? ----------------------------------

10. Magnōrum spēs praemiōrum Gallōs permōvit. ----------------------------------

B. Translate the English words into Latin.

1. magnitūdō *of the island* ----------------------------------

2. *the boy's* equus ----------------------------------

3. *the soldiers'* castra ----------------------------------

4. pater *of the children* ----------------------------------

5. negōtium *of great difficulty* ----------------------------------

6. *Julia's* soror ----------------------------------

7. adventus *of the army* ----------------------------------

8. *the men's* togae ----------------------------------

9. cupiditās *of the kingdom* ----------------------------------

10. vōx *of peace* ----------------------------------

11. tempus *of the year* ----------------------------------

12. *their* spēs (spēs *of them*) ----------------------------------

13. lātitūdō *of Italy* ----------------------------------

14. *the consuls'* cōnsilia ----------------------------------

15. *the slave's* beneficium ----------------------------------

Lesson 56—THE DATIVE CASE

1. The *indirect object* of a verb is in the dative.

Ducī respondit. He replied to the general.
Mihi togam dedit. He gave me a toga.

2. The dative is also used with certain *adjectives*, such as **amīcus** (friendly), **inimīcus** (unfriendly), **fīnitimus** (neighboring), **idōneus** (suitable), **propinquus** (near), and **similis** (like). In English, these adjectives are usually followed by the word *to* or *for*.

Estne inimīcus **Rōmānīs?** Is he unfriendly to the Romans?
Locus erat idōneus **castrīs.** The place was suitable for a camp.
Domus propinqua **flūminī** mea est. The house near the river is mine.

Note

The dative of the indirect object is used with verbs of giving, telling, and showing. However, with verbs of motion, **ad** with the accusative is used.

Puerō librum dedit. He gave a book to the boy.
But
Ad **puerum** contendit. He hurried to the boy.

EXERCISES

A. Underline the correct translation in parentheses.

1. He gave water *to the horses.* (equīs, ad equōs)
2. We are hastening *to the town.* (ad oppidum, oppidō)
3. They ran *to the river.* (flūminī, ad flūmen)
4. Did he speak *to you?* (ad tē, tibi)
5. Report the victory *to the allies.* (sociīs, ad sociōs)
6. When did they sail *to Greece?* (Graeciae, ad Graeciam)
7. She replied at once *to her friend.* (ad amīcum, amīcō)
8. The general led his men *to the camp.* (castrīs, ad castra)
9. He read a story *to the children.* (ad līberōs, līberīs)
10. They drove the enemy *to the mountain.* (ad montem, montī)

B. Underline all the words in the dative, and then translate them into English.

1. Eī fīliam suam dat. _____
2. Caesar barbarīs respondit. _____
3. Propinquī sunt Germānīs. _____
4. Puer similis suō patrī est. _____
5. Populō perīculum nūntiābit. _____
6. Locum idōneum castrīs dēlēgit. _____
7. Omnibus rem ēnūntiābam. _____
8. Eratne amīcus magistrō nostrō? _____
9. Duōbus cōnsulibus vēra dīxit. _____
10. Erāmus aequī negōtiō difficilī. _____

135

C. Translate the English words into Latin.

1. Erat inimīcus *to the woman*. _____

2. Amīcitiam *to the allies* ēnūntiāvit. _____

3. Collis *for a battle* nōn idōneus fuit. _____

4. Pecūniam *to the wretched slaves* dedī. _____

5. Puella *to herself* dīcēbat. _____

6. Erāmus amīcī *to the good general*. _____

7. *To his master* respondit. _____

8. Castra erant fīnitima *the forest*. _____

9. Campum *to the horsemen* dēmōnstrāvit. _____

10. Dēbetne *me* magnam cōpiam frūmentī? _____

Lesson 57—THE ACCUSATIVE CASE

1. The *direct object* of a verb is in the accusative.

Aciem īnstrūxit.	He drew up a line of battle.
Cōnstituērunt **pācem** petere.	They decided to seek peace.

2. Certain *prepositions* take the accusative. Among them are **ad, ante, apud, inter, ob, per, post, propter,** and **trāns.**

Ante **castra** exspectāvit.	He waited in front of the camp.
Trāns **flūmen** contendērunt.	They hurried across the river.

3. *Extent of time or space* is expressed by the accusative.

Paucās hōrās manēbit.	He will stay a few hours.
Magnum spatium nāvigāvērunt.	They sailed a great distance.

4. *Place to which* is expressed by **ad** or **in** with the accusative.

Ad **īnsulam** vēnit.	He came to the island.
Nāvem in **aquam** mōvērunt.	They moved the ship into the water.

Note. The preposition is omitted with **domum** and *names of towns.*

Domum pervēnit.	He arrived home.
Rōmam contendit.	He hurried to Rome.

5. The *subject of an infinitive* is in the accusative.

Virōs pugnāre iussit.	He ordered the men to fight.
Nūntiāvit **ducem** discessisse.	He announced that the general had left.

EXERCISES

A. In each sentence, underline the word or words that go in the accusative, and then translate them into Latin.

1. The war was waged for many years.
2. Caesar attacked the enemy.
3. The children hastened home.
4. He said that the army was drawn up.
5. The wall extended ten feet.
6. We ordered the slaves to return.
7. On account of the danger they fled.
8. Did the citizens praise the consul?
9. They sailed toward Italy.
10. The horsemen will travel across the mountain.
11. Who found the supply of grain?
12. He carried the boy through the forest.
13. They had seen him in the river.
14. He urges on the swift horses.
15. Whom did we frighten?

137

B. Translate into English.

1. Portā frūmentum ad aquam. ---

2. Magister līberōs dīmittit. --

3. Omnēs domum contendērunt. --

4. Perīculum vīdī. ---

5. Virōs manēre iussit. --

6. Trēs diēs bellum gessimus. ---

7. Dīxit cīvēs discēdere. ---

8. Cōpiae ductae sunt mīlle pedēs. --------------------------------------

9. Petīvistīne pācem? --

10. Inter montēs erat flūmen. --

11. Rōmam excessērunt. --

12. Quis pugnam vīderat? --

13. In fīnēs hostium exercitum dūxit. ------------------------------------

14. Cōnsuētūdinēs barbarōrum cognōvit. ----------------------------------

15. Aciem post castra īnstruet. --

The Eagle and S.P.Q.R.

The eagle was used by the Romans to signify courage, strength, and invincibility. The abbreviation S.P.Q.R. (senātus populusque Rōmānus) was a symbol of Roman power and influence. In 1776, the Continental Congress adopted the emblem of the eagle for the seal of the newly formed United States of America. Today in Italy, the government employs the initials S.P.Q.R. on buildings, buses, documents, etc.

Lesson 58—THE ABLATIVE CASE

1. Certain *prepositions* take the ablative. Among them are **ab, cum, dē, ex, prō,** and **sine.**

Prō **patriā** pugnāvit.	He fought for his country.
Sine **proeliō** vīcit.	He conquered without a battle.

2. *Accompaniment* is expressed by the ablative with **cum.** This ablative usually refers to a person and answers the question: *In company with whom?*

Labōrat cum **patre.**	He works with his father.
Mānsit cum **servīs.**	He stayed with the slaves.

Note. When **cum** is used with a pronoun, it is attached to it as an enclitic: **mēcum** (with me), **tēcum** (with you), **nōbīscum** (with us), **quōcum** (with whom).

Pāx **vōbīscum!**	Peace be with you!
Quibuscum iter facit?	With whom is he traveling?

3. The *means* by which something is done is expressed by the ablative without a preposition. This ablative refers to a thing and answers the question: *By what means?*

Armīs pugnāvērunt.	They fought with arms.
Gladiō sē dēfendit.	He defended himself by means of a sword.

4. *Personal agent* is expressed by the ablative with **ā** or **ab.** It is used with passive verbs to indicate the person by whom the action is done.

Ab **mīlite** servātus est.	He was saved by the soldier.
Ā **cōnsulibus** līberābantur.	They were freed by the consuls.

5. *Place where or in which* is expressed by the ablative with the preposition **in.**

In **silvīs** sunt.	They are in the woods.
In **Italiā** mānsit.	He remained in Italy.

6. *Place from which* is expressed by the ablative with the preposition **ab, dē,** or **ex.**

Mīles ex **castrīs** excessit.	The soldier left camp.
Ab **omnibus partibus** convēnērunt.	They assembled from all directions.

7. *Time when or within which* is expressed by the ablative without a preposition.

Aestāte nōn labōrāmus.	In summer we don't work.
Negōtium **tribus diēbus** cōnfectum est.	The task was finished within three days.

8. The ablative of *specification* is used without a preposition to answer the question: *In what respect?*

Virtūte superant.	They excel in courage.
Sunt paucī **numerō.**	They are few in number.

9. *Separation* is expressed by the ablative, with or without the preposition **ab** or **ex.**

Hostēs ab **oppidō** prohibuit.	He kept the enemy from the town.
Patriam **perīculō** līberābit.	He will free his country from danger.

10. *Manner* is expressed by the ablative with **cum,** and answers the question: *How?*

Cum **dīligentiā** labōrat.	He works carefully (with care).
Cum **virtūte** pugnāverunt.	They fought courageously (with courage).

Note. **Cum** may be omitted if an adjective modifies the noun. If expressed, **cum** usually stands between the adjective and the noun.

Magnā (cum) **celeritāte** pervēnit.	He arrived with great speed.
Maximā (cum) **difficultāte** sē dēfendērunt.	They defended themselves with the greatest difficulty.

Copyright 1963 by Amsco School Publications, Inc.

11. The *ablative absolute* construction is used to denote the *time or circumstances* of an action. It consists of a noun or pronoun in the ablative, with a participle agreeing with it. Sometimes an adjective or another noun is used instead of the participle. The ablative absolute is usually translated into English by using the word *after*, *when*, or *since*.

Signō datō, mīlitēs cessērunt.	After the signal was given, the soldiers retreated.
Caesare duce, Rōmānī hostēs vīcērunt.	When Caesar was general, the Romans defeated the enemy.
Barbarī, **oppidō captō,** pācem petēbant.	Since their town was captured, the natives sought peace.

Note

1. The ablative absolute can often be detected by commas that set it off from the rest of the sentence.

2. The dative and ablative are frequently confused because of their identical spellings in most instances. A word referring to a person is likely to be in the dative. A word referring to a thing is more often in the ablative.

Puerīs (*dative*) locum dēmōnstrāvit.	He showed the place to the boys.
Armīs (*ablative*) pūgnāvērunt.	They fought with arms.

3. It is common to find in Latin a genitive followed by an ablative. When this occurs, translate first the ablative and then the genitive.

Cīvium auxiliō, hostēs superāvimus.	With the aid of the citizens, we defeated the enemy.
Eius adventū proelium commissum est.	At his arrival (At the arrival of him) the battle started.

EXERCISES

A. Underline the correct answer in parentheses.

1. They fought *with swords*.   (gladiīs, cum gladiīs)

2. He works hard *in winter*.   (hieme, in hieme)

3. She was frightened *by her brother*.   (frātre, ā frātre)

4. We hurried *down the mountain*.   (monte, dē monte)

5. He was playing *with his friend*.   (amīcō, cum amīcō)

6. I shall arrive *in four hours*.   (quattuor hōrīs, in quattuor hōrīs)

7. They stayed *in the water*.   (aquā, in aquā)

8. He escaped *from the Gauls*.   (Gallīs, ab Gallīs)

9. She is outstanding *in height*.   (altitūdine, in altitūdine)

10. We left *with fear*.   (timōre, cum timōre)

B. In each sentence, underline the word or words that are in the ablative, and then translate them into English. Include prepositions in your translation.

1. Prō patriā pugnant. _____

2. Ex eō oppidō pōns pertinet. _____

3. Cum fīliā servīsque suīs nāvigat. _____

4. Oppidum ā Rōmānīs occupātum est. _____

5. Diē cōnstitūtā discessērunt. _____

140

6. In fīnibus Belgārum bellum gerunt. -----------------------------------

7. Fugā sē servāvērunt. ---

8. Hīs pulsīs, Rōmānī cōpiās prōdūxērunt. ----------------------------

9. Hī omnēs linguā lēgibusque differunt. ------------------------------

10. Suīs fīnibus eōs prohibent. --

11. Pōns duōbus annīs factus est. --

12. Mēcum fugam temptat. --

13. Rēgnī cupiditāte adductus, amīcitiam cōnfīrmāvit. -----------------

14. Flūmen prōvinciam ab Helvētiīs dīvidit. ------------------------------

15. Hōc modō aciem īnstrūxit. --

C. Translate the following ablatives absolute into idiomatic English:

1. omnibus rēbus comparātīs --

2. hīs locīs occupātīs --

3. eō negōtiō perfectō --

4. rēge interfectō --

5. meō amīcō vīsō --

6. senātū dīmissō --

7. aciē īnstrūctā --

8. bellō factō --

9. cōpiīs multīs coāctīs --

10. castrīs relictīs --

D. Translate the italicized words into Latin.

1. *On the same day* he saw his friends. ---------------------------------

2. *When the town had been captured,* they left. ---------------------

3. The army stayed *in camp* all day. -------------------------------------

4. He traveled *with his allies.* ---

5. We received them *from the province.* -----------------------------

6. Caesar defeated them *within a few years.* ---------------------------

7. Few were killed *by the enemy.* -------------------------------------

8. They crossed *by means of ships.* -----------------------------------

9. He excelled all *in speed.* ---

10. They fought *with hope* of victory. -----------------------------------

11. They sailed *without us.* ---

12. They sailed *with us.* ---

13. He kept his country *from war.* -------------------------------------

14. I will go *with you,* Marcus. ---

15. I don't know *with whom* you live. ---------------------------------

141

Lesson 59—REVIEW OF ALL CASES

A. Underline the correct translation in parentheses.

1. A reward was given *to the consul*.   (cōnsulī, ad cōnsulem)
2. He reported it *with a signal*.   (signō, cum signō)
3. The soldier was *very brave*.   (fortissimus, fortissimum)
4. They hurried *to the senate*.   (senātuī, ad senātum)
5. He told *the children* a story.   (līberīs, ad līberōs)
6. She lived *with her sister*.   (sorōre, cum sorōre)
7. We saw *a crowd*.   (multitūdō, multitūdinem)
8. The *king's* daughter was married.   (Rēx, Rēgis)
9. He was helped *by his father*.   (patre, ab patre)
10. *At that time* I was in Rome.   (Eō tempore, In eō tempore)
11. The flight *of the citizens* was reported.   (cīvēs, cīvium)
12. They stood *in front of the camp*.   (prō castra, prō castrīs)
13. I lived here *many years*.   (multōs annōs, multīs annīs)
14. *On account of the danger* we fled.   (Ob perīculum, Ob perīculō)
15. He decided to go *to Rome*.   (Rōmam, ad Rōmam)
16. The *children's* courage was outstanding.   (līberī, līberōrum)
17. The girl was like *her father*.   (patrī, patrem)
18. He said that *the city* was destroyed.   (urbs, urbem)
19. *Whom* did you defend?   (Quis, Quem)
20. He surpassed his father *in influence*.   (auctōritāte, in auctōritāte)

B. Translate the following expressions into English:

1. vir magnae auctōritātis; oppidō captō

----

2. propter hoc; multōs diēs

----

3. in silvam; in agrīs

----

4. dē montibus; cum eius frātre

----

5. ex librīs; quattuor hōrīs

----

6. quibus rēbus gestīs; hieme

----

7. trāns flūmen; sine perīculō

----

8. hōc factō; magnā cum virtūte

----

9. paucīs annīs; eōdem tempore

----

10. quā de causā; hīs rēbus cognitīs

C. Complete the following Latin sentences by translating the words in parentheses:

1. (At that time) excessērunt.

2. Puer est similis (his father).

3. (With swords) pugnāvērunt.

4. Dīxit (that the allies) venīre.

5. (With his sister) pervēnit.

6. (The enemy's) castra capta sunt.

7. Praemia (to the citizens) dedit.

8. Hominēs erant (wretched).

9. Spem (of freedom) habēmus.

10. (By the horsemen) vulnerātī erant.

11. Ante (the camp) aciem īnstrūxit.

12. Puer (home) contendit.

13. (From the town) vēnerat.

14. Virōs (to the fields) addūxit.

15. Bellum (for many years) gestum est.

D. Using the ablative absolute construction, express the following in Latin:

1. after the enemy had been defeated

2. when they had found out the plan

3. after capturing the towns

4. having decided upon these things

5. since everything had been prepared

6. the place being suitable

7. when they had heard the slave

8. after receiving many wounds

9. having handed over all the arms

10. when Galba was king

E. Translate into English.

1. Brevī tempore līberī iter fēcērunt. -

2. Trāns flūmen castra posuerat. -

3. Quot puerī prō patriā pugnābunt? -

4. Aquā frūmentōque servī miserī servātī sunt. -

5. Docēbanturne puellae ab magistrō? -

6. Multīs interfectīs, prīncipēs rēgnī pācem petīvērunt. -

7. Dux omnibus virīs praemia dederat. -

8. Fortūna bellī equitibus inīqua erat. -

9. Cōpiās multa mīlia passuum praemīsit. -

10. Mīles nūntiāvit hostēs venīre. -

11. Propter perīculum sociī sēsē in fugam dedērunt. -

12. In forum rēx ab cōnsule addūcētur. -

13. Nocte imperātor ex castrīs contendit. -

14. Eōdem tempore patria perīculō līberāta est. -

15. Celeritāte omnēs puerōs puellāsque superābat. -

F. Translate into Latin.

1. They are conquered by the arms of the Romans. -

2. Because of the memory of this thing, he will fight. -

3. With his sister he hastened into the forest. _____

_____

4. The boys were taught by the teacher in the forum. _____

_____

5. Without help he had carried the grain out of the camp. _____

_____

6. In winter the slaves will work a long time. _____

_____

7. The general reported the victory to the people. _____

_____

8. He ordered the soldiers to surround the town. _____

_____

9. The leader chose a place suitable for a camp. _____

_____

10. The foreigners surpass all in size of body. _____

_____

G. Rewrite the sentences below, making *all* changes required by the directions in parentheses.

1. Ad Italiam contendērunt. (substitute *Rome*)

_____

2. Cum hostibus pugnant. (substitute *swords*)

_____

3. Urbe captā, Rōmānī excessērunt. (change to the plural)

_____

4. Post flūmen castra posuit. (change to **Prō**)

_____

5. Sex hōrās iter fēcit. (substitute *two*)

_____

6. Puella **ā patre** servābātur. (change to *a plan*)

_____

7. Erat **vir** magnae virtūtis. (change to the plural)

_____

8. Mīlitis socius fortis est. (change to *the soldiers'*)

_____

9. Puer virō **dīxit.** (substitute the equivalent form of **venīre**)

_____

10. Homō manet. (start the sentence with **Putō**)

_____

Lesson 60—AGREEMENT

1. A *verb* agrees with its *subject* in person and number.

Ego negōtium **confēcī.**	I finished the task.
Puerī **labōrābant.**	The boys were working.

2. An *adjective* or a *participle* agrees with its *noun* in gender, number, and case.

Equum **celerem** dēlēgit.	He chose the swift horse.
Paucī nautae aderant.	Few sailors were present.
Hōc perīculō **perterritae,** mātrēs discessērunt.	Terrified by this danger, the mothers left.

Note. In the passive of the perfect system, the *participle* agrees with the *subject*.

Mīlitēs **circumventī** sunt.	The soldiers were surrounded.
Vōx **audīta** erat.	A voice had been heard.

3. A *predicate noun* or *predicate adjective* (one used with the verb **sum**) is in the same case as the *subject*.

Galba est **rēx.**	Galba is king.
Puellae **parvae** erant.	The girls were small.

4. A noun used in *apposition* with another noun agrees with it in case.

Prīnceps, fortis **vir,** diū pugnāvit.	The chief, a brave man, fought for a long time.
Equum amīcō, **cōnsulī,** dedit.	He gave a horse to his friend, the consul.

5. A *relative pronoun* agrees with its *antecedent* in gender and number; its case, however, depends on its use in its own clause.

Aciēs **quam** īnstrūxit prīma erat.	The battle line which he drew up was the first.
Locus ā **quō** vēnit Rōma erat.	The place from which he came was Rome.

6. The possessive adjective **suus, -a, -um** is reflexive; that is, it refers to the subject. Its *meaning* therefore is determined by the subject.

Puer suam patriam laudat.	The boy praises *his* country.
Puella suam patriam laudat.	The girl praises *her* country.
Līberī suam patriam laudant.	The children praise *their* country.

The *form* of **suus, -a, -um** depends upon the word it modifies, not the subject. In the three examples above, the word **suam** modifying **patriam** remains the same, even though the subject varies.

7. Distinguish between the use of **suus, -a, -um** and the genitive of the pronouns is, **hic,** and **ille.** The former refers to the subject, the latter to someone other than the subject.

Magister **suum** librum legit.	The teacher is reading his (*own*) book.
Magister **eius / huius / illīus** librum legit.	The teacher is reading his (*someone else's*) book.
Fēmina **suam** vōcem audit.	The woman hears her (*own*) voice.
Fēmina **eius / huius / illīus** vōcem audit.	The woman hears his or her (*someone else's*) voice.
Virī in **suīs** agrīs labōrant.	The men are working in their (*own*) fields.
Virī in **eōrum / hōrum / illōrum** agrīs labōrant.	The men are working in their (*other people's*) fields.

146

Note

Observe the difference in meaning in the following three sentences:

Mīles **suum** gladium capit.   The soldier is taking *his* (*own*) sword.
Mīles **eius** gladium capit.   The soldier is taking *his* (*someone else's*) sword.
Mīles **eum** gladium capit.   The soldier is taking *this* (or *that*) sword.

EXERCISES

A. Underline the correct answer in parentheses.

1. Mīlitēs erant (fortissimī, fortissimōs).

2. Iter hodiē (factus est, factum est).

3. Meum amīcum (Mārcus, Mārcum) vīdī.

4. Hominēs auxilium (petēbat, petēbant).

5. Quis erat (victor, victōrem)?

6. Puer (quī, quem) scrībēbat erat Sextus.

7. (Permōtus, Permōtī) morte cōnsulis, cīvēs diū mānsērunt.

8. Tū omnēs rēs nōn (cognōvistī, cognōvistis).

9. Nautae dē celeritāte flūminis (monitī, monitae) erant.

10. Servus (quī, cui) equus datus est dīligenter labōrābat.

11. (Expōnēbatne, Expōnēbantne) prīncipēs lēgēs?

12. (Maxima, Maximam) spem victōriae habēbat.

13. Vulnerāvit virum (quī, quem) gladium tenuit.

14. (Eadem, Eandem) patriam amāvērunt.

15. Castra sub monte mūnīta (est, sunt).

B. Make each adjective agree with its noun.

1. nocte—is   ---------------------
2. equīs—celer   ---------------------
3. domus—magnus   ---------------------
4. diem—longior   ---------------------
5. cīvitātum—īdem   ---------------------
6. iter—brevior   ---------------------
7. hominum—līber   ---------------------
8. flūmen—altus   ---------------------

9. genere—hic   ---------------------
10. agricolās—miser   ---------------------
11. pācis—vērus   ---------------------
12. poenās—ācer   ---------------------
13. virīs—trēs   ---------------------
14. rēgis—ipse   ---------------------
15. exercituī—ille   ---------------------

C. Write the correct form of the verb in parentheses, using the tense and voice indicated. Then translate the sentence into English.

1. Equitēs (maneō, imperfect active). --

----

2. Ego (veniō, perfect active). --

----

3. Tū (videō, future passive). --

147

4. Puer puellaque (doceō, present passive). _____

_____

5. Nōs (labōrō, pluperfect active). _____

_____

6. Ōrātiōnēs (habeō, perfect passive). _____

_____

7. Populus (pugnō, future active). _____

_____

8. Vōs (vincō, perfect active). _____

_____

9. Hostēs (iubeō, pluperfect passive). _____

_____

10. Castra (capiō, perfect passive). _____

_____

11. Ego atque pater (nāvigō, future active). _____

_____

12. Senātus (conveniō, present active). _____

_____

13. Et fēminae et virī (perterreō, perfect passive). _____

_____

14. Numerus mīlitum magnus (sum, imperfect). _____

_____

15. Arma (trādō, pluperfect passive). _____

_____

D. Translate into Latin the words in italics.

1. Imperātor erat _brave._ _____

2. Cōnsulem, _a noble man_, laudābant. _____

3. Virī, _to whom_ praemia dedit, aberant. _____

4. Līberī erant _sons_ cōnsulum. _____

5. Servus, _whom_ scīvimus, interfectus est. _____

6. Equitibus, _allies_ Rōmae, gratiās ēgit. _____

7. Mīles, _by whom_ servātī erāmus, vulnerātus est. _____

8. Timōre _alarmed_, cīvēs urbem relīquērunt. _____

9. Rēx, _whose_ adventus nūntiātus est, amīcus appellābātur. _____

10. Aciem, _drawn up_ in campō, vīdī. _____

148

E. Translate into English.

1. Hostēs illō tempore ab mīlitibus vīsī sunt. _____

_____

2. Sextus, agricola Rōmānus, cum duōbus fīliīs semper labōrābat. _____

_____

3. Post longum bellum populus pācem vēram cupiēbat. _____

_____

4. Multī servī Rōmānī miserrimī erant. _____

_____

5. Britannī Gallīs, sociīs suīs, auxilium multum dant. _____

_____

6. Rōmānī barbarōs proeliīs ācribus iam superābunt. _____

_____

7. Virī, quōs cōnsul interficī iussit, nōn Rōmānī erant. _____

_____

8. Castra nostra in aequō locō posita erant. _____

_____

9. Timōre poenae commōta, puella urbem relīquit. _____

_____

10. Cūr in eādem lībertāte quam ā patribus accēpimus manēre nōn possumus? _____

_____

F. Translate into Latin.

1. The shortest route was more difficult than the longest. _____

_____

2. The wars which the Romans waged with the Gauls were severe. _____

_____

3. Influenced by the danger of war, the general collected his troops. _____

_____

4. The boy, to whom they gave the reward of victory, was Marcus. _____

_____

5. I saw boys, friends of Galba, in the Roman army. _____

_____

6. That night the leader had drawn up a long line of battle. _____

_____

7. The camp has been defended by many brave soldiers. _____

_____

8. The children are playing with their friends in the wide street. _____

_____

149

9. The good farmer was praised by all the citizens. -

- -

10. Noble women had been seen on the small island. -

- -

    G. Underline the correct answer in parentheses.

1. The father punished *his* fīlium.   (suum, eius)

2. They love *their* patriam.   (suam, suās)

3. She knew *his* cōnsilium.   (suum, huius)

4. The farmers live in *their own* vīllā.   (suīs, suā)

5. Caesar accepts *their* condiciōnēs.   (hās, eōrum)

6. The horseman drove *that* equum.   (illum, illīus)

7. They sold *his* frūmentum.   (id, eius)

8. The girls carried *their own* librōs.   (illārum, suōs)

9. The king admired *her* virtūtem.   (eius, eam)

10. The chief noticed *their* perīculum.   (hōrum, suum)

11. He told the story to *his* sorōrī.   (suae, eī)

12. They traveled with *her* amīcīs.   (suīs, illīus)

13. All feared *this* proelium.   (hoc, huius)

14. He was pleased with *their* victōriā.   (suā, hōrum)

15. He worshipped *those* deōs.   (suōs, illōs)

Lesson 61—INFINITIVES

1. Some verbs, such as **possum** (be able), **incipiō** (begin), **cupiō** (wish), **dubitō** (hesitate), require another verb in the infinitive to complete their meaning (*complementary infinitive*). The subject for both verbs is the same.

Senātus pācem **cōnfīrmāre** potuit.   The senate was able to establish peace.
Incipiunt animum **āmittere.**   They begin to lose courage.

2. Some verbs, such as **iubeō** (order), **cōgō** (compel), **prohibeō** (prevent), take the infinitive of another verb as *object*. Each verb has a different subject, with the subject of the infinitive always in the accusative case.

Caesar virōs **pugnāre** iussit.   Caesar ordered the men to fight.
Dominus servum **labōrāre** nōn cōget.   The master will not compel the slave to work.

Note. Complementary and *object* infinitives are used only in the *present* tense.

3. Verbs of *knowing, thinking, telling,* and *perceiving,* such as **sciō, putō, dīcō, sentiō,** are often followed by an infinitive in *indirect statement.* The subject of the infinitive is in the accusative case. The conjunction *that,* expressed or implied in English, is never translated into Latin.

a. The *present* infinitive is used if the action takes place *at the same time* as that of the main verb.

Dīcit virōs **pugnāre.**   He says that the men are fighting.
Dīxit virōs **pugnāre.**   He said that the men were fighting.

b. The *perfect* infinitive is used if the action takes place *before* that of the main verb.

Dīcit virōs **pugnāvisse.**   He says that the men fought.
Dīxit virōs **pugnāvisse.**   He said that the men had fought.

c. The *future* infinitive is used if the action takes place *after* that of the main verb.

Dīcit virōs **pugnātūrōs esse.**   He says that the men will fight.
Dīxit virōs **pugnātūrōs esse.**   He said that the men would fight.

Note

When the subject of an infinitive is the same as the subject of the main verb, the reflexive **sē** is used. When the subject is different, the accusative of **is, ille,** or **hic** is used.

Mārcus dīcit **sē** manēre.   Marcus says that he (Marcus) is staying.
Mārcus dīcit **eum** manēre.   Marcus says that he (Sextus) is staying.

EXERCISES

A. Translate into English the following sentences:

1. Omnia comparāre cōnstituērunt.

----

2. Id facere temptant.

----

3. Ad Italiam excēdere contendit.

----

4. Duōs annōs satis esse putāvērunt.

----

5. Eum causam dīcere coēgērunt.

----

6. Diū manēre nōn poterant.

----

7. Pācem et amīcitiam cōnfīrmāre cōnstituimus.

----

8. Cupiō mē esse parātum.

----

9. Dīcō tē ad mē eā nocte vēnisse.

----

10. Eum esse hostem cognōvistī.

----

11. Vidēs eum ducem bellī futūrum esse.

----

12. Circumvenīre castra incēpērunt.

----

13. Eum in castrīs exspectārī sentīs.

----

14. Ad Americam nāvigāre dubitāvimus.

----

15. Respondit sē oppidum occupāvisse.

----

16. Caesar iussit suōs fortiter pugnāre.

----

17. Senātum convenīre prohibet.

----

18. Scit eōs perventūrōs esse.

----

19. Servōs līberāre dēbent.

----

20. Renūntiat urbem occupātam esse.

B. Underline the correct translation in parentheses for the italicized English words.

1. Nōn possunt *work*.   (labōrant, labōrāre)

2. Castra *to fortify* incēpērunt.   (mūnīre, mūnīvisse)

3. Sociōs *to remain* iussit.   (manēre, mānsisse)

4. Dīxit ducem bellum *was waging*.   (gerere, gerī)

5. Audit agricolās *will come together*.   (conventūrōs esse, conventōs esse)

6. Cīvēs *to leave* coēgit.   (discēdere, discessūrōs esse)

7. Putāvit fīliōs suōs *had been wounded*.   (vulnerāvisse, vulnerātōs esse)

8. Hodiē dēbēmus *to write*.   (scrībere, scrībī)

9. Scīvit oppidum *was being seized*.   (occupārī, occupātum esse)

10. Sagittās *to throw* temptāvit.   (iacere, iēcisse)

11. Cognōvit hostēs oppidum *had surrounded*.   (circumvēnisse, circumventōs esse)

12. Nūntiat Caesarem *will wait*.   (exspectābit, exspectātūrum esse)

13. Vīdit eōs *were being hard pressed*.   (premere, premī)

14. *To send* auxilium cōnstituit.   (Mittere, Mīsisse)

15. Scrīpsit omnia *was* parāta.   (esse, fuisse)

Peristyle of a Roman House

The peristȳlium, or garden court with columns, was located in the rear of the house, and thus afforded greater privacy for the family. Today in Italy, Spain, and our own California, there are gardens, terraces, and patios designed for outdoor living.

Lesson 62—PARTICIPLES

A *participle* is a verbal adjective agreeing in gender, number, and case with the noun or pronoun it modifies. It is often best translated into English by a clause.

a. The *present* participle exists only in the *active* voice, and denotes action occurring *at the same time* as that of the main verb.

Pugnantēs ācriter, Rōmānī hostēs vīcērunt.   Fighting fiercely, the Romans defeated the enemy.

Puellam **lūdentem** perterruit.   He frightened the girl while she was playing.

Note. Being a verb form, a present participle may take an object.

Spectāvī hominēs **patriam** relinquentēs.   I watched the men abandoning their country.

b. The *perfect* participle exists only in the *passive* voice, and denotes action occurring *before* the time of the main verb.

Timōre **permōtae,** puellae sēsē in fugam dedērunt.   Moved by fear, the girls fled.

Omnēs servōs **līberātōs** vīdit.   He saw all the slaves who had been freed.

Note. The frequent use of participles in the *ablative absolute* construction has been discussed on page 140.

EXERCISES

A. Underline each participle and then translate into English the following sentences:

1. Ab mātre relictī, puerī in silvam contendērunt. ------------------------------

2. Animōs virōrum dubitantium cōnfīrmāvit. ------------------------------

3. Rēgnī cupiditāte adductus, bellum gessit. ------------------------------

4. Adventū hostium perterritī, in castrīs mānsērunt. ------------------------------

5. Dominus servum lībertātem petentem cēpit. ------------------------------

6. Auctōritāte eius permōtī, cōnstituunt discēdere. ------------------------------

7. Armīs pulsī, hostēs victī sunt. ------------------------------

8. Graviter commōtus, puer domum contendit. ------------------------------

9. Librum legēns, puella ad amīcum appropinquāvit. ------------------------------

10. Equitēs vim hostium sustinentēs, Caesarī auxilium dabant. ------------------------------

B. Translate the English words into Latin participles.

1. Magistrum *as he was teaching* spectābam. ------------------------------

2. Ā patre *sent*, puer ad vīllam pervēnit. ------------------------------

3. Spē victōriae *influenced*, ācriter pugnābant. ------------------------------

4. Perīculō bellī *alarmed*, fēminae urbem relīquērunt. ------------------------------

5. Dux *while preparing* bellum, pācem cupiēbat. ------------------------------

6. Monuit puerum *who was frightening* puellās. ------------------------------

7. Spē lībertātis *led*, servī dīligenter labōrābant. ------------------------------

8. Mīlitī *who was leaving* praemium dedērunt. ------------------------------

9. Timōre *seized*, imperātor sē trādidit. ------------------------------

10. Castra *which had been fortified* dux occupāvit. ------------------------------

154

Lesson 63—REVIEW OF GRAMMAR

A. Underline the word or expression in parentheses which makes the sentence grammatically correct.

1. Imperātor in (castra, castrīs) vēnit.
2. Puerī (silvae, ad silvam) contendērunt.
3. (Nocte, In nocte) signum dedit.
4. (Servus, Servum) in agrō esse putō.
5. Puella (amīcō, ab amīcō) vulnerāta est.
6. Vir (frātre, cum frātre) perveniet.
7. Mīlitēs in (oppidum, oppidō) sunt.
8. Iter (duās hōrās, duābus hōrīs) iam fēcit.
9. Praemium (optimō puerō, ad optimum puerum) dedit.
10. Cognōvit hostēs (discēdunt, discēdere).
11. Terra rēgis (magna, magnam) est.
12. Populus audīvit rēgem (interfectus esse, interfectum esse).
13. Mīlitēs (cum gladiīs, gladiīs) pugnant.
14. Hominem trāns (flūmine, flūmen) vīdit.
15. Amīcōs (virtūte, in virtūte) superāvit.
16. Cōnsul (virīs, virōs) discēdere iussit.
17. Oppidum (monte, montī) dēfenditur.
18. Mārcus (ad frātrem, frātrī) similis est.
19. Hostēs (vī, ā vī) armōrum victī sunt.
20. Prīncipēs fortēs (laudātus est, laudātī sunt).
21. Dīxit cōnsulem (ventūrus esse, ventūrum esse).
22. Fuērunt apud (Rōmānōs, Rōmānīs) duo cōnsulēs.
23. Potuērunt (mūnīre, mūnīvisse) castra.
24. Servī ex (terram, terrā) contendērunt.
25. (Eō diē, Eum diem) servōs līberāvit.
26. Sine (iniūriās, iniūriīs) pervēnerant.
27. (Quibus, Ad quōs) cōnsilium dedistī?
28. Fēminae (proelium, ad proelium) spectābant.
29. Laudāvērunt virum (quem, quī) interfectus est.
30. Hīs rēbus (cognitus, cognitīs), dux pācem petīvit.
31. Agricolae (bonae, bonī) in agrīs labōrant.
32. Barbarī (Rōmānīs, ad Rōmānōs) inimīcī sunt.
33. Propter (hoc, hōc) aciem īnstrūxit.
34. Omnēs ducēs erant (ēgregiōs, ēgregiī).
35. Hostēs sē (trādere, trādidisse) coēgit.
36. Post (victōriam, victōriā) veniunt praemia.
37. Oppidum (populō, ā populō) dēfēnsum est.
38. Puellae per (silvīs, silvās) contendēbant.
39. (Difficultāte, Cum difficultāte) factum est.
40. Dēbent (manent, manēre) in īnsulā.
41. Discēdisne ab (agrīs, agrōs)?
42. Ante (castrīs, castra) aciem īnstrūxit.
43. Virīs (quibus, quī) adsunt dīcit.
44. Fīnēs sunt fīnitimī (Germānīs, ad Germānōs).
45. Hominēs ad (flūmen, flūmine) contendēbant.
46. Dominus servum (labōrāns, labōrantem) vocāvit.
47. Magister dē (victōriam, victōriā) renūntiāvit.
48. Exīstimāvit (fēmina, fēminam) in vīllā esse.
49. Mīlitēs (excēdere, excessisse) prohibuit.
50. Negōtium (illō diē, in illō diē) cōnfēcit.
51. Puerum (Galba, Galbam) vīdī.
52. Germānī sunt propinquī (flūminī, ad flūmen).
53. Hostibus (captus, captīs), bellum cōnfectum est.

54. Post (multōs annōs, multīs annīs) frātrem vīdit.
55. Puellae mātrem (petit, petunt).
56. Vir (cui, quī) pecūniam dō est meus frāter.
57. Cōnsul fīlium (videt, vidēre) nōn potest.
58. Servī (perīculō, perīculī) līberābantur.
59. (Ad Rōmam, Rōmam) contendērunt.
60. Dīxit (rēx, rēgem) appropinquāre.
61. Līberī (inventus, inventī) erant.
62. (Ab equite, Equite) vulnerātus est.
63. Rōmānī (pugnāns, pugnantēs) interfectī sunt.
64. Imperātor scit Germānōs (sunt, esse) fortēs.
65. Iussit equōs (ēdūcēbantur, ēdūcī).
66. Hostēs castra (magna, magnam) cēpērunt.
67. Omnēs Britannī erant (barbarōs, barbarī).
68. Amīcōs (altitūdine, in altitūdine) superat.
69. Meus pater (trēs diēs, tribus diēbus) perveniet.
70. Ex (castrīs, castra) excessērunt.
71. Sine (praemium, praemiō) labōrant.
72. (Duōs mēnsēs, Duōbus mēnsibus) manēbit.
73. Nauta (rīpae, ad rīpam) contendit.
74. Ob (perīculum, perīculō) nōn respondit.
75. Cōnsilium (ducī, ad ducem) nūntiant.
76. Erat homō (magna auctōritās, magnae auctōritātis).
77. (Cum sociīs, Sociīs) discēdent.
78. Līberī in (īnsulā, īnsulam) mānsērunt.
79. Hāc rē (adductus, adductī), mīlitēs bene pugnāvērunt.
80. Puer (cuius, quī) pater erat cōnsul laudābātur.

B. Rewrite the sentences below, making *all* changes required by the directions in parentheses.

1. Campus **mīlle passūs** pertinuit.   (change to *three miles*)

----

2. Caesar est fortis.   (start the sentence with **Dīcunt**)

----

3. Omnēs ad **oppidum** contendērunt.   (change to *home*)

----

4. Puerō gladium **dant**.   (substitute equivalent form of **portāre**)

----

5. Līberī magistrum laudant.   (express the same idea in the passive voice)

----

6. **Dominus** servōs **docet**.   (change to direct address and command)

----

7. **Vir** auxilium dedit.   (change to the plural)

----

8. **Dē** monte vēnērunt.   (substitute **Trāns**)

----

9. Cicerō cōnsulem **audīvit**.   (substitute equivalent form of **esse**)

156

10. Puerī adductī sunt.   (substitute *girls*)

---

11. Trēs diēs nāvigābit.   (change to *within three days*)

---

12. Ab **amīcō** servātus est.   (substitute *signal*)

---

13. Gladiō pugnāvit.   (substitute *with the horseman*)

---

14. Eadem **oppida** vīdimus.   (change to the singular)

---

15. Nūntiāvī eōs urbem **dēfendere.**   (change to the past)

---

16. Timōre permōtī, **mīlitēs** proelium nōn fēcērunt.   (change to the singular)

---

17. Erat meus **frāter** quī exspectābat.   (substitute *sister*)

---

18. Cōnsul ad senātum **contendet.**   (substitute equivalent form of **dīcere**)

---

19. Scit exercitum **superāre.**   (change to the future)

---

20. Nautam nāvigantem monuī.   (change to the plural)

C. After each number below appear two sentences. Rewrite them, combining them into one sentence according to the instructions. Make whatever changes are necessary.

EXAMPLE: *Use the proper form of the relative pronoun:*

Calpurnia est bona.   Calpurnia est mea fīlia.

ANSWER: Calpurnia quae est mea fīlia est bona.

1. *Use et . . . et:*

Mārcus frātrem habet. Mārcus sorōrem habet.

---

2. *Use the proper form of the relative pronoun:*

Poēta est meus amīcus. Poēta est nōtus.

---

3. *Use an ablative absolute:*

Barbarī victī sunt. Rōmānī discessērunt.

---

4. *Use nec . . . nec:*

Nautam nōn videō. Nāvem nōn videō.

----

5. *Use the proper form of the relative pronoun:*

Silvās spectāmus. Silvās amāmus.

----

6. *Change to an indirect statement:*

Mīles est fortis. Hoc sciō.

----

7. *Use a complementary infinitive:*

Hodiē incipit. Hodiē labōrat.

----

8. *Use a noun in apposition:*

Caesarem laudāmus. Caesar est dux.

----

9. *Use a participle:*

Puer perterrēbātur. Puer in fugam sēsē dedit.

----

10. *Change to one interrogative sentence:*

Invēnī librum. Cuius est liber?

----

11. *Use an object infinitive:*

Iussit mīlitēs. Mīlitēs oppidum mūniunt.

----

12. *Use a present participle:*

Puellae lūdunt. Puellae sibi dīcunt.

----

13. *Use aut . . . aut:*

Līberī legent. Līberī scrībent.

----

14. *Use an ablative absolute:*

Sextus est cōnsul. Pāx erit.

----

15. *Change to an indirect statement:*

Prīnceps dēlēctus erat. Hoc audīvimus.

Unit X—*Passages for Comprehension*

Lesson 64

GROUP I

Do *not* write a translation of the following passages; read them through carefully several times and then answer in English the questions below. Use *everything* in the text that will make your answers clear and complete.

A

[Sacred geese save Rome]

Interim Rōma Capitōliumque in magnō perīculō erant. Gallī collem ascendere nocte temptābant, nam Capitōlium in locō altissimō erat. Rōmānī magnopere permovēbantur. Omnia in silentiō erant. In Capitōliō M. Manlius, quī anteā cōnsul fuerat, praeerat. Etiam in Capitōliō erant ānserēs (*geese*) sacrī. Manlius Gallōs advenientēs nōn audīvit, sed ānserēs Gallōs audiēbant. Incipiēbant clangere (*cackle*) et Manlium excitāvērunt (*awakened*). Manlius, vir bellō ēgregius, armīs captīs, Gallōs ab Capitōliō prohibuit. Hōc modō ānserēs Rōmam servāvērunt.

1. What were in great danger? _____

_____

2. What were the Gauls trying to do, and when did they make the attempt? _____

_____

3. Where was the Capitolium situated? _____

_____

4. How did the Roman people feel? _____

_____

5. What position had Manlius previously held? _____

_____

6. How did the geese warn Manlius? _____

_____

7. What kind of man was Manlius? _____

_____

8. What two things did Manlius do? _____

_____

B

[The courage of Regulus]

Ōlim Rōmānī cum Poenīs (*Carthaginians*) bellum longum et ācre gerēbant. Dux Rōmānōrum, nōmine M. Regulus, ab Poenīs captus est. Poenī, iam bellō dēfessī (*exhausted*), pācem cōnfīrmāre cum Rōmānīs cupiēbant. Hoc cōnsilium cēpērunt. Regulō dīxērunt, "Discēde ad senātum Rōmānum et iubē cīvēs tuōs pācem facere. Sī impetrābis (*gain your request*), līberāberis; sī nōn impetrābis, interficiēris." Regulus domum nāvigāvit. Cīvibus suīs ipse dīxit, "Poenī pācem cupiunt. Nōlīte (*Do not*) pācem facere. Pugnāte fortius et ācrius. Tum, Poenīs victīs, pāx erit." Hīs dictīs, Regulus ad Poenōs contendit et interfectus est.

1. Describe the war carried on between the Romans and the Carthaginians. _____

_____

2. What happened to Regulus? ---------------------------------

----

3. Why did the Carthaginians want peace? -----------------------

----

4. What two things did they tell Regulus to do? ----------------

----

5. What would happen to him if he succeeded in his mission? -----

----

6. What two things did Regulus urge his countrymen to do? -------

----

7. When did he say there would be peace? -----------------------

----

8. What finally happened to Regulus? ---------------------------

----

C

[Hannibal crosses the Alps]

Nōnō diē Hannibal cum cōpiīs suīs ad Alpēs pervēnit. Castrīs positīs, omnēs mīlitēs quiētī (*to rest*) sē dedērunt. Casus nivis (*falling of snow*) etiam magnum terrōrem adiēcit. Hannibal in prōmontōriō stāns mīlitibus Italiam ostendit. Sed iter ad Italiam difficillimum fuit. Arboribus magnīs dēiectīs, via facta est per quam mīlitēs ductī sunt. Etiam elephantī per viam dēdūcī poterant. Hōc modō in Italiam pervēnērunt. Aliī auctōrēs (*some authors*) scrībunt fuisse in exercitū Hannibalis centum mīlia peditum (*infantry*), vīgintī mīlia equitum; aliī scrībunt fuisse vīgintī mīlia peditum, sex mīlia equitum.

1. When did Hannibal arrive at the Alps? ----------------------

----

2. After pitching camp, what did the soldiers do? -------------

----

3. How did the falling of snow affect the soldiers? ----------

----

4. While standing on a promontory, what did Hannibal do? -----

----

5. Describe the journey to Italy. ----------------------------

----

6. What did the soldiers do to make a road through the Alps? --

----

7. What animals accompanied the soldiers? -------------------

----

8. How many infantrymen and cavalrymen were in Hannibal's army, according to the first group of

writers? --

----

9. According to the second group of writers, how many infantrymen were there?_____

_____

GROUP II

Read the following passages carefully, but do *not* write a translation. Below each passage you will find five questions. Each question has four answers, one of which is correct. Underline the correct answer.

A

[The murder of Gracchus]

Decem annīs interpositīs (*having elapsed*), īdem furor (*passion*) quī Ti. Gracchum, Gāium frātrem eius occupāvit. Gāius enim omnibus Italicīs (*Italians*) cīvitātem dabat, extendēbat eam paene (*almost*) ad Alpēs, agrōs dīvidēbat, prohibuit quemquam (*each*) cīvem plūs quīngentīs iugeribus (*500 acres*) habēre, iudicia (*law courts*) ā senātū trānsferēbat ad equitēs, frūmentum plēbī darī iussit. Hunc L. Opimius cōnsul armīs petīvit, dēnique (*finally*) interfēcit. Corpus eius in Tiberim iactum est.

1. What was the relationship between Tiberius and Gaius? They were

    a. enemies   *c.* friends
    b. brothers   *d.* strangers

2. What happened after a lapse of ten years?

    a. Gaius seized his brother.   *c.* The same passion seized Gaius.
    b. Gracchus seized Gaius.   *d.* Tiberius seized Gracchus.

3. What was one of the reforms accomplished by Gaius?

    a. He transferred the law courts to the senate.
    b. He prevented each citizen from having less than 500 acres.
    c. He refused citizenship to the Italians.
    d. He ordered grain to be given to the common people.

4. How did Lucius Opimius react to these reforms?

    a. He attacked Gaius and killed him.   *c.* He killed the consul with arms.
    b. He sought arms and fought.   *d.* He asked the consul for arms.

5. How was the body of Gaius disposed of?

    a. It was given to Tiberius.   *c.* It was buried by Tiberius.
    b. It was thrown into the river.   *d.* It was carried away on the Tiber.

B

[Scipio is accused by Naevius]

M. Naevius, tribūnus plēbis, accūsāvit Scīpiōnem ad populum, dīxitque eum accēpisse ā rēge Antiochō pecūniam. Scīpiō prōmīserat sē cum Antiochō pācem condiciōnibus mollibus (*easy*) populī Rōmānī nōmine factūrum esse. Tum Scīpiō respondit, "Memoriā teneō hodiē esse diem quō Hannibalem, imperiō vestrō inimīcissimum, magnō proeliō in terrā Africā vīcī, pācemque et victōriam vōbīs obtinuī. Deīs ingrātī (*ungrateful*) nōn dēbēmus esse. Iovī (*To Jupiter*) optimō maximō grātiās agere dēbēmus omnēs." Hīs dictīs, contendere ad Capitōlium incēpit.

1. What did Naevius accuse Scipio of doing?

    a. He had received money for King Antiochus.
    b. He had given money to the people.
    c. He had received money from King Antiochus.
    d. He had received money from the people's tribune.

2. What had Scipio promised to do?

    a. To make peace by easy terms.
    b. To make known the name of the Roman people.
    c. To make peace easy for Antiochus.
    d. To make easy terms for the Roman people.

3. What did Scipio remember about this day?

    a. Hannibal was victorious in Africa.
    b. Scipio was conquered in a great battle.
    c. Hannibal obtained peace and victory.
    d. Scipio defeated Hannibal and obtained peace and victory.

4. What reference is made to the gods?

    a. The gods ought not to be ungrateful.
    b. The Romans ought not to be ungrateful to the gods.
    c. All ought to erect a statue to Jupiter.
    d. The greatest and best gods ought to be thanked.

5. What did Scipio do after he made these remarks?

    a. He attacked the Capitolium.
    b. He began to fight for the Capitolium.
    c. He started to hasten towards the Capitolium.
    d. He began to withdraw from the Capitolium.

GROUP III

Read the following passages carefully, but do *not* write a translation. Below each passage you will find five incomplete Latin statements. Complete each statement by underlining one of the four choices given.

A

[Horatius defends the bridge]

Tarquinius rēx, Rōmā expulsus, in Etrūriam sēsē in fugam dedit. Ibi Lars Porsena, rēx, temptāvit Tarquiniō auxilium dare eīque rēgnum Rōmae obtinēre. Cum exercitū magnō ad (*near*) Rōmam vēnit Porsena. Senātus Rōmānus magnopere perterrēbātur, nam nōmen Porsena maximum erat. Rōmānī praesidiīs urbem mūniēbant. Pōns autem in Tibere erat quī iter Rōmam dedit. Horātius Coclēs, vir fortissimus, dīxit sē cum duōbus amīcīs pontem dēfēnsūrum esse. Hostēs sagittās multās in Horātium coniciēbant, sed Horātius pontem nōn relīquit. Dēnique (*Finally*) Rōmānī pontem rescidērunt (*cut down*), Horātius in flūmen dēsiluit (*jumped*) et ad rīpam trānāvit (*swam*). Ita Rōma servāta est.

1. Tarquinius, Rōmā expulsus,

    a. temptāvit vincere Porsenam.   *c.* auxilium ab Porsenā petīvit.
    b. Rōmam magnō cum exercitū occupāvit.   *d.* rēgnum Rōmae obtinuit.

2. Rōmānī perterritī sunt quod

    a. urbem mūnīre nōn poterant.   *c.* Tarquinius magnum exercitum habuit.
    b. spem nōn habēbant.   *d.* Porsena potentissimus erat.

3. Horātius pontem dēfendit

    a. cum exercitū magnō.   *c.* multīs cum amīcīs.
    b. cum duōbus sociīs.   *d.* cum senātū Rōmānō.

4. Hostibus sagittās conicientibus, Horātius

    a. in ponte mānsit.   *c.* multās sagittās cēpit.
    b. pontem relīquit.   *d.* pontem rescidit.

5. Dēnique virtūs Horātī

a. pontem servāvit.
b. Rōmam cōnservāvit.

c. mortem eius effēcit.
d. Rōmam dēfēcit.

B

[Fabricius refuses to be bribed]

Pyrrhus, Graecus imperātor, bellum cum Rōmānīs gerēbat et Rōmam contendere cōnstituit. Exercitus Rōmānus perterrēbātur et in Campāniam sēsē in fugam dedit. Lēgātī (*Envoys*) ad Pyrrhum missī sunt quod captīvōs redimere (*to ransom*) cupiēbant. Ūnum ex lēgātīs Rōmānōrum, Fabricium, Pyrrhus sollicitāre (*to bribe*) temptāvit, quartā parte rēgnī prōmissā, sed frūstrā (*in vain*). Posteā Pyrrhus lēgātum nōbilem virum, Cineam nōmine, ad Rōmānōs mīsit et pācem aequīs condiciōnibus petīvit. Partem Italiae, quam iam armīs occupāverat, obtinēre cupīvit. Hoc Rōmānīs nōn grātum (*pleasing*) erat. Fabricius contrā (*against*) Pyrrhum missus est. Dē eō Pyrrhus ōlim dīxit, "Ille est Fabricius quī difficilius ab honestāte (*uprightness*) quam sōl ā cursū (*course*) suō removērī potest."

1. Exercitus Rōmānus sēsē in fugam dedit quod Pyrrhus

a. ad Campāniam contendit.
b. Rōmam appropinquābat.

c. Rōmam occupāvit.
d. erat Graecus imperātor.

2. Pyrrhus prōmīsit quartam partem rēgnī sī Fabricius

a. Pyrrhō auxilium dederit.
b. captīvōs redēmerit.

c. ad Rōmānōs remissus erit.
d. lēgātōs Rōmānōrum remīserit.

3. Pyrrhus partem Italiae obtinēre cupīvit

a. armīs.
b. per lēgātōs nōbilēs.

c. proeliō.
d. aequīs condiciōnibus pācis.

4. Rōmānī Pyrrhō cēdere nōn cupiēbant, itaque

a. arma eius occupāvērunt.
b. dīxērunt eum nōn grātum esse.

c. Fabricium contrā eum mīsērunt.
d. lēgātī contrā eum missī sunt.

5. Pyrrhus ōlim dīxit, "Fabricius ab honestāte removērī potest

a. sine difficultāte."
b. facile."

c. maximā cum difficultāte."
d. cursū sōlis."

C

[Tacitus, a Roman historian, describes the ancient Germans]

Tacitus, scrīptor Rōmānus, dē Germāniā et vītā Germānōrum scrīpsit. Dīxit Germāniam silvās multās magnāsque habēre. Quā dē causā virī dē aliīs terrīs timēbant, neque bellum gerēbant. Cōpiās in Germāniam nōn indūcēbant. Germānī erant mīlitēs fortissimī atque pugnās amābant. Fēminīs Germāniae quidem agrōs committēbant.

Tacitus etiam dē deīs Germānōrum scrīpsit. Rōmānī deīs templa multa faciēbant et statuās deōrum in templīs pōnēbant. Germānī autem deōs in silvīs colēbant (*worshipped*). Omnium deōrum maximē Mercurium colēbant, deārum Terram.

Germānī exīstimābant deam Terram in īnsulā habitāre (*lived*). Ea currum (*chariot*) habēbat. Quotannīs (*Every year*) dea populum Germānum vīsēbat (*came to visit*). Eō tempore omnēs arma dēpōnēbant. Bella nōn erant, sed pāx et amīcitia.

1. Tacitus scrīpsit

a. vītam Germānōrum magnam esse.
b. in Germāniā multās silvās esse.

c. Germāniam patriam magnam esse.
d. Germānōs multōs esse.

2. Propter hoc virī dē aliīs terrīs

a. bellum gerunt.
b. cōpiās in Germāniam dūcunt.

c. proelia nōn timent.
d. perterritī sunt.

163

3. Germānī, virī fortissimī,

    a. pugnāre cupiunt.
    b. in agrīs labōrant.

    c. fēminās Germāniae amant.
    d. mīlitibus agrōs committunt.

4. Deī Germānōrum

    a. statuās in templīs habēbant.
    b. in templīs pōnēbantur.

    c. in silvīs colēbantur.
    d. in silvīs templa habēbant.

5. Deā Terrā in Germāniā vīsā, virī

    a. arma nōn capiēbant.
    b. in īnsulā habitāre cupiēbant.

    c. pācem et amīcitiam āmīsērunt.
    d. Mercurium tum colēbant.

D

[Terms of peace after the battle of Zama]

Scīpiō, imperātor Rōmānus, Hannibalem ad Zamam vīcit. Carthāginiēnsēs ad Scīpiōnem lēgātōs (*envoys*) mīsērunt quī dē pāce agēbant (*discussed*).

Tum Scīpiō eīs dūrās (*harsh*) condiciōnēs pācis imposuit. Carthāginiēnsēs poterant occupāre urbēs agrōsque quōs ante bellum habēbant. Sed omnēs captīvōs (*prisoners*) Rōmānīs trādere dēbēbant. Omnēs nāvēs longās (*battleships*) et elephantōs etiam Rōmānīs trādere dēbēbant. Praetereā (*In addition*) Scīpiō multam pecūniam et centum obsidēs (*hostages*) petīvit.

Eae condiciōnēs pācis paucīs Carthāginiēnsibus nōn idōneae erant. Hannibal autem dīxit aequās necessariāsque esse. Itaque Carthāginiēnsēs eās accēpērunt.

Scīpiō propter suam victōriam in Africā appellātus est *Africānus.* Hannibal autem ad Antiochum, rēgem Syriae, sēsē in fugam dedit, et posteā in terrā Bīthȳniā sē interfēcit.

1. Lēgātī Carthāginiēnsium

    a. pācem petīvērunt.
    b. ad Zamam vīcērunt.

    c. Hannibalem ad Scīpiōnem mīsērunt.
    d. cum Hannibale dē pāce agēbant.

2. Carthāginiēnsēs victī

    a. imposuērunt dūrās condiciōnēs pācis.
    b. bellum gerere poterant in urbēs agrōsque.

    c. habēbant urbēs agrōsque Rōmānōrum.
    d. dūrās condiciōnēs pācis accēpērunt.

3. Rōmānī Carthāginiēnsēs coēgērunt

    a. ab Rōmānīs elephantōs petere.
    b. captīvōs, nāvēs, elephantōs trādere.

    c. obsidibus nāvēs longās trādere.
    d. multōs captīvōs Scīpiōnī dare.

4. Condiciōnēs pācis

    a. erant idōneae omnibus Carthāginiēnsibus.
    b. ab Carthāginiēnsibus acceptae sunt.

    c. inīquae erant.
    d. Hannibalī nōn idōneae erant.

5. Post victōriam Zamae

    a. Hannibal in Syriā sē interfēcit.
    b. Scīpiō ad Antiochum contendit.

    c. Scīpiō cognōmen *Africānum* accēpit.
    d. Scīpiō appellātus est *Africānus* ab Bīthȳniā.

Unit XI—Derivation and Word Study

Lesson 65—PREFIXES AND VERB FAMILIES

Compound verbs in Latin are formed by adding prefixes, many of which are prepositions, to simple verbs. In most cases there is no change in spelling. However, for ease of pronunciation, the following changes in spelling do occur in some verbs:

1. *Assimilation.* The final letter of a prefix may change to the first letter of the simple verb. The letter **n** before **p** is changed to **m.**

$$\text{con + moveō = commoveō}$$
$$\text{in + pellō = impellō}$$

2. *Contraction.* A letter may be dropped completely.

$$\text{co + agō = cōgō}$$
$$\text{con + iaciō = coniciō}$$

3. *Weakening of vowel.* The vowel **a** or **e** of the simple verb is weakened to **i** in the compound.

$$\text{in + capiō = incipiō}$$
$$\text{con + teneō = contineō}$$

Note

1. A compound verb may undergo *two* changes in spelling, such as assimilation and weakening of vowel.

$$\text{ad + capiō = accipiō}$$
$$\text{ob + faciō = officiō}$$

2. The force of the prefix usually gives added meaning to the simple verb.

dūcō, lead	**prōdūcō,** lead forth
mittō, send	**remittō,** send back

3. Sometimes a compound verb takes on a new meaning.

faciō, do	**interficiō,** kill
habeō, have	**prohibeō,** prevent

PREFIXES

ab (ā), from, away
ad, to, toward, near
circum, around
con (co, com), with, together, deeply, completely
dē, from, down

dis (dī), apart, away
ex (ē), out
in, in, on, upon
inter, between
ob, against, toward

per, through, thoroughly
prae, ahead
prō, forth
re (red), back, again
sub (sus), under, up from under
trāns (trā), across, over

COMMON VERB FAMILIES

agō, drive
  cōgō, drive together, gather

capiō, take
  accipiō, receive
  incipiō, take on, begin

cēdō, go, retreat
  discēdō, go away
  excēdō, go out

dō, give
  reddō, give back
  trādō, hand over

dūcō, lead
  addūcō, lead to, influence
  prōdūcō, lead forth

faciō, make, do
  cōnficiō, do completely, finish
  dēficiō, fail, revolt
  interficiō, kill
  perficiō, do thoroughly, finish

habeō, have, hold
  prohibeō, keep off, prevent

iaciō, throw
  coniciō, throw together

legō, choose, read
  dēligō, choose (from), select

mittō, send, let go
  āmittō, send away, lose
  committō, bring together, join, entrust
  dīmittō, send off, dismiss
  intermittō, interrupt, stop
  permittō, let go, allow, entrust
  praemittō, send ahead
  remittō, send back

moveō, move
  commoveō, move deeply, alarm
  permoveō, move thoroughly, alarm
  removeō, move back, withdraw

nūntiō, report
  ēnūntiō, speak out, proclaim
  renūntiō, bring back word

parō, prepare
  comparō, get together, arrange

pōnō, put
  expōnō, put out, set forth
  prōpōnō, set forth, offer

scrībō, write
  cōnscrībō, enlist, enroll

servō, keep, save
  cōnservō, keep together, preserve

spectō, look at
  exspectō, look out for, await

sum, be
  absum, be away
  adsum, be near
  possum, be able
  praesum, be at the head of

teneō, hold
  contineō, hold together
  obtineō, obtain, hold
  pertineō, pertain, extend
  sustineō, hold up

veniō, come
  circumveniō, surround
  conveniō, come together
  inveniō, come upon, find
  perveniō, arrive, reach

EXERCISES

A. Separate the following compound verbs into their component parts (prefix and simple verb), and give the meaning of each part:

	PREFIX	MEANING	SIMPLE VERB	MEANING
1. cōnservō				
2. renūntiō				
3. sustineō				
4. circumveniō				
5. trādō				
6. praemittō				
7. adsum				
8. prōpōnō				
9. exspectō				
10. perficiō				

B. Using your knowledge of prefixes, what would you judge to be the meaning of the following compound verbs?

1. trānsportō ....

2. indūcō ....

3. expellō ....

4. permaneō ....

5. accēdō ....

6. dēpōnō ....

7. intersum ....

8. prōvideō ....

166

9. convocō ---------------------------------
10. praedīcō -------------------------------
11. abiciō ----------------------------------
12. redigō ----------------------------------
13. suscipiō --------------------------------
14. distineō -------------------------------
15. recipiō ---------------------------------
16. praeficiō ------------------------------
17. reprimō --------------------------------

18. interveniō ----------------------------
19. circumdūcō --------------------------
20. ēvocō -----------------------------------
21. trānsmittō --------------------------
22. dēsum -----------------------------------
23. reficiō ---------------------------------
24. opprimō -------------------------------
25. adiciō ----------------------------------

C. Form compound verbs by combining the following prefixes and simple verbs. Make changes in spelling where necessary.

1. dē + dūcō -----------------------------
2. in + pōnō ------------------------------
3. ad + faciō -----------------------------
4. ob + ferō ------------------------------
5. re + teneō -----------------------------

6. per + capiō ----------------------------
7. prō + iaciō ----------------------------
8. prae + nūntiō -------------------------
9. con + legō -----------------------------
10. inter + cēdō -------------------------

D. Give the meaning of the following English compound verbs, all derived from Latin:

1. compose ------------------------------
2. produce ------------------------------
3. remit ---------------------------------
4. eject ----------------------------------
5. circumscribe -------------------------

6. intervene ----------------------------
7. precede ------------------------------
8. transport ----------------------------
9. impel ---------------------------------
10. perfect ------------------------------

Triremes

Triremes, war-galleys equipped with three banks of oars, were propelled by oars and sails. They attained a speed nearly equal to that of a modern steamboat. The rostrum, or beak, below the prow was used to ram another vessel.

Lesson 66—LATIN ROOTS USED IN ENGLISH WORDS

ROOT	MEANING	EXAMPLES
aequ (*equ*)	even, just	equality
ag, act	do, perform	agent, action
am, amat	love	amiable, amatory
aqu	water	aqueous
aud	hear	audience
bene	well	benefit
cap, cip, cept	take, seize	captive, recipient, accept
capit	head	capital
ced (*ceed*), cess	move, yield	recede, proceed, concession
corp, corpor	body	corpulent, corporal
cup	desire, wish	cupidity
de	god	deity
dict	say, speak	diction
doc, doct	teach	docile, doctor
duc, duct	lead	induce, product
fac, fic, fact, fect	do, make	facility, efficient, factor, effect
fid	trust, belief	fidelity
fin	end	infinite
grat	pleasing	gratitude
hab, hib	have, hold	habit, prohibit
iect (*ject*)	throw	reject
iur (*jur*)	right, law	jury
iust (*just*)	just, fair	justice
leg, lect	read, choose	legible, elect
liber	free	liberate
libr	book	library
loc, locat	place	local, locate
luc	light	lucid
magn	large, great	magnitude
mal	bad	malice
mitt, miss	send, let go	remittance, mission
monstrat	show, point out	demonstrate
mort	death	mortal
mov, mot	move	remove, motion
mult	much, many	multitude
naut	sailor	nautical
nav	ship	naval
nomin	name	nominate
nov	new	novelty
omn	all	omnibus
ped	foot	pedal
pell (*pel*), puls	drive	repellent, compel, compulsive
pet	seek, ask	compete
pon, pos, posit	put, place	component, compose, position
port	carry	import
press	press	oppression
pug, pugn	fight	pugilist, pugnacious
sc	know	science
scrib, script	write	describe, scripture
serv	save	preserve
simil	like	simile
spec, spic, spect	look	specimen, despicable, inspect
stru, struct	build	instrument, construct

168

tempor	time	temporary
ten (*tain*), tin, tent	hold	tenure, retain, continent, content
tim	fear	timid
un	one	unify
urb	city	urban
ven, vent	come	convene, convent
ver	true	verify
vid, vis	see	evident, revise
vinc, vict	conquer	invincible, victor
vit	life	vital
voc (*voke*), vocat	call	vocal, revoke, vocation

EXERCISES

A. In the space before each word in column *A*, write the letter of its meaning in column *B*.

	Column A		Column B
-------	**1.** confide	*a.*	hearing
-------	**2.** magnify	*b.*	easily taught
-------	**3.** infinite	*c.*	allowing light through
-------	**4.** repulse	*d.*	undying
-------	**5.** illegible	*e.*	call out
-------	**6.** audition	*f.*	extreme desire
-------	**7.** gratify	*g.*	trust
-------	**8.** novice	*h.*	drive back
-------	**9.** translucent	*i.*	endless
-------	**10.** veracious	*j.*	lawful power
-------	**11.** evoke	*k.*	enlarge
-------	**12.** similitude	*l.*	unbeatable
-------	**13.** docile	*m.*	truthful
-------	**14.** invincible	*n.*	worship as a god
-------	**15.** concupiscence	*o.*	unable to be read
-------	**16.** inequity	*p.*	delay in time
-------	**17.** temporize	*q.*	beginner
-------	**18.** deify	*r.*	please
-------	**19.** immortal	*s.*	likeness
-------	**20.** jurisdiction	*t.*	injustice

B. Next to each italicized word, of Latin derivation, are four words, one of which gives a clue to the meaning of the derivative. Underline the correct clue.

1. *conspicuous*	(*a*) heard	(*b*) seen	(*c*) felt	(*d*) thought
2. *retentive*	(*a*) yielding	(*b*) turning	(*c*) holding	(*d*) bending
3. *infidel*	(*a*) believe	(*b*) play	(*c*) start	(*d*) follow
4. *indoctrinate*	(*a*) injure	(*b*) capture	(*c*) poison	(*d*) teach
5. *projection*	(*a*) throw	(*b*) abandon	(*c*) run	(*d*) hate

6. *decapitate*	(*a*) body	(*b*) head	(*c*) foot	(*d*) hand
7. *pellucid*	(*a*) light	(*b*) dark	(*c*) heavy	(*d*) colored
8. *denomination*	(*a*) number	(*b*) crowd	(*c*) picture	(*d*) name
9. *repugnant*	(*a*) hear	(*b*) feel	(*c*) fight	(*d*) touch
10. *contemporaneous*	(*a*) hatred	(*b*) time	(*c*) city	(*d*) call

C. For each English derivative, give the Latin root and its meaning.

	LATIN ROOT	MEANING
1. infinity	----------------------	-------------------------------
2. circumspect	----------------------	-------------------------------
3. impediment	----------------------	-------------------------------
4. elucidate	----------------------	-------------------------------
5. recession	----------------------	-------------------------------
6. deportment	----------------------	-------------------------------
7. convince	----------------------	-------------------------------
8. impulsive	----------------------	-------------------------------
9. suburban	----------------------	-------------------------------
10. beneficent	----------------------	-------------------------------

Lesson 67—SUFFIXES

A suffix is an addition to a stem and serves to define its meaning. By learning the meaning of common suffixes, we can arrive at the meaning of new words, both Latin and English, based on familiar stems. Following is a list of common Latin suffixes with the English equivalents in parentheses:

FORMING NOUNS

-tās (*-ty*), **-tia** (*-ce, -cy*), **-tūdō** (*-tude*), **-tūs** (*-tude*), denote quality, condition, act of

veri**tās**	veri*ty*	condition of being true
clēmen**tia**	clemen*cy*	act of showing mercy
magni**tūdō**	magni*tude*	quality of being large

-or (*-or*), denotes physical or mental state

horr**or**	horr*or*	state of fear

-tor (*-tor*), denotes one who does something

vic**tor**	vic*tor*	one who conquers

-iō (*-ion*), **-tiō** (*-tion*), denote an act or the result of an act

reg**iō**	reg*ion*	result of limiting an area
ōrā**tiō**	ora*tion*	act of speaking

-ellus, -olus, denote small or little

agellus (ager + ellus) = a little field
gladiolus (gladius + olus) = a small sword

FORMING ADJECTIVES

-ōsus (*-ous, -ose*), denotes full of

perīcul**ōsus**	peril*ous*	full of danger

-ālis (*-al*), **-ānus** (*-an*), **-āris** (*-ar, -ary*), **-ēlis** (*-el*), **-icus** (*-ic, -ical*), **-idus** (*-id*), **-ilis** (*-ile*), **-ius** (*-ious*), **-ter** (*-trian*), **-timus** (*-time*), denote belonging to or pertaining to

vīt**ālis**	vit*al*	pertaining to life
urb**ānus**	urb*an*	belonging to a city
aquā**ticus**	aquat*ic*	pertaining to water

FORMING VERBS

-tō, denotes repeated or intense action

agitō (agō + tō) = drive or move violently

EXERCISES

A. Separate the following compound words into their component parts (simple word and suffix), and give the meaning of each part:

	SIMPLE WORD	MEANING	SUFFIX	MEANING
1. celeritās	----------	----------------	--------	------------------------------
2. amīcitia	----------	----------------	--------	------------------------------
3. altitūdō	----------	----------------	--------	------------------------------

171

----------	----------------	--------	-------------------------------------
----------	----------------	--------	-------------------------------------

6. cupidus

7. facilis

8. maritimus

9. imperātor

10. lībertās

B. Using your knowledge of suffixes, what would you judge to be the meaning of the following Latin words?

1. mīlitāris _____

2. mūnītiō _____

3. hostilis _____

4. montānus _____

5. doctor _____

6. nātūrālis _____

7. fīliolus _____

8. animōsus _____

9. equester _____

10. populāris _____

11. iactō _____

12. domesticus _____

13. patrius _____

14. cīvicus _____

15. sententia _____

16. nōbilitās _____

17. servitūs _____

18. libellus _____

19. amor _____

20. viator _____

21. bellicōsus _____

22. fidēlis _____

23. fortitūdō _____

24. bonitās _____

25. ostentō _____

26. pueritia _____

27. amābilis _____

28. levitās _____

29. mortālis _____

30. audītor _____

C. Give the meaning of the following English words, all derived from Latin, paying particular attention to suffixes:

1. servitude _____

2. demonstrator _____

3. appellation _____

4. timorous _____

5. portal _____

6. celerity _____

7. terror _____

8. potency _____

9. magnitude _____

10. sylvan _____

11. maritime _____

12. aquatic _____

13. pecuniary --
14. verity --
15. lucid --
16. facility --
17. puerile --
18. verbose --
19. arboreal --
20. generic --

Roman Dress

The toga, the formal garment of the Romans, has become associated with tradition, dignity, and authority. Today the academic gowns worn at commencement exercises and the judicial robes worn in court are reminiscent of the Roman toga.

Lesson 68—RELATED WORDS

The following is a list of words in groups which are related in meaning and resemble one another in spelling:

ācer, sharp; **ācriter,** sharply; **aciēs,** sharp edge, battle line

aequus, even; **inīquus (in + aequus),** uneven

altus, high; **altitūdō,** height

amīcus, friend; **amīcitia,** friendship; **inimīcus (in + amīcus),** unfriendly; **amō,** love

ante, before; **anteā,** previously

celer, swift; **celeriter,** swiftly; **celeritās,** swiftness

cīvis, citizen; **cīvitās,** citizenship, state

cupiō, desire; **cupidus,** desirous; **cupiditās,** desire

decem, ten; **decimus,** tenth

diēs, day; **hodiē (hōc diē),** today; **merīdiēs (medius diēs),** midday, noon

dūcō, lead; **dux,** leader

equus, horse; **eques,** horseman; **equitātus,** cavalry

faciō, do; **factum,** deed; **facultās,** ability to do, opportunity; **facilis,** able to be done, easy; **facile,** easily; **difficilis (dis + facilis),** not able to be done, difficult; **difficultās,** difficulty

fīlius, son; **fīlia,** daughter

fīnis, boundary; **fīnitimus,** neighboring, bordering

fortis, brave; **fortiter,** bravely

imperium, command; **imperātor,** commander

inter, between; **interim,** time between, meanwhile

lātus, wide; **lātitūdō,** width

līber, free; **līberō,** set free; **lībertās,** freedom; **līberī,** (freeborn) children

magnus, great; **magnopere,** greatly; **magnitūdō,** greatness; **magis,** in a greater degree; **magister,** one with greater learning, teacher

mare, sea; **maritimus,** pertaining to the sea

multus, much; **multitūdō,** great number

nāvis, ship; **nāvigō,** sail; **nauta,** sailor

novem, nine; **nōnus,** ninth

octō, eight; **octāvus,** eighth

pater, father; **patria,** fatherland

possum, have power, be able; **potēns,** powerful; **potestās,** power

post, after; **posteā,** afterwards

prīmus, first; **prīnceps (prīmus + capiō),** holding first place, chief

puer, boy; **puella,** girl

pugna, fight; **pugnō,** fight

quattuor, four; **quārtus,** fourth

quīnque, five; **quīntus,** fifth

relinquō, leave behind; **reliquus,** remaining

rēx, king; **rēgīna,** queen; **rēgnum,** kingdom

septem, seven; **septimus,** seventh

sex, six; **sextus,** sixth

timeō, fear; **timor,** fear; **timidus,** fearful

trēs, three; **tertius,** third

veniō, come; **adventus (ad + veniō),** coming toward, arrival

vērus, true; **vērō,** truly

videō, see; **prūdēns (prō + vidēns),** foreseeing, wise

vincō, conquer; **victor,** conqueror; **victōria,** victory

vir, man; **virtūs,** manliness

vocō, call; **vōx,** voice

vulnerō, wound; **vulnus,** wound

EXERCISES

A. In the space before each word in column *A*, write the letter of its related word in column *B*.

	Column A		Column B
-------	**1.** faciō	*a.*	prīnceps
-------	**2.** dux	*b.*	adventus
-------	**3.** quārtus	*c.*	rēgnum
-------	**4.** prīmus	*d.*	inīquus
-------	**5.** reliquus	*e.*	nauta
-------	**6.** veniō	*f.*	prūdēns
-------	**7.** possum	*g.*	magis
-------	**8.** rēx	*h.*	difficilis
-------	**9.** aciēs	*i.*	relinquō
-------	**10.** magnitūdō	*j.*	inimīcus
-------	**11.** diēs	*k.*	indūcō
-------	**12.** nāvis	*l.*	potestās
-------	**13.** aequus	*m.*	ācer
-------	**14.** amīcitia	*n.*	hodiē
-------	**15.** videō	*o.*	quattuor

B. In each group, underline the word *not* related to the word in italics.

1. *vērus*   (vērō, vir, vēritās, vērum)
2. *possum*   (sum, potēns, potestās, pōnō)
3. *rēgnum*   (rēs pūblica, rēx, rēgīna, regō)
4. *līber*   (lībertās, līberō, liber, līberī)
5. *equus*   (eques, aequus, equitātus, equester)
6. *faciō*   (facultās, difficilis, facilis, familia)
7. *cupiō*   (cupidus, cupiditās, corpus, concupiēns)
8. *fortis*   (fortūna, fortiter, fortitūdō, fortissimus)
9. *nāvis*   (nāvigō, nauta, nātūra, nāvālis)
10. *vincō*   (convincō, victor, vīta, victōria)

Lesson 69—SYNONYMS

VERBS

agō, faciō, do
āmittō, dīmittō, send away
appellō, vocō, call
capiō, occupō, seize
cognōscō, sciō, know
committō, permittō, entrust
commoveō, permoveō, perterreō, alarm

cōnficiō, perficiō, finish
contendō, pugnō, fight
dēmōnstrō, ostendō, show
discēdō, excēdō, relinquō, leave
exīstimō, putō, think
expōnō, prōpōnō, set forth
habeō, teneō, have

iaciō, coniciō, throw
legō, dēligō, choose
nūntiō, ēnūntiō, renūntiō, report
parō, comparō, prepare
servō, cōnservō, save
spectō, videō, see
superō, vincō, conquer

NOUNS

amīcus, socius, friend
animus, mēns, mind
beneficium, grātia, favor
cīvitās, rēs pūblica, state
collis, mōns, mountain
cōnsilium, ratiō, plan

dux, imperātor, general
equitātus, equitēs, cavalry
fīnēs, terra, land
homō, vir, man
hostis, inimīcus, enemy
imperium, potestās, power

iter, via, road
iūs, lēx, law
līberī, puerī, children
oppidum, urbs, town
proelium, pugna, battle

PRONOUNS

hic, ille, is, he

ADJECTIVES

aequus, pār, equal
commūnis, pūblicus, public

fīnitimus, propinquus, neighboring
hic, is, this

ille, is, that
nōbilis, nōtus, famous
novus, recēns, new

ADVERBS

iam, nunc, now

quidem, vērō, indeed

PREPOSITIONS

ab, dē, ex, from

ante, prō, before
apud, inter, among

ob, propter, on account of

CONJUNCTIONS

autem, tamen, however

enim, nam, for

et, -que, atque, and

EXERCISES

A. Underline the synonym of the word in italics.

1. *prō:*   propter, ante, ab
2. *pugnō:*   contendō, committō, cōnficiō
3. *ratiō:*   iūs, cōpia, cōnsilium
4. *recēns:*   novus, pār, omnis
5. *tamen:*   atque, quidem, autem

6. *occupō:*   cupiō, capiō, cōgō
7. *mēns:*   homō, animus, modus
8. *pār:*   inīquus, ōrdō, aequus
9. *faciō:*   agō, parō, premō
10. *potestās:*   fortis, virtūs, imperium

176

B. In the space before each word in column *A*, write the letter of its synonym in column *B*.

	Column A		Column B
_____	**1.** nōtus	*a.*	mōns
_____	**2.** iūs	*b.*	socius
_____	**3.** oppidum	*c.*	vincō
_____	**4.** collis	*d.*	inimīcus
_____	**5.** ob	*e.*	publicūs
_____	**6.** dēmōnstrō	*f.*	teneō
_____	**7.** amīcus	*g.*	urbs
_____	**8.** enim	*h.*	vocō
_____	**9.** superō	*i.*	nōbilis
_____	**10.** commoveō	*j.*	inter
_____	**11.** commūnis	*k.*	ostendō
_____	**12.** dē	*l.*	nam
_____	**13.** hostis	*m.*	videō
_____	**14.** grātia	*n.*	vērō
_____	**15.** habeō	*o.*	lēx
_____	**16.** proelium	*p.*	ab
_____	**17.** quidem	*q.*	propter
_____	**18.** appellō	*r.*	pugna
_____	**19.** spectō	*s.*	beneficium
_____	**20.** apud	*t.*	perterreō

C. Write a synonym of the italicized word.

1. Puer negōtium *cōnfēcit.* _____

2. *Hominēs* auxilium dabant. _____

3. *Hoc* cōnsilium vīdī. _____

4. Erat ēgregius *inter* amīcōs. _____

5. Pugnābant *quidem* fortissimē. _____

6. Caesar Gallōs *vīcit.* _____

7. *Potestās* eius lātē pertinēbat. _____

8. Fēminae *tamen* nōn pervēnērunt. _____

9. Terrae fuērunt *propinquae.* _____

10. Hostēs fortiter *contendērunt.* _____

D. Write *two* Latin translations for each of the following words:

1. cavalry _____   _____

2. I think _____   _____

3. for
4. I leave
5. road
6. children
7. general
8. I prepare
9. land
10. now

Diana, identified by the Romans with the Greek Artemis, was the goddess of the chase and the moon. As a huntress, she carries a bow, quiver, and arrows. As the goddess of the moon, she wears a long robe reaching down to her feet. A veil covers her head, and above her forehead rises the crescent of the moon.

Lesson 70—ANTONYMS

VERBS

absum, be away	**adsum,** be present
accipiō, receive	**dō,** give
āmittō, lose	**inveniō,** find
appropinquō, approach	**excēdō,** leave
cognōscō, find out	**nūntiō,** inform
cōnficiō, finish	**incipiō,** begin
conveniō, come together	**discēdō,** depart
dīmittō, send away	**remittō,** send back
labōrō, work	**lūdō,** play

NOUNS

aestās, summer	**hiems,** winter
amīcus, friend	**inimīcus,** enemy
aqua, water	**terra,** land
bellum, war	**pāx,** peace
beneficium, kindness	**iniūria,** harm
cīvis, citizen	**barbarus,** foreigner
cōpia, abundance	**inopia,** scarcity
diēs, day	**nox,** night
fēmina, woman	**vir,** man
fīlia, daughter	**fīlius,** son
frāter, brother	**soror,** sister
homō, human being	**rēs,** thing
hostis, enemy	**socius,** ally
māter, mother	**pater,** father
mors, death	**vīta,** life
poena, punishment	**praemium,** reward
puella, girl	**puer,** boy
rēgīna, queen	**rēx,** king
timor, fear	**virtūs,** courage

PRONOUNS

hic, this	**ille,** that

ADJECTIVES

aequus, even	**inīquus,** uneven
bonus, good	**malus,** bad
brevis, short	**longus,** long
dexter, right	**sinister,** left
facilis, easy	**difficilis,** hard
fortis, brave	**timidus,** timid
gravis, heavy	**levis,** light
magnus, large	**parvus,** small
multī, many	**paucī,** few
nōtus, well-known	**novus,** strange

ADVERBS

anteā, previously	**posteā,** afterwards
bene, well	**male,** badly
maximē, most of all	**minimē,** least of all
nunc, now	**tum,** then

PREPOSITIONS

ab, from

ante, before

cum, with

ex, out of

ad, to

post, after

sine, without

in, into

CONJUNCTIONS

et, and

neque, and not

EXERCISES

A. In the space before each word in column *A*, write the letter of its nearest opposite in column *B*.

Column A	Column B
_____ 1. incipiō	*a.* facilis
_____ 2. aqua	*b.* inveniō
_____ 3. difficilis	*c.* hostis
_____ 4. ex	*d.* nox
_____ 5. socius	*e.* sinister
_____ 6. āmittō	*f.* cōnficiō
_____ 7. accipiō	*g.* in
_____ 8. diēs	*h.* pāx
_____ 9. dexter	*i.* terra
_____ 10. bellum	*j.* dō

B. Underline the word which is most nearly the opposite of the italicized word.

1. *magnus:* longus, parvus, bonus, malus

2. *lūdō:* vulnerō, gerō, dēligō, labōrō

3. *vīta:* mors, fēmina, terra, vīs

4. *nunc:* ubi, ad, tum, bene

5. *brevis:* aequus, longus, miser, pār

6. *aestās:* hiems, virtūs, inīquus, mēns

7. *praemium:* pāx, bellum, pugna, poena

8. *ante:* in, post, posteā, tum

9. *nūntiō:* nāvigō, dēfendō, cognōscō, dēbeō

10. *virtūs:* fēmina, timor, homō, mors

C. Write the opposite of the italicized words.

1. Omnēs hominēs *aderant.* _____

2. Portae erant *magnae.* _____

3. Cōpiae *ante* castra īnstrūctae sunt. _____

4. Dux praemium *dedit.* _____

5. Equitātum *maximē* timēbāmus. _____

6. Erat *cōpia* frūmentī. _____

180

7. *Cum* amīcīs discessērunt. ----------------------------

8. Gladius *levis* erat. ----------------------------

9. Mīles tubam *āmīsit*. ----------------------------

10. *Hanc* togam cupiō. ----------------------------

D. Write the feminine of each of the following:

1. pater ----------------------------

2. frāter ----------------------------   **4.** rēx ----------------------------

3. puer ----------------------------   **5.** vir ----------------------------

E. Write the opposite of:

1. hiems ----------------------------   **6.** rēs ----------------------------

2. nunc ----------------------------   **7.** paucī ----------------------------

3. sinister ----------------------------   **8.** posteā ----------------------------

4. conveniō ----------------------------   **9.** labōrō ----------------------------

5. ab ----------------------------   **10.** cīvis ----------------------------

Bridges

The Tiber was crossed by eight bridges, some of which were so expertly built that they are functioning to this very day. The Fabrician Bridge is one of the most famous of these arched bridges. Similar bridges span countless rivers throughout the world.

Lesson 71—SPELLING OF ENGLISH WORDS

Many English words owe their spelling to the Latin stems from which they are derived. If the Latin word is a noun or adjective, the stem is found in the genitive singular; if the Latin word is a verb, then the second or fourth principal part determines the spelling of the English derivative. For example, *temporary* comes from **temporis**, the genitive of **tempus**; *evident* comes from the second and *vision* from the fourth principal part of **video**.

Latin verbs also determine whether English words end in *-ant* or *-ent; -able* or *-ible*. To obtain the correct spelling, note the present participle stem of the Latin verb from which the English word is derived. If it is a verb of the first conjugation, then the English word in all probability ends in *-ant;* otherwise in *-ent*. Similarly, a word derived from a verb of the first conjugation is likely to end in *-able;* from other conjugations, in *-ible*. For example, *expectant* comes from **spectāre**, while *competent* comes from **petere**. Similarly, *portable* comes from **portāre**, while *invincible* comes from **vincere**.

EXERCISE

Complete the spelling of each word below by underlining the missing letter or letters in parentheses. Then write the Latin stem from which each word is derived.

1. ben-fit (i, e) ....
2. co-otion (m, mm) ....
3. conveni-nt (e, a) ....
4. itin-rary (a, e) ....
5. repugn-nt (e, a) ....
6. lib-ary (er, r) ....
7. a-ept (c, cc) ....
8. aud-ble (i, a) ....
9. occup-nt (e, a) ....
10. conten-ion (s, t) ....
11. compar-ble (a, i) ....
12. invis-ble (i, a) ....
13. a-ual (n, nn) ....
14. correspond-nt (e, a) ....
15. laud-ble (i, a) ....
16. admoni-ion (s, t) ....
17. belliger-nt (a, e) ....
18. di-icult (f, ff) ....
19. nom-nate (e, i) ....
20. mi-ion (s, ss) ....
21. intermitt-nt (a, e) ....
22. vi-ion (s, ss) ....
23. vulner-ble (i, a) ....
24. excep-ion (t, s) ....
25. incipi-nt (e, a) ....

26. te-ify (r, rr) ....
27. reduc-ble (a, i) ....
28. corp-ral (e, o) ....
29. expon-nt (e, a) ....
30. import-nt (e, a) ....
31. fi-ial (l, ll) ....
32. inim-cal (a, i) ....
33. audi-nce (e, a) ....
34. sep-ration (e, a) ....
35. rep-titious (e, i) ....
36. pe-imist (s, ss) ....
37. expect-nt (a, e) ....
38. cap-talize (i, u) ....
39. lun-r (a, e) ....
40. de-imal (c, s) ....
41. tradi-ion (s, t) ....
42. insup-rable (a, e) ....
43. t-rtiary (e, u) ....
44. cog-nt (a, e) ....
45. fe-inine (m, mm) ....
46. mil-tary (e, i) ....
47. a-imation (n, nn) ....
48. necess-ry (a, e) ....
49. temp-ral (e, o) ....
50. appe-ation (l, ll) ....

182

Lesson 72—REVIEW OF DERIVATION AND WORD STUDY

A. In the space *before* each word in column *A*, write the letter of its definition in column *B*. Then in the space *after* each word in column *A*, give a Latin word associated with it by derivation,

	Column A		Column B
-------	1. repel	-----------------------	*a.* compelling
-------	2. amicable	-----------------------	*b.* horn of plenty
-------	3. indubitably	-----------------------	*c.* pertaining to a shore
-------	4. impecunious	-----------------------	*d.* relating to a forest
-------	5. sorority	-----------------------	*e.* friendly
-------	6. riparian	-----------------------	*f.* beginning
-------	7. cogent	-----------------------	*g.* small number
-------	8. sylvan	-----------------------	*h.* all-knowing
-------	9. decapitate	-----------------------	*i.* drive back
-------	10. cornucopia	-----------------------	*j.* poor
-------	11. facilitate	-----------------------	*k.* course of a trip
-------	12. paucity	-----------------------	*l.* behead
-------	13. imperious	-----------------------	*m.* without a doubt
-------	14. omniscient	-----------------------	*n.* pertaining to land
-------	15. incipient	-----------------------	*o.* keen desire
-------	16. inimical	-----------------------	*p.* make easy
-------	17. octave	-----------------------	*q.* a women's club
-------	18. cupidity	-----------------------	*r.* unfriendly
-------	19. terrestrial	-----------------------	*s.* commanding
-------	20. itinerary	-----------------------	*t.* eight musical notes

B. Underline the Latin word with which each of the following English words is associated by derivation:

1. EQUALITY   equus, aequus, aqua
2. PENALTY   poena, pōnō, pōns
3. MONITOR   maneō, mūniō, moneō
4. COMPOSITION   pōnō, campus, possum
5. TERRIFY   terra, perterreō, tertius
6. VISION   videō, vīs, virtūs
7. MISSION   miser, mēnsis, mittō
8. OPPRESSION   praesum, premō, praesidium
9. INNUMERABLE   iniūria, numerus, nūntiō
10. LUCID   lūna, locus, lūx

C. Next to each Latin word are four English words. Three of these words are correct derivatives. Underline the one that does *not* belong.

1. *audiō:*   audience, audacity, audible, auditorium
2. *bellum:*   belle, bellicose, belligerent, belligerence

183

3. *fuga:*   fugitive, refuge, fugue, frugal
4. *gladius:*   gladiator, glade, gladiolus, gladiatorial
5. *mittō:*   remit, mission, mitten, admission
6. *labōrō:*   lavatory, laborious, laboratory, labor
7. *pōnō:*   postpone, deposit, pony, component
8. *līber:*   liberal, library, liberty, liberate
9. *portō:*   portable, import, portal, report
10. *īnsula:*   insulate, peninsula, insular, insult
11. *celer:*   celerity, accelerate, celery, accelerator
12. *dīcō:*   diction, dice, predict, dictate
13. *mīles:*   mile, militate, militia, militarize
14. *magnus:*   magnitude, magnolia, magnify, magnificent
15. *pēs:*   pedal, pediment, pessimist, impede

D. Underline the correct meaning in parentheses of each of the capitalized English words, and give a Latin word associated with it by derivation.

1. (a vegetable, speed, fame)   CELERITY   ------------------------------
2. (friendship, friendly, friend)   AMITY   ------------------------------
3. (long-winded, famous, unrehearsed)   EXTEMPORANEOUS   ------------------------------
4. (great number, large size, majority) MULTITUDE   ------------------------------
5. (oration, curse, bad deed)   MALEDICTION   ------------------------------
6. (tall, stout, big-hearted)   MAGNANIMOUS   ------------------------------
7. (dead, undying, of short duration)   IMMORTAL   ------------------------------
8. (seize, abandon, enjoy)   RELINQUISH   ------------------------------
9. (modest, rude, foresighted)   PRUDENT   ------------------------------
10. (truthfulness, shamelessness, greed) VERACITY   ------------------------------

E. For each of the following sentences, (1) write a Latin word with which the italicized word is associated by derivation, and (2) underline the word or expression in the accompanying list that best expresses the meaning of the italicized word.

1. She had an *amiable* disposition. ------------------------------
    (a) gentle   (b) likable   (c) calm   (d) determined

2. The lawyer gave *cogent* arguments in the case. ------------------------------
    (a) forceful   (b) weak   (c) easily understood   (d) adequate

3. He was a *contemporary* of ours. ------------------------------
    (a) friend   (b) descendant   (c) ancestor   (d) one living at the same time

4. He was *expatriated* by law. ------------------------------
    (a) given citizenship   (b) exiled   (c) honored   (d) imprisoned

5. I shall *elucidate* his position in the trial. ------------------------------
    (a) examine   (b) attack   (c) make clear   (d) defend

6. Can you *alleviate* his suffering? ------------------------------
    (a) reduce   (b) eliminate   (c) appreciate   (d) condemn

7. The senators voted for *agrarian* reform. ------------------------------
    (a) labor   (b) prison   (c) land   (d) housing

184

8. They tried to *ameliorate* conditions. --------------------------------

    (*a*) analyze   (*b*) examine   (*c*) stabilize   (*d*) improve

9. I was convinced the boy was *veracious*. --------------------------------

    (*a*) truthful   (*b*) lying   (*c*) deceiving   (*d*) content

10. The principal *admonished* the students. --------------------------------

    (*a*) praised   (*b*) punished   (*c*) warned   (*d*) rewarded

11. He realized the *gravity* of the situation. --------------------------------

    (*a*) shame   (*b*) honor   (*c*) seriousness   (*d*) slowness

12. He was a *docile* creature. --------------------------------

    (*a*) stupid   (*b*) easily taught   (*c*) stubborn   (*d*) pathetic

13. They tried an *innovation*. --------------------------------

    (*a*) something new   (*b*) old custom   (*c*) debate   (*d*) game

14. The substance was very *tenacious*. --------------------------------

    (*a*) hard   (*b*) sticky   (*c*) soft   (*d*) easy-flowing

15. They *suppressed* the conspiracy. --------------------------------

    (*a*) revealed   (*b*) started   (*c*) crushed   (*d*) learned about

16. The speaker made some very *pertinent* remarks. --------------------------------

    (*a*) fresh   (*b*) insulting   (*c*) new   (*d*) appropriate

17. He urged *malice* toward none. --------------------------------

    (*a*) punishment   (*b*) evil   (*c*) assistance   (*d*) love

18. The circus clown was very *corpulent*. --------------------------------

    (*a*) fat   (*b*) thin   (*c*) funny   (*d*) quick

19. The farmers were sometimes *dejected*. --------------------------------

    (*a*) delighted   (*b*) exhausted   (*c*) downcast   (*d*) deceived

20. He was an *associate* of mine. --------------------------------

    (*a*) client   (*b*) pupil   (*c*) ancestor   (*d*) companion

21. The situation was *aggravated* by his arrival. --------------------------------

    (*a*) remedied   (*b*) made worse   (*c*) explained   (*d*) simplified

22. The students took *copious* notes. --------------------------------

    (*a*) few   (*b*) careful   (*c*) many   (*d*) difficult

23. The man displayed great *fortitude*. --------------------------------

    (*a*) intelligence   (*b*) thought   (*c*) honesty   (*d*) courage

24. His *levity* annoyed me. --------------------------------

    (*a*) weakness   (*b*) calmness   (*c*) lack of seriousness   (*d*) attitude

25. They had *pecuniary* difficulties. --------------------------------

    (*a*) financial   (*b*) trade   (*c*) social   (*d*) moral

26. His motives were very *laudable*. --------------------------------

    (*a*) dangerous   (*b*) praiseworthy   (*c*) cruel   (*d*) questionable

185

27. We used to take a *nocturnal* stroll. ------------------------------

    (*a*) daily (*b*) leisurely (*c*) nightly (*d*) weekly

28. He overcame *insuperable* difficulties. ------------------------------

    (*a*) very many (*b*) unbearable (*c*) unconquerable (*d*) long established

29. The *propinquity* to school was convenient. ------------------------------

    (*a*) nearness (*b*) walking (*c*) driving (*d*) distance

30. They *unified* the transport system. ------------------------------

    (*a*) developed (*b*) controlled (*c*) reduced (*d*) made into one

F. Give the meaning of each italicized word in the following passage, and write a Latin word associated with it by derivation:

Science has recently made great strides in man's conquest of space. Scientists are *collaborating* on projects which only a *decade* ago were considered impractical. Guided *missiles* and rockets are being *propelled* at ever increasing weights and speeds. One cannot *minimize* the problems involved, but a *lunar* probe is *envisaged* as an *event* soon to be realized. The *circumnavigators* of yesterday are the *astronauts* of today.

	MEANING	LATIN WORD
1. *collaborating*	---	-------------------------------
2. *decade*	---	-------------------------------
3. *missiles*	---	-------------------------------
4. *propelled*	---	-------------------------------
5. *minimize*	---	-------------------------------
6. *lunar*	---	-------------------------------
7. *envisaged*	---	-------------------------------
8. *event*	---	-------------------------------
9. *circumnavigators*	---	-------------------------------
10. *astronauts*	---	-------------------------------

Unit XII—Roman Civilization and Culture

Lesson 73—HISTORY, GOVERNMENT, AND ROMAN SOCIETY

PERIODS IN ROMAN HISTORY

Monarchy (from the founding of Rome, 753 B.C., to 509 B.C.). There were seven kings, the first being Romulus, and the last Tarquinius Superbus (Tarquin the Proud), a member of the Etruscan family. Supreme authority of the king was symbolized by a bundle of rods with an ax, called **fascēs,** which is the origin of the term *fascism.* The cruel despotism of Tarquin drove the Romans to rebel, to overthrow the rule of kings, and to establish a republic.

Republic (from 509 B.C. to 27 B.C.). This was the period of struggle and growth. At first it was marked by civil wars and wars against Rome's immediate neighbors, such as the Etruscans, the Volscians, and the Aequians. Later came wars of conquest in Italy itself: against the Samnites, the most warlike people of central Italy, and against the Greek cities of southern Italy defended by Pyrrhus, the famous Greek general. The conquered territories embracing the entire Italian peninsula became incorporated into the Roman state as colonies or as allies, both having limited self-government.

Rome then engaged in wars of conquest outside Italy. In the Punic Wars of the third century B.C., the Romans under Scipio defeated the brilliant Carthaginian general, Hannibal, establishing Rome as the only power in the western Mediterranean. Rome annexed the islands of Sicily, Sardinia, and Corsica, and instituted the system of provinces whereby conquered lands were controlled by Roman governors. In the Macedonian Wars, which ended in 168 B.C., Macedonia was subjugated and reduced to a province. Rome acquired in quick succession the provinces of Greece, Africa, and Spain. Even the little kingdom of Pergamum in Asia Minor became a province, bequeathed to Rome in 133 B. c. by its last king, Attalus III.

Finally Rome's victories were climaxed in the first century B.C. by Julius Caesar's conquest of Gaul and his invasion of Germany and Britain. Despite the civil wars that shook the Roman state during this period (the conflicts between Marius and Sulla, and between Caesar and Pompey), Rome nevertheless became the dominant world power, and the Mediterranean Sea was aptly called by the Romans **Mare Nostrum** (Our Sea).

Empire (from 27 B.C. to 476 A.D.). Gaius Octavius, Caesar's grandnephew and adopted son, defeated his rival Antony and became Rome's first emperor with the title Augustus. He reigned from 27 B.C. until 14 A.D., a period marked by the flowering of Roman genius in art and literature. It has truly been said that Augustus "found Rome a city of brick and left it a city of marble."

Rome had over twenty-five emperors before its fall in 476 A.D., some famous, others infamous. Tiberius, Augustus' immediate successor, was able though cruel and tyrannical. Nero not only "fiddled while Rome burned," but was notorious for persecuting the Christians. The fame of Titus rests on his destruction of the sacred city of Jerusalem. Under Trajan, in the second century A.D., Rome reached its greatest territorial extent, spreading from the Atlantic on the west to the Caspian Sea on the east, from Africa on the south to Britain and the borders of Germany on the north.

Marcus Aurelius was known as the philosopher emperor, and Constantine the Great was the first Christian emperor. The last of the emperors was Romulus Augustulus.

Many reasons have been given for the fall of Rome and, with it, the collapse of civilization and social order. Among them are: (1) the system of slavery and serfdom that demoralized a large segment of the population, (2) the decay and corruption of the ruling class and the imperial court, (3) heavy taxation, and (4) the inroads made by the enemies of Rome, such as the Visigoths and the Vandals.

An eminent historian has said that "the history of Rome is in truth the same as the history of the world."

ITALIA, C. 200 B.C.

100 MILES

Mediolanum (Milan)
LIGURIA
Genua
SINUS LIGUSTICUS
Patavium
VENETIA
GALLIA
PADUS (PO)
APPEN
Ravenna
RUBICO
Faesulae
Pisae
ARNUS
Florentia
Sentinum
UMBRIA
PICENUM
ETRURIA
Tarquinii
SABINI
Reate
ROMA
TIBERIS
Ostia
LATIUM
VIA APPIA
Capua
CAMPANIA
SAMNIUM
APULIA
Neapolis (Naples)
VESUVIUS
Pompeii
LUCANIA
Paestum
Brundisium
CALABRIA
Heraclea
SINUS TARENTINUS

ILLYRICUM
MARE
HADRIATICUM

CORSICA

SARDINIA

MARE TYRRHENUM

BRUTTIUM
MAGNA GRAECIA

Messana
AETNA
Rhegium
SICILIA
Syracusae

MARE MEDITERRANEUM

Carthago
NUMIDIA AFRICA

GOVERNMENT

The Senate. The most powerful body in ancient Rome was the Senate. It consisted of about 600 members, mostly former officials, who held office for life. It managed foreign affairs, declared war, and controlled taxation. The power of the Senate was symbolized by the abbreviation **S.P.Q.R. (senātus populusque Rōmānus),** found on buildings, coins, and standards.

Popular Assemblies. Two assemblies administered the elective and legislative business of the Roman state. One assembly, called the **Comitia Centūriāta,** elected the higher magistrates—consuls, praetors, and censors. The other assembly, called the **Comitia Tribūta,** elected the tribunes, quaestors, aediles, and minor officials.

Cursus Honōrum. This was the order in which the various important offices might be held according to law. The highest official was the consul. Before one could become consul, he had to serve as praetor. Before being praetor, he had to serve as quaestor.

Consul. Two consuls, elected annually, held office for one year only. They were the chief executives, and each served as a check upon the other.

Praetor. Eight praetors were elected annually for one year. Their chief duty was to serve as judges in court.

Quaestor. Twenty quaestors were elected annually for one year. They served as public treasurers.

Aedile. Although not in the *cursus honōrum,* the aedile used his position to gain popularity for election to higher office. He was in charge of public games and amusements, public works, markets, streets, etc. There were four aediles in Rome elected annually for one year.

Tribune of the People. Ten tribunes were elected annually for one year. They had the extraordinary right to veto any decree or law passed by the Senate or the assemblies.

Censor. There were two censors elected every five years for a term of eighteen months. Their duties were to assess property, determine the order of society to which each citizen belonged, fix the eligibility of senators, raise revenue for public works, and maintain high standards of morality.

Dictator. In times of extreme public danger, a dictator was appointed with supreme power for a period of six months.

CLASSES OF SOCIETY

The Senatorial Order, also called the **Patricians** or **Optimātēs,** consisted of officeholders (magistrates) and their descendants.

The Equestrian Order, or **Equitēs,** was the wealthy class, consisting of those whose possessions were equivalent to at least $20,000.

The Plebeian Order, the working class embracing the vast majority of the population, consisted of those free-born citizens who possessed less than $20,000.

Below these three orders of society were the **slaves,** who had no rights whatsoever; and the **freedmen** (former slaves), who had the right to vote and own property, but not to hold office.

EXERCISES

A. In the following statements, if the italicized term is incorrect, write the correct term. If the italicized term is correct, write *true.*

1. Another name for the Optimātēs was *Equitēs.*

2. The *Republic* lasted from 509 B.C. to 27 B.C.

3. The first Roman emperor was *Romulus Augustulus.*

4. The *freedmen* had the right to vote and own property.

5. There were two censors elected every *five* years.

189

6. The consul, praetor, quaestor, and aedile were *all* in the cursus honōrum.

----

7. To be in the Equestrian Order, one had to possess the equivalent of at least *$2000*.

----

8. Two consuls were elected annually for a period of only *one* year.

----

9. The *Senate* had the power to declare war and control taxation.

----

10. The *quaestors* served as public treasurers.

B. In the following passage, ten words or expressions are italicized and repeated in the questions below. Underline the alternative that best explains each of these ten words or expressions as it is used in the passage.

Historically, Rome *began* as a monarchy and ended as an *empire*. There were seven kings whose symbol of authority was a *bundle of rods* with an ax. This symbol still appears on the American dime.

Civil wars and wars of conquest kept Rome in a state of turmoil during the Republic. Rome's greatest threat was removed when Scipio defeated the brilliant *general* sent by Carthage. Because of Rome's vast conquests by Scipio, Pompey, Caesar, and other outstanding generals, the Mediterranean became practically a *Roman lake*.

Caesar's *heir* became the first Roman emperor with the title Augustus. His reign was marked by a period of peace and the development of the arts. Not all of Augustus' successors, however, were famous. One *emperor* was notorious for persecuting the Christians. The Emperor Titus destroyed a *famous city*.

Rome reached its *greatest extent* under Trajan in the second century A.D. Many emperors followed, and finally, because of internal slavery and corruption, Rome became an easy target when her *enemies* invaded her territory in the fifth century A.D.

1. *began*

1. 509 B.C.
2. 27 B.C.
3. 753 B.C.
4. 1000 B.C.

2. *empire*

1. 27 B.C.–476 A.D.
2. 509 B.C.–500 A.D.
3. 100 A.D.–1000 A.D.
4. 1 B.C.–500 A.D.

3. *bundle of rods*

1. vigilēs
2. ratiōnēs
3. ōrdinēs
4. fascēs

4. *general*

1. Pyrrhus
2. Hannibal
3. Attalus
4. Philip

5. *Roman lake*

1. Mare Nōtum
2. Mare Rōmānus
3. Mare Nostrum
4. Mare Vestrum

6. *heir*

1. Octavius
2. Antonius
3. Tiberius
4. Pompeius

7. *emperor*

1. Aurelius
2. Constantine
3. Nero
4. Augustulus

8. *famous city*

1. Carthage
2. Alexandria
3. Athens
4. Jerusalem

9. *greatest extent*

1. from the Atlantic to the Pacific
2. from Spain to Greece
3. from the Atlantic to the Caspian Sea
4. from Britain to Gaul

10. *enemies*

1. Goths
2. Britons
3. Greeks
4. Egyptians

C. In the space before each item in column *A*, write the letter of the matching item in column *B*.

	Column A		Column B
_____	1. Rome founded		*a.* Patricians
_____	2. wealthy class		*b.* quaestor
_____	3. right to veto decrees		*c.* 509 B.C.
_____	4. elected the higher magistrates		*d.* Romulus
_____	5. beginning of the Republic		*e.* Comitia Tribūta
_____	6. magistrates		*f.* 753 B.C.
_____	7. public treasurer		*g.* Comitia Centūriāta
_____	8. elected minor officials		*h.* Equitēs
_____	9. first Roman king		*i.* Tarquinius Superbus
_____	10. last of the kings		*j.* tribune of the people

D. Complete the following statements:

1. The chief duty of a praetor was to serve as a _____.
2. The abbreviation S.P.Q.R. stood for _____.
3. Under the emperor _____, the Roman Empire reached its greatest extent.
4. A dictator was appointed for a period of _____.
5. Before running for the praetorship, one had to serve as _____.
6. The man in charge of public games and amusements was called _____.
7. _____ was the name given to the Mediterranean by the Romans.
8. The bundle of rods with an ax, symbolizing supreme power, was called _____.
9. The highest Roman official was called a _____.
10. The _____ Order was the wealthy class of Rome.

E. In the space before each name in column *A*, write the letter of the matching item in column *B*.

	Column A		Column B
_____	1. Marcus Aurelius		*a.* succeeded Augustus
_____	2. Trajan		*b.* conquered Carthage
_____	3. Nero		*c.* first Christian emperor
_____	4. Scipio		*d.* bequeathed land to Rome
_____	5. Constantine the Great		*e.* philosopher emperor
_____	6. Hannibal		*f.* last Roman king
_____	7. Tiberius		*g.* Rome's first emperor
_____	8. Attalus		*h.* greatest expansion of Rome
_____	9. Tarquinius Superbus		*i.* Carthaginian general
_____	10. Octavius		*j.* persecuted the Christians

Lesson 74—ROME, ITS ROADS AND HOUSES

THE CITY OF ROME

Founding. Legend has it that Rome was founded in 753 B.C. by Romulus, after whom the city was named. Romulus and his twin brother, Remus, who were reared by a she-wolf, were the sons of Rhea Silvia and Mars, the god of war.

Location. Situated on the Tiber River near the west central coast of Italy, Rome encompassed seven hills. The most famous were the **Capitoline** hill, on which were located the Temple of Jupiter and the citadel; and the **Palatine** hill, which contained the homes of prominent, wealthy Romans.

The area in which Rome was situated was called **Latium,** which is the origin of the word *Latin*. Rome's outlet to the sea was at Ostia, a seaport about sixteen miles away. Because of its strategic location—on a group of hills, on an important river, and almost in the center of Italy—Rome obtained military and commercial advantages that contributed greatly to her rapid growth in wealth and power.

The Forum. The Forum was the marketplace of Rome and the center of civic life. Besides shops, it contained temples, law courts **(basilicae),** the senate house **(cūria),** the speaker's platform **(rōstra),** and other public buildings. The Forum, where so much argumentation and wrangling in the courts took place, has given us the word "forensic."

STREETS AND ROADS

Streets were narrow and crooked, often unpaved. At corners, stepping stones were placed at intervals to assist in crossing to the other side. Streets were unlighted, and **vigilēs** (police-firemen) carrying small lanterns walked the dark alleys to afford protection.

The Romans constructed an extensive system of highways connecting the principal cities of Italy with Rome. Hence the expression, "All roads lead to Rome." The most famous road was the **Via Appia** (the Appian Way), also called **Rēgīna Viārum,** connecting Rome with Brundisium on the southeastern coast of Italy. Others roads were the **Via Flāminia,** leading northeast toward Umbria; and the **Via Aurēlia,** a military road running along the west coast toward Gaul.

THE HOUSE

ātrium—the spacious front hall beyond the entrance used as a reception room.

compluvium—the opening in the ceiling of the atrium to admit light and air, since the Roman house usually had no windows.

impluvium—the marble basin built directly beneath the compluvium, to catch the rainwater that came through the opening.

tablīnum—the study or office of the master of the house, located opposite the entrance in full view of the atrium.

peristÿlium—the open courtyard, usually with garden and columns, entered by a passageway from the atrium. The peristyle was the center of family living.

trīclīnium—the dining room adjoining the peristyle, containing a dining table flanked by three couches.

Bedrooms, kitchen, and bath were built around the peristyle.

The above is a description of a city house belonging to a wealthy Roman, many of whom also had elaborate country homes called **vīllae.**

Most Romans, however, lived in tenement or apartment houses called **īnsulae** (islands), a name originally applied to city blocks, detached from one another. Tenements were usually five or six stories high and were unsafe, especially in the event of fire.

Fires were frequent, and, before the system of **vigilēs** was established, private fire companies were organized. When a fire broke out, these companies would buy up burning buildings at prices far below their value and then extinguish the fire before much damage was done.

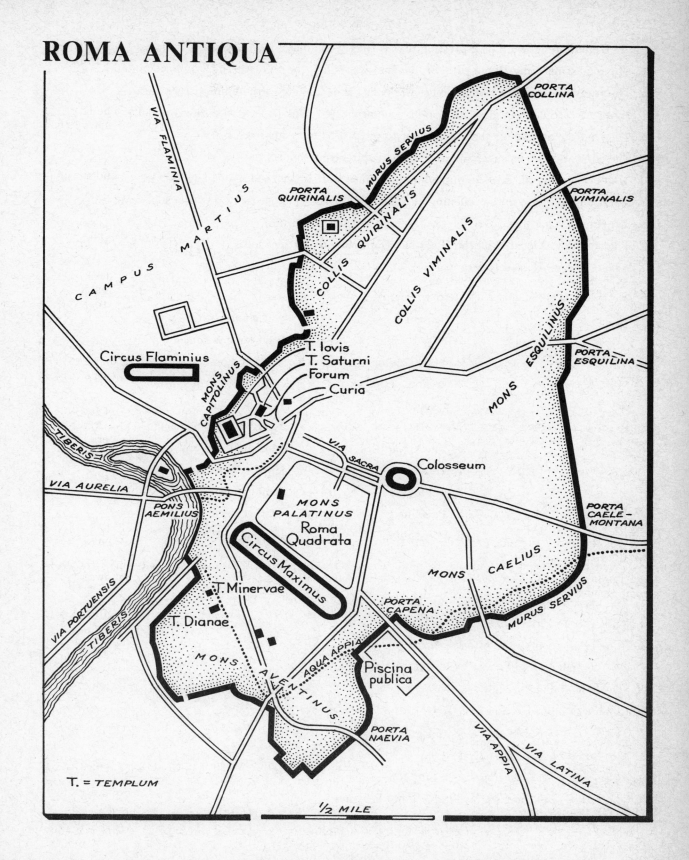

ROMA ANTIQUA

Circus Flaminius

T. Iovis
T. Saturni
Forum
Curia

VIA FLAMINIA

CAMPUS MARTIUS

PORTA QUIRINALIS

MURUS SERVIUS

PORTA COLLINA

COLLIS QUIRINALIS

COLLIS VIMINALIS

PORTA VIMINALIS

MONS ESQUILINUS

PORTA ESQUILINA

MONS CAPITOLINUS

TIBERIS

VIA SACRA

Colosseum

VIA AURELIA

PONS AEMILIUS

MONS PALATINUS
Roma Quadrata

MONS CAELIUS

PORTA CAELE-MONTANA

Circus Maximus

T. Minervae

VIA PORTUENSIS

T. Dianae

TIBERIS

MONS AVENTINUS

PORTA CAPENA

MURUS SERVIUS

AQUA APPIA

Piscina publica

PORTA NAEVIA

VIA APPIA

VIA LATINA

T. = TEMPLUM

½ MILE

193

EXERCISES

A. Underline the word or expression that correctly completes the sentence.

1. The road connecting Rome with Brundisium was called the Via (Aurēlia, Appia, Flāminia).

2. The study or office in a Roman house was called the (tablīnum, trīclīnium, peristȳlium).

3. Īnsulae was the name given to (country homes, apartment houses, reception rooms).

4. The traditional date for the founding of Rome is (753 B.C., 509 B.C., 476 B.C.).

5. The cūria was the (speaker's platform, law court, senate house).

6. Men performing the services of modern policemen were known as (vīgintī, vigilēs, virī).

7. The compluvium was the (opening in the ceiling, basin to catch rainwater, spacious front hall).

8. The dining room was called the (impluvium, ātrium, trīclīnium).

9. The citadel was located on the (Palatine, Capitoline, Aventine) hill.

10. A law court was called (rōstra, basilica, vīlla).

B. In the space before each item in column *A*, write the letter of the matching item in column *B*.

	Column A		Column B
_____	1. rōstra	*a.*	road leading south
_____	2. Via Flāminia	*b.*	country home
_____	3. ātrium	*c.*	open courtyard
_____	4. basilica	*d.*	marble basin
_____	5. Forum	*e.*	road leading northeast
_____	6. Via Appia	*f.*	front hall
_____	7. vīlla	*g.*	speaker's platform
_____	8. impluvium	*h.*	famous hill
_____	9. Palatine	*i.*	marketplace
_____	10. peristȳlium	*j.*	law court

C. In the following statements, if the italicized term is incorrect, write the correct term. If the italicized term is correct, write *true*.

1. The most famous Roman road was the *Via Appia*. _____

2. Most Romans lived in *vīllae*. _____

3. Roman tenements were often *firetraps*. _____

4. The Temple of Jupiter was located on the *Palatine* Hill. _____

5. Streets in Roman times were *well lighted*. _____

6. Rome was built on *seven* hills. _____

7. The *ātrium* was used as a reception room. _____

8. The Roman house generally had *many* windows. _____

9. The *peristyle* was the center of family living. _____

10. The *Forum* contained shops, temples, and law courts. _____

Lesson 75—FAMILY LIFE

THE FAMILY

The Latin word **familia,** although generally translated "family," more accurately meant "household." In addition to the father, mother, and children, the familia often included the wives of sons, relatives, slaves, and clients. The father **(pater familiās)** was supreme in his own home. He had absolute power over his children and commanded complete obedience.

The mother **(māter familiās)** held a position of honor and influence in the home. She managed the usual household affairs, supervised the slaves, conducted the early training of her children, and was a helpmate to her husband in matters of business and politics.

Families descended from a common ancestor often formed a clan, called **gēns.** Like the family, the gēns was united by common religious rites and was governed by a common ruler.

NAMES

A Roman citizen generally had three names: a **praenōmen,** a **nōmen,** and a **cognōmen.**

praenōmen—corresponded to our given name. The Romans had very few given names and often abbreviated them in writing. Some common ones were:

A.	Aulus	P.	Pūblius
C.	Gāius	Q.	Quīntus
D.	Decimus	S.	Sextus
L.	Lūcius	T.	Titus
M.	Mārcus	Ti.	Tiberius

nōmen—the family name, indicated the clan (gēns).

cognōmen—indicated the particular branch of the gēns.

Thus, in the name Gāius Iūlius Caesar, Gāius is the praenōmen, Iūlius is the nōmen, and Caesar is the cognōmen.

An honorary cognōmen was sometimes given a person for some noteworthy accomplishment. Thus, Pompey received the title *Magnus* for his military exploits. Scipio, after destroying Carthage, was surnamed *Africānus*, and the cognōmen *Augustus* was bestowed upon Octavian by the Roman senate.

EDUCATION

Up to the age of seven, children received their training in the home. They were taught obedience, reverence, patriotism, and respect for the law.

There was no compulsory public education. At the age of seven, the Roman boy was sent to a private elementary school **(lūdus),** where the teacher **(litterātor)** taught him reading, writing, and simple arithmetic. He often had an educated slave, called a **paedagōgus,** who served as tutor and accompanied him to school.

Upon completing elementary school, the Roman boy went to a grammar school, where the teacher **(grammaticus)** taught him Latin and Greek literature. After school hours, the father taught his son the manly sports of horseback riding, swimming, boxing and wrestling, and the use of arms.

Next came the school of rhetoric, or college, where the boy received training in oratory and politics. Finally, as a youth, he could complete his education by traveling abroad to Greece, Rhodes, or Asia Minor to study philosophy, law, and oratory under famous teachers.

The Roman girl rarely attended school. As a rule, she received all her training at home. From her mother she learned to sew, spin, and weave, and the details of housekeeping.

Books, as we know them today, did not exist in Roman times. Instead, writing of permanent value was done with pen and ink on parchment, which was rolled up for convenience in handling. Letters were written on papyrus, a kind of paper made from a reed which grew on the banks of the Nile River. The Romans also wrote on wax tablets **(tabellae** or **tabulae),** made with wooden boards covered with a thin layer of wax. Writing was done by scratching the wax with a pointed instrument called a **stilus** (stylus).

DRESS

FOR MEN

tunica (tunic)—a short-sleeved, woolen shirt reaching to the knees. It was the usual garment for indoor wear.

toga—a large, white, woolen cloth draped gracefully around the body and extending to the feet. It was worn over the tunic. The toga was the formal garment of Roman citizens.

toga candida—a pure white toga worn by a man seeking public office (hence our word "candidate").

FOR WOMEN

Over a tunic, women wore the

stola—a long, full garment extending to the feet and fastened by a girdle at the waist. It was worn indoors.

palla—a woolen, shawl-like wrap for use outdoors.

FOR CHILDREN

toga praetexta—a toga with a purple border, worn by a boy of aristocratic family until about the age of 16. The adolescent then assumed the **toga virīlis,** or adult male toga. Priests and magistrates also wore the toga praetexta.

Other articles of clothing worn by the Romans were sandals and shoes. Stockings were unknown. Hats were rarely used.

Roman women were very fond of jewelry. Necklaces, earrings, bracelets, and rings, all made of expensive materials, were some of the ornaments worn by wealthy matrons. Styles in hairdressing were varied and often elaborate. Some women even dyed their hair and wore wigs.

MEALS

ientāculum—a light breakfast consisting chiefly of bread and wine. Cheese and olives were sometimes added.

prandium—lunch eaten around noon. Among the foods served were bread, wine, cheese, olives, fruit, cold cuts, vegetables, and nuts.

cēna—the dinner or principal meal eaten in the evening. It was usually a hot meal consisting of soup, fish, fowl or meat, vegetables, and fruit.

Foods eaten by the Romans were similar to those eaten today. However, there were some exceptions. Instead of sugar the Romans used honey for sweetening purposes. Olive oil was used instead of butter. In fact, olive oil had a variety of uses besides being a food. It was used as an ointment after bathing, as fuel for lamps, and as an ingredient in the making of perfume.

The following foods, which are very common today, were unknown to the Romans: oranges, potatoes, tomatoes, tea, and coffee. Wine, usually mixed with water, was the favorite drink of the Romans.

Instead of sitting on chairs while eating, guests at banquets reclined on couches. Food was generally picked up with the fingers, since table knives and forks were unknown. Slaves would provide water and towels for the diners to wash their hands.

EXERCISES

A. In the following passage, ten words or expressions are italicized and repeated in the questions below. Underline the alternative that best explains each of these ten words or expressions as it is used in the passage.

L. Appulēius Sāturnīnus, son of a prominent Roman family, started his education at a private *elementary school* with an excellent *teacher*. He was fortunate also in having a *Greek slave* who accompanied him to school and helped him in his studies. He went on to grammar school and then to college, where he excelled in the *subjects* usually taught there. Having *relinquished his toga praetexta*, he now assumed the *adult male toga*. He completed his education by *studying abroad* under famous teachers.

1. *L.*

1. Lepidus
2. Lūcius
3. Līvius
4. Laelius

2. *Appulēius*

1. nōmen
2. praenōmen
3. cognōmen
4. gēns

3. *Sāturnīnus*

1. familia
2. cognōmen
3. praenōmen
4. nōmen

4. *elementary school*

1. schola
2. tabula
3. lūdus
4. prandium

5. *teacher*

1. grammaticus
2. magister
3. pontifex
4. litterātor

6. *Greek slave*

1. plēbs
2. servus
3. paedagōgus
4. stilus

7. *subjects*

1. oratory and politics
2. history and drama
3. music and psychology
4. economics and sociology

8. *relinquished his toga praetexta*

1. at age 12
2. at age 16
3. at age 21
4. at age 40

9. *adult male toga*

1. toga praetexta
2. toga candida
3. toga virīlis
4. toga antīqua

10. *studying aboard*

1. Britain
2. Gaul
3. Germany
4. Greece

B. In the space before each item in column *A*, write the letter of the matching item in column *B*.

	Column A	Column B
-------	**1.** palla	*a.* lunch
-------	**2.** T.	*b.* a pointed instrument
-------	**3.** prandium	*c.* worn by a magistrate
-------	**4.** stilus	*d.* stands for Titus
-------	**5.** stola	*e.* stands for Tiberius
-------	**6.** ientāculum	*f.* a woolen wrap for outdoors
-------	**7.** toga candida	*g.* a writing board
-------	**8.** toga praetexta	*h.* worn by an office seeker
-------	**9.** Ti.	*i.* a garment for indoors
-------	**10.** tabella	*j.* breakfast

C. Complete the following statements:

1. Letters were written on _____, a kind of paper made from reeds.

2. The abbreviation P. stood for _____.

3. The Latin word "familia" is most accurately translated _____.

4. A man's short-sleeved, knee-length shirt was called _____.

5. The principal meal eaten in the evening was called in Latin _____.

6. A Roman citizen usually had a nōmen, a praenōmen, and a _____.

7. Roman tabellae were covered with a thin layer of _____.

8. Instead of sugar, the Romans used _____.

9. As far as education was concerned, the Roman girl received most of her training _____ _____.

10. In the name Mārcus Tullius Cicerō, Tullius was called the _____.

D. In the following statements, if the italicized term is incorrect, write the correct term. If the italicized term is correct, write *true*.

1. Instead of butter, the Romans used *margarine*. _____

2. The abbreviation L. stood for *Lucullus*. _____

3. Hats were *rarely worn* by the ancient Romans. _____

4. The pater familiās had *absolute power* over his children. _____

5. The toga was the *formal garment* of Roman citizens. _____

6. The *cognōmen* corresponded to our given name. _____

7. The māter familiās held a very *inferior* position in the home. _____

8. *Wine mixed with water* was the favorite drink of the Romans. _____

9. Public education in ancient Rome *was compulsory*. _____

10. The *cēna* was usually a light meal consisting of bread, wine, and cheese. _____

Lesson 76—AMUSEMENTS, RELIGION, ROMAN CONTRIBUTIONS

AMUSEMENTS

The Romans were very fond of games of excitement. Their chief public amusements took place in the circus, the theater, and the amphitheater. To pacify the mob, the government provided free amusements and bread lines, exemplified by the expression **"pānem et circēnsēs"** (bread and circus games). The most popular amusements were gladiatorial combats, chariot races, and theatrical performances. A visit to the baths was also a favorite pastime of the Romans.

The **Colosseum,** completed in 80 A.D., was the greatest amphitheater in Rome and the scene of combats between gladiators, or between gladiators and wild beasts. These contests were often spectacles of human suffering, and served to brutalize the populace. Schools for training gladiators were established in various parts of Italy, and slaves were selected for their skill as fighters. Perhaps the most famous gladiator in Roman history was a Thracian slave named **Spartacus,** who led a formidable uprising of slaves against the Roman state.

In imperial times, the amphitheater was also the scene of religious and political persecutions. Sometimes the Colosseum was flooded with water, and sensational naval battles were fought to amuse the crowd.

The **Circus Maximus,** the most famous arena in Rome, was used chiefly for chariot races. It was about two thousand feet long and six hundred feet wide. In the center, for about two-thirds of its length, was a dividing wall called the **spīna** around which the chariots raced. The number of horses harnessed to a chariot varied, but the four-horse team was the most popular. There were usually seven laps to a race, with sharp turns at each end of the arena. The reckless driving of the charioteers and the frequent accidents that occurred provided the thrills and excitement that the Romans were so fond of.

The **Campus Martius** was a large area set aside for athletic exercises and military training. Here the young men of Rome were participants rather than spectators, as at the Colosseum and the Circus. They engaged in track and field athletics, such as running, jumping, discus throwing, archery, wrestling, and boxing.

Theatrical performances, mainly pantomimes, comedies, and dances, were held in open-air theaters in the daytime, since there were no lighting facilities. The actors were all slaves, and men played the roles of women.

In 55 B.C. Pompey the Great erected the first permanent theater at Rome. It was built of stone and was supposed to accommodate about twenty thousand people. The seats in front were assigned to the senators. The first fourteen rows behind them were reserved for the knights **(equitēs).** The common people occupied the rest of the seats.

Thermae or **balneae** were elaborate baths corresponding to our country clubs. In addition to all sorts of bathing facilities, the buildings contained gymnasiums, libraries, lounging rooms, and gardens. Among the most famous were the Baths of Caracalla, after which the Pennsylvania Railroad Terminal in New York City is modeled.

RECREATION

Children's games, similar to those of today, were played with dolls, marbles, jacks, tops, kites, hoops, and various other toys. Hide-and-seek, blindman's buff, and leapfrog were also played by Roman children.

Older children and adults played board games, not much different from our chess and checkers. Among the outdoor sports were handball, fishing, hunting, running, jumping, swimming, discus throwing, boxing, wrestling, and fencing.

RELIGION

The Romans lived constantly in the presence of the gods, and their numerous festivals, offerings, and prayers testified to their eagerness to please their deities and obtain favors. From earliest times, the imagination of the Romans saw gods everywhere in nature, and *polytheism*, or the belief in many gods, was universally practiced. There were gods who protected the crops and herds, gods of the weather and seasons, gods of the earth and sky. Gods had to be appeased, and when a disaster struck it proved that some god was offended.

Festivals were held all the year round, the most famous being the **Saturnalia,** dedicated to the god Saturn. This holiday took place at about the time we celebrate Christmas. It was a period of riotous merrymaking when even slaves were allowed their freedom.

Since religion was the function of the state, all temples, statues, and altars to the gods were built by the government. A very important temple was the temple of **Vesta,** where six Vestal Virgins kept the sacred fire forever burning. The priests, including the **pontifex maximus** (chief priest), were government officials, not necessarily trained for the priesthood.

After the conquest of Greece, the Romans identified their own gods with those of Greece. Below is a list of Roman deities with their Greek equivalents.

ROMAN		GREEK
Jupiter	king of the gods	**Zeus**
Juno	queen of the gods	**Hera**
Mercury	messenger of the gods	**Hermes**
Mars	god of war	**Ares**
Neptune	god of the sea	**Poseidon**
Saturn	god of the harvest	**Cronus**
Apollo	god of the sun, song, and prophecy	**Apollo**
Vulcan	god of fire	**Hephaestus**
Bacchus	god of wine	**Dionysus**
Cupid	god of love	**Eros**
Venus	goddess of love and beauty	**Aphrodite**
Minerva	goddess of wisdom	**Athena**
Diana	goddess of the chase and moon	**Artemis**
Ceres	goddess of agriculture	**Demeter**
Vesta	goddess of the hearth	**Hestia**
Janus	strictly a Roman god; the god of beginnings and doorways. He is always represented with two faces.	
Larēs and **Penātēs**	gods of the household	

ROMAN CONTRIBUTIONS TO CIVILIZATION

1. **Language.** The Roman alphabet, derived originally from the Phoenicians, is in use today throughout most of the world. Latin is the basis of the Romance languages, the chief ones being Italian, Spanish, French, Portuguese, and Roumanian. English, though not a Romance language, has been profoundly influenced by Latin. Roman numerals are still in limited use: as chapter headings in books, as hours on the face of a clock, and as dates on the cornerstones of buildings.

2. **Law.** Considered by many to be Rome's most valuable gift to the modern world, Roman law forms the basis of many legal systems today. The **Laws of the Twelve Tables,** engraved on bronze tablets and displayed in the Forum, were the foundation of Roman law.

Rome's greatest jurists recognized the equality of man before the law and the need for equal protection of the rights of person and property. Our own Declaration of Independence has embodied these ideas of justice. The Emperor Justinian codified the great mass of laws and thus facilitated the transmission of Roman law to the modern world.

3. **Literature.** In prose and poetry, Roman writers have left us a rich legacy, outstanding in the field of world literature. We need but mention Caesar and Livy in the field of history; Cicero in the field of oratory, philosophy, and letters; and Vergil and Horace in the field of poetry. These authors are still read and enjoyed today in schools throughout the world, and have exercised a profound influence upon modern writers.

4. **Government.** In the organization and administration of the republic, the Romans have left their imprint on modern political systems. With the expansion of her territory and the formation and administration of her provinces, Rome showed a genius for organization that became a model for many modern governments.

5. **Engineering and Architecture.** The Romans were famous for their construction of roads, aqueducts, and bridges. They also perfected the rounded arch and the dome.

In imperial times Rome became an imposing city of magnificent public buildings, temples, aqueducts, basilicas, theaters, columns, triumphal arches, and tombs. Today's tourist can still see the ancient Roman Forum with its ruins, the Colosseum, the Pantheon, the mausoleum of Hadrian, the arches of Titus, Severus, and Constantine, and other monuments of a bygone day.

6. **The Calendar.** The calendar in use today is based essentially on the calendar revised by Julius Caesar. It was thus known as the *Julian calendar*. In the sixteenth century, Pope Gregory XIII made some further minor corrections, whence the term *Gregorian calendar*.

EXERCISES

A. In the following passage, ten words or expressions are italicized and repeated in the questions below. Underline the alternative that best explains each of these ten words or expressions as it is used in the passage.

It was the time of the *Saturnalia*. Lucius and I decided to go to the *arena* to watch the chariot races. We would have preferred to see a gladiatorial contest in Rome's greatest *amphitheater*, but none was scheduled for that day. On the way, we passed the *Thermae* Caracallae and the *Campus Martius*, which was named after the *god of war*. In the arena itself, the charioteers were getting ready for their seven-lap race. Enthusiasm ran high, and the joys of *Bacchus* and *Venus* were in evidence everywhere. One charioteer, making a sharp turn around the *dividing wall*, suffered a spill and had to be carried off the track. This accident, plus the fact that the arena was so *long*, delayed the close of the contest until after sundown.

1. *Saturnalia*

1. February
2. May
3. July
4. December

2. *arena*

1. Colosseum
2. Circus Maximus
3. Campus Martius
4. Comitium

3. *amphitheater*

1. Cūria
2. Thermae
3. Campus Martius
4. Colosseum

4. *Thermae*

1. amphitheater
2. baths
3. arena
4. temple

5. *Campus Martius*

1. athletic exercises
2. gladiatorial combats
3. chariot races
4. theatrical performances

6. *god of war*

1. Vulcan
2. Janus
3. Mars
4. Saturn

7. *Bacchus*

1. god of fire
2. god of the household
3. god of love
4. god of wine

8. *Venus*

1. Aphrodite
2. Eros
3. Athena
4. Hera

9. *dividing wall*

1. mūrus
2. spīna
3. vāllum
4. circēnsēs

10. *long*

1. 200 feet
2. 500 feet
3. 2000 feet
4. 5000 feet

B. Complete the following statements:

1. Latin is the basis of the _____ languages.

2. The chief priest was called by the Romans _____

3. The translation of pānem et circēnsēs is _____

4. The Larēs and Penātēs were _____

5. The calendar in use today is essentially the one revised by the Roman _____.

6. Vulcan was the god of _____.

7. The Roman goddess of wisdom was called _____.

8. The Greek god Hermes was called _____ by the Romans.

9. The god with two faces was called _____.

10. Roman baths corresponded to our _____.

C. In the following statements, if the italicized term is incorrect, write the correct term. If the italicized term is correct, write *true*.

1. The Laws of the Twelve Tables formed the foundation of *Roman* law.

   _____

2. Penn Station in New York City is modeled after the *Colosseum.*

   _____

3. The Romans practiced polytheism, the belief in *gladiatorial combats.*

   _____

4. Saturn was the god of the *harvest.*

   _____

5. Poseidon was the Greek counterpart of *Apollo.*

   _____

6. Children's games in ancient Rome were *similar* to those of today.

   _____

7. The Romans perfected the dome and the *pointed* arch.

   _____

8. *Diana* was the goddess of the chase and of the moon.

   _____

9. Theatrical performances in Rome were held in open-air theaters in the *daytime.*

   _____

10. Eros among the Greeks corresponded to *Cupid* among the Romans.

   _____

Lesson 77—REVIEW OF CIVILIZATION

A. In the following statements, if the italicized term is incorrect, write the correct term. If the italicized term is correct, write *true*.

1. The period of the Republic was marked by *civil* wars.

   ----

2. Conquered lands were governed by Roman *consuls*.

   ----

3. Marius was a bitter enemy of *Sulla*.

   ----

4. *Parchment and papyrus* were used by the Romans for writing.

   ----

5. *Antony* found Rome a city of brick and left it a city of marble.

   ----

6. The *impluvium* was the opening in the ceiling of the ātrium.

   ----

7. The pontifex maximus was *one of the Roman deities*.

   ----

8. The system of slavery was one of the reasons for the *growth* of Rome.

   ----

9. Romulus and Remus were the sons of *Mercury*.

   ----

10. The *trīclīnium* was an open courtyard with garden and columns.

    ----

11. Rome was located practically in the *center* of Italy.

    ----

12. The traditional date of the founding of Rome is *753* B.C.

    ----

13. *Pompey* was given the cognōmen Augustus.

    ----

14. Guests usually *sat on chairs* while eating.

    ----

15. Vergil and Horace were outstanding in the field of *prose* writing.

B. In the space before each item in column *A*, write the letter of the matching item in column *B*.

	Column A		Column B
-------	1. Vulcan	*a.*	god of the sun
-------	2. Mercury	*b.*	goddess of the hearth
-------	3. Apollo	*c.*	god of the sea
-------	4. Diana	*d.*	goddess of wisdom
-------	5. Vesta	*e.*	god of fire
-------	6. Neptune	*f.*	goddess of agriculture
-------	7. Mars	*g.*	god of wine
-------	8. Minerva	*h.*	god of war
-------	9. Ceres	*i.*	messenger of the gods
-------	10. Bacchus	*j.*	goddess of the chase

203

C. Underline the word or expression in parentheses that best completes each statement.

1. The stilus was used as a (sword, dagger, writing instrument, spear).
2. The spacious reception room in a Roman house was the (tablīnum, ātrium, impluvium, compluvium).
3. A common drink at a Roman meal was (wine, water, milk, beer).
4. Gladiatorial combats took place in the (Thermae, Circus Maximus, Campus Martius, Colosseum).
5. The senate house was called the (basilica, rōstra, cūria, balnea).
6. The road that connected Rome with Brundisium was the Via (Flāminia, Appia, Aurēlia, Latīna).
7. The class of society that connoted wealth was the (patrician, plebeian, equestrian, senatorial).
8. The highest official in government was the (consul, praetor, quaestor, aedile).
9. The consul held office for (1 year, 2 years, 3 years, 4 years).
10. Mare Nostrum referred to the (Atlantic Ocean, Black Sea, Adriatic Sea, Mediterranean Sea).
11. Tenement houses were known as (vīllae, īnsulae, silvae, pallae).
12. The stola was worn by (men, magistrates, women, priests).
13. The man who accompanied the child to school was called (grammaticus, lūdus, litterātor, paedagōgus).
14. The first or given name of a Roman was called the (cognōmen, praenōmen, nōmen, gēns).
15. The Romans annually elected (one, two, three, four) consul(s).
16. The Roman girl received most of her training (in school, at temple, at home, with a private tutor).
17. The freedman was not permitted to (hold office, vote, hold property, marry).
18. The aedile was a (judge, treasurer, censor, administrator of public works).
19. The power to veto any law was exercised by the (quaestor, tribune, aedile, praetor).
20. The first Roman emperor was (Caesar, Augustus, Tarquinius, Romulus).

D. Complete the following sentences by supplying the missing words:

1. The Larēs and Penātēs were Roman gods of the _____.
2. The god _____ is always pictured with two faces.
3. Priests and magistrates wore the toga _____.
4. In New York City, _____ is modeled after the Baths of Caracalla.
5. Rome is said to have been founded in 753 B.C. by _____.
6. The police-firemen who patrolled the streets at night were called _____.
7. The three orders of society were the senatorial, the equestrian, and the _____.
8. The three officials in the cursus honōrum in descending order were the consul, the praetor, and the
   _____.
9. Rome reached its greatest territorial extent during the reign of Emperor _____.
10. The initials S.P.Q.R. and the fascēs both symbolized Roman _____.
11. Apollo was the god of the sun, song, and _____.
12. The three names of a Roman citizen were called the praenōmen, the nōmen, and the _____.
13. Q. is the abbreviation for the Roman name _____.
14. The wax tablet used for writing purposes was called a _____.
15. The pure white toga worn by a man seeking public office was called a toga _____.

E. In the following statements, if the italicized term is incorrect, write the correct term. If the italicized term is correct, write *true.*

1. In Roman theatrical performances *men* played the parts of women. _____

2. Latin is the basis of the *Romance* languages, such as French, Spanish, and Portuguese.

$\text{-----------------------------}$

3. The *Colosseum* was used principally for chariot racing.

$\text{-----------------------------}$

4. Spartacus was a *gladiator* who led a revolt against the Roman state.

$\text{-----------------------------}$

5. The spīna was the *arena* in the Circus Maximus.

$\text{-----------------------------}$

6. *In back of* the equitēs in a Roman theater sat the senators.

$\text{-----------------------------}$

7. The Emperor *Justinian* put Roman law into a complete codified form.

$\text{-----------------------------}$

8. *Pompey* erected the first permanent theater at Rome in 55 B.C.

$\text{-----------------------------}$

9. During the *Saturnalia*, slaves were permitted temporary freedom.

$\text{-----------------------------}$

10. Rome's outlet to the sea was at *Naples*.

$\text{-----------------------------}$

F. In the space before the name of each Roman deity in column *A*, write the letter of the Greek equivalent in column *B*.

	Column A		Column B
-------	**1.** Mars	*a.*	Eros
-------	**2.** Jupiter	*b.*	Demeter
-------	**3.** Cupid	*c.*	Poseidon
-------	**4.** Minerva	*d.*	Hera
-------	**5.** Ceres	*e.*	Ares
-------	**6.** Mercury	*f.*	Dionysus
-------	**7.** Bacchus	*g.*	Athena
-------	**8.** Juno	*h.*	Aphrodite
-------	**9.** Neptune	*i.*	Zeus
-------	**10.** Venus	*j.*	Hermes

G. The English words in column *A* are derived from the names of Romans gods or goddesses. In the space *before* each word in column *A*, write the name of the deity connected with the word. Then in the space *after* each word in column *A*, write the letter of its meaning in column *B*.

	Column A		Column B
-------------------------	**1.** vulcanize	-------	*a.* lively, fickle
-------------------------	**2.** martial	-------	*b.* pertaining to drunken revelry
-------------------------	**3.** cereal	-------	*c.* chaste, pure
-------------------------	**4.** janitor	-------	*d.* treat with high temperature
-------------------------	**5.** mercurial	-------	*e.* queenly, haughty
-------------------------	**6.** bacchanalian	-------	*f.* gloomy, grave
-------------------------	**7.** vestal	-------	*g.* warlike
-------------------------	**8.** jovial	-------	*h.* a grain
-------------------------	**9.** junoesque	-------	*i.* doorkeeper, porter
-------------------------	**10.** saturnine	-------	*j.* favorable, merry

205

H. In the following passage, ten words or expressions are italicized and repeated in the questions below. Underline the alternative that best explains each of these ten words or expressions as it is used in the passage.

Ancient Rome has made many contributions to modern civilization, and her influence still continues. When the *Rēgīna Viārum* was built in the 4th century B.C., who would have realized that it would still be used in the 20th century A.D.? The great *amphitheater* in Rome is still in use, and operatic performances can be seen today in the *Baths of Caracalla*. The *foundations of Roman law* still serve as a guide to modern legal systems. The *Romance languages* spoken today have their origin in Latin. In literature Rome's influence is still felt in the writings of her *most illustrious orator* and her *poets*. In architecture the *structures* dedicated to the Emperors Titus, Severus, and Constantine still stand as a reminder of Roman grandeur. Even our calendar underwent reform by a *famous Roman*. In its *long history* Rome has been called the epitome of Western civilization.

1. *Rēgīna Viārum*

    1. Via Aurēlia   3. Via Appia
    2. Via Flāminia   4. Via Sacra

2. *amphitheater*

    1. Colosseum   3. Circus Maximus
    2. Campus Martius 4. Capitōlium

3. *Baths of Caracalla*

    1. basilicae   3. comitia
    2. thermae   4. rōstra

4. *foundations of Roman law*

    1. cūria   3. Twelve Tables
    2. familia   4. balneae

5. *Romance languages*

    1. English and French
    2. Spanish and German
    3. Greek and French
    4. Italian and Portuguese

6. *most illustrious orator*

    1. Cicero   3. Augustus
    2. Demosthenes 4. Pompey

7. *poets*

    1. Caesar and Livy
    2. Cato and Octavius
    3. Vergil and Horace
    4. Cicero and Scipio

8. *structures*

    1. domes   3. aqueducts
    2. arches   4. columns

9. *famous Roman*

    1. Pliny   3. Hadrian
    2. Gregory   4. Caesar

10. *long history*

    1. 500 years   3. 2000 years
    2. 1200 years   4. 3000 years

Lesson 78—FAMOUS PEOPLE AND MYTHS IN ROMAN HISTORY

FAMOUS PEOPLE

Aeneas—Trojan leader and reputed ancestor of the Romans. He displayed exemplary devotion to father, country, and the gods.

Brutus—Rome's first consul. He was known for his heroic devotion to duty by putting to death his own sons for plotting treason.

Cato the Elder—Roman censor famed for his frugality, self-sacrifice, and devotion to duty.

Cincinnatus—Roman farmer-patriot who was called from his plow to lead the Roman army. After defeating the enemy, he modestly returned to his farm, rather than continue in high position.

Cornelia—devoted mother of the Gracchi brothers, who, pointing to her sons, exclaimed, "These are my jewels."

Decius Mus—Roman consul and general. He rushed into the midst of the enemy and sacrificed his life, thereby bringing victory to the Romans.

Fabricius—displayed integrity of character by refusing to be bribed by Pyrrhus, the famous Greek general.

Gracchi brothers (Gaius and Tiberius)—sons of Cornelia. As tribunes of the people, both showed sympathy for the underprivileged and tried to enact laws in their favor. In the course of duty, they were slain by their opponents.

Horatius—courageous Roman who defended a bridge over the Tiber to delay the Etruscans who were advancing on Rome.

Mucius Scaevola—Roman patriot. Ordered to be burnt alive by King Porsena, Mucius showed extreme physical endurance and open defiance of the Etruscans by thrusting his right hand into the fire prepared for his execution. Subsequently, he was nicknamed "Scaevola" (left-handed), since he lost the use of his right hand.

Regulus—Roman general captured in the First Punic War. He kept his word of honor to return to his Carthaginian captors, even though he knew that it meant death.

Remus—twin brother of Romulus.

Romulus—legendary founder of Rome.

FAMOUS MYTHS

Baucis and **Philemon**—an aged couple who, having hospitably entertained Jupiter and Mercury in disguise, were later rewarded by the gods.

Ceres and **Proserpina**—Ceres was the goddess of agriculture whose daughter, Proserpina, was carried off by Pluto to the underworld. Through the intervention of Jupiter, it was arranged that Proserpina spend one-third of the year with Pluto and the remaining part on earth with her mother.

Daedalus and **Icarus**—Daedalus, a craftsman, made the first successful flight by using wings fastened with wax. His son Icarus, despite his father's warning, flew so near the sun that the wax melted. Icarus fell into the sea and drowned.

Hercules—Greek hero noted for his strength. He performed the "Twelve Labors."

Medusa—one of three Gorgons, pictured with wings and claws and a head covered with serpents. Until finally beheaded by Perseus, the famous Greek hero, she could turn to stone anyone who looked at her.

Midas—King of Phrygia, renowned for his wealth. Whatever he touched turned to gold.

Orpheus and **Eurydice**—Orpheus, a celebrated Greek poet, enchanted with his lyre wild beasts, trees, and even rocks. When his wife Eurydice died, he was able, with the charm of his music, to enter Hades and bring her back, only to lose her again for gazing back.

Perseus and **Andromeda**—Perseus, a Greek hero, slew a sea monster which threatened the life of Andromeda, chained to a rock as a sacrifice. Perseus later married the girl he had saved. He also cut off the head of Medusa.

Pyramus and **Thisbe**—famous lovers whose parents refused to give consent to their marriage. Their young lives ended in tragic death.

Theseus and the **Minotaur**—Theseus, a Greek hero, slew the Minotaur, a monster half-man and half-bull. Theseus was aided by Ariadne, daughter of King Minos.

EXERCISES

A. Name the person referred to in each of the following statements:

1. He was called from his farm to lead the Roman army._____

2. He kept his word of honor after being released by his Carthaginian captors. _____

3. He performed the famous "Twelve Labors." _____

4. He was the legendary founder of Rome. _____

5. He defended a bridge against the enemy. _____

6. By thrusting his right hand into a fire, he showed his defiance of King Porsena. _____

7. He was a king famous for his golden touch. _____

8. She was the devoted mother of the Gracchi brothers. _____

9. His own sons were put to death by this consul. _____

10. He was a Trojan leader and reputed ancestor of the Romans. _____

B. Each incomplete statement below is followed by four words or expressions in parentheses. Underline the one that will complete the statement correctly.

1. Perseus slew a sea monster, thereby saving the life of (Eurydice, Andromeda, Helen, Proserpina).

2. Daedalus is famous in mythology for having fashioned (wings, sandals, precious stones, wax tablets).

3. Medusa is always pictured with a head full of (serpents, jewels, curls, thorns).

4. Pyramus and Thisbe were famous (consuls, lovers, craftsmen, heroes).

5. Theseus slew the Minotaur with the aid of (Minos, Andromeda, Proserpina, Ariadne).

6. Baucis and Philemon were (an aged couple, young lovers, a god and goddess, a craftsman and his son).

7. The girl carried off by Pluto to the underworld was (Medusa, Cornelia, Proserpina, Ceres).

8. Eurydice was almost rescued from Hades by (Orpheus, Perseus, Theseus, Hercules).

9. Decius Mus is famous in Roman history for having (enacted good laws, sacrificed his life, saved a Roman's life, defended a bridge).

10. The Roman who showed integrity of character by refusing to be bribed by Pyrrhus was (Cato, Brutus, Fabricius, Regulus).

C. In the following statements, if the italicized term is incorrect, write the correct term. If the italicized term is correct, write *true*.

1. Scaevola was so called because he lost the use of his *right hand*. _____

2. Whatever King *Midas* touched turned to gold. _____

3. Daedalus' son, *Baucis*, fell into the sea and drowned.

  ----

4. The Minotaur was a monster, half-man and *half-goat*.

  ----

5. Medusa was beheaded by *Perseus*.

  ----

6. *Julia* was the mother of the Gracchi brothers.

  ----

7. Pyramus and Thisbe were a pair of famous *lovers*.

  ----

8. Orpheus was almost successful in bringing *Eurydice* out of Hades.

  ----

9. Cato the Elder was known for his *lavish spending*.

  ----

10. Brutus *refused* to put to death his own sons accused of treason.

  ----

ad infinitum, without end

ad nauseam, to the point of disgust

alma mater, college (nourishing mother)

ante bellum, before the war

ars artis gratia, art for art's sake

ars longa, vita brevis, art is long, life is short

bona fide, in good faith

carpe diem, seize the opportunity (day)

cave canem, beware of the dog

corpus delicti, the facts (body) of a crime

cum grano salis, with a grain of salt

de facto, in fact; actually

de jure, by right; legally

de mortuis nil nisi bonum, speak only good of the dead

errare humanum est, to err is human

et tu, Brute! even you, Brutus!

exit; exeunt, he goes out; they go out

ex libris, from the books (of)

ex officio, by virtue of office

ex post facto, enacted after the fact; retroactive

ex tempore, on the spur of the moment

festina lente, make haste slowly

in absentia, in absence

in hoc signo vinces, by this sign you will conquer

in loco parentis, in the place of a parent

in medias res, into the midst of things

in memoriam, in memory (of)

in re, in the matter of; concerning

in toto, entirely

ipso facto, by the very fact itself

lapsus linguae, a slip of the tongue

mens sana in corpore sano, a sound mind in a sound body

multum in parvo, much in something small

pater patriae, father of his country

pax vobiscum, peace be with you

per annum, by the year

per capita, by heads

per diem, by the day

per se, by itself; essentially

persona non grata, an unwelcome person

post mortem, after death

prima facie, on first sight or appearance

pro and con(tra), for and against

pro bono publico, for the public welfare

pro tempore, for the time being

quid pro quo, something for something

semper fidelis, always faithful

semper paratus, always prepared

sic transit gloria mundi, thus passes the glory of the world

sine die, indefinitely, without setting a day

sine qua non, indispensable; a necessity

status quo, the existing state of affairs

te Deum laudamus, we praise thee, O Lord

tempus fugit, time flies

terra firma, solid ground

vade mecum, a constant companion (go with me)

veni, vidi, vici, I came, I saw, I conquered

verbatim, word for word

via, by way of

vice versa, the other way around

viva voce, by spoken word

vox populi, vox Dei, the voice of the people is the voice of God

EXERCISES

A. Give the meaning of each of the following Latin quotations:

1. carpe diem _____

2. festina lente _____

3. ad infinitum _____

4. cum grano salis _____

5. lapsus linguae _____

6. in loco parentis _____

7. in medias res _____

8. de jure _____

211

9. quid pro quo _____

10. in re _____

11. sine qua non _____

12. pro bono publico _____

13. ad nauseam _____

14. ars artis gratia _____

15. semper paratus _____

16. tempus fugit _____

17. cave canem _____

18. ars longa, vita brevis _____

19. errare humanum est _____

20. bona fide _____

B. Complete the following statements:

1. Congress passed an **ex post** _____ law.

2. The ambassador was called **persona non** _____.

3. An excellent motto to follow is **mens sana in** _____.

4. The motto of the United States Marine Corps is _____ **fidelis.**

5. When the patient died, the hospital conducted a **post** _____ examination.

6. Upon receiving the gift, she exclaimed, "**Multum in** _____."

7. In court the lawyer produced **prima** _____ evidence.

8. After graduation, we called our college our **alma** _____.

9. Without thinking, he jumped **in medias** _____."

10. She greeted her friends with the expression, "**Pax** _____."

C. Each incomplete statement below is followed by four words or expressions in parentheses. Underline the one that will complete the statement correctly.

1. A legally recognized government is a government (ex officio, de facto, ex tempore, de jure).

2. The motto "make haste slowly" is expressed in Latin by the words (viva voce, tempus fugit, festina lente, carpe diem).

3. The expression "de mortuis nil nisi bonum" refers to the (brave, mighty, dead, poor).

4. If a person calls off a list of items almost endlessly, he is said to do it (cum grano salis, ad infinitum, de facto, ad nauseam).

5. "By virtue of office" is expressed in Latin by the words (vice versa, ars artis gratia, ex officio, quid pro quo).

6. On being stabbed, Caesar is said to have exclaimed (cave canem; post mortem; et tu, Brute; exit Caesar).

7. When Congress adjourns indefinitely, it does so (sine qua non, in re, sine die, in toto).

8. The Latin expression "vade mecum" refers to (a greeting, a lake, a road, a constant companion).

9. The evidence in a crime is expressed by the Latin words (corpus delicti, de jure, ex officio, bona fide).

10. A person appointed to office at a meeting at which he is not present is appointed (viva voce, pro tempore, in absentia, prima facie).

Lesson 80—LATIN ABBREVIATIONS USED IN ENGLISH

A.D.	*annō Dominī*, in the year of our Lord
ad lib.	*ad libitum*, at pleasure
A.M.	*ante merīdiem*, before noon
cf.	*cōnfer*, compare
e.g.	*exemplī grātiā*, for example
et al.	*et aliī (aliae, alia)*, and others
etc.	*et cētera*, and the rest, and so forth
ibid.	*ibīdem*, in the same place
i.e.	*id est*, that is
M.D.	*Medicīnae Doctor*, Doctor of Medicine
N.B.	*notā bene*, note well
op. cit.	*opere citātō*, in the work mentioned
per cent	*per centum*, by the hundred
P.M.	*post merīdiem*, after noon
pro tem.	*pro tempore*, for the time being
P.S.	*post scrīptum*, postscript, written afterwards
q.v.	*quod vidē*, which see
℞	*recipe*, take (as directed)
viz.	*vidēlicet (vidēre licet)*, one may see, namely
vs.	*versus*, against

EXERCISES

A. Give the English meaning for each of the following Latin abbreviations:

1. etc. _____
2. P.M. _____
3. viz. _____
4. q.v. _____
5. P.S. _____

6. vs. _____
7. ibid. _____
8. et al. _____
9. A.D. _____
10. ℞ _____

B. Give the familiar Latin abbreviation for each of the following English expressions:

1. that is _____
2. for example _____
3. at pleasure _____
4. before noon _____
5. note well _____

6. compare _____
7. for the time being _____
8. doctor of medicine _____
9. namely _____
10. in the work mentioned _____

C. In the passage below, write the English meaning of each Latin abbreviation.

My friend Henry became a _____ (*M.D.*) after a long period of hard work. He was in competition _____ (*vs.*) students from Harvard, Yale, Princeton, _____ (*et al.*). When the president of his class became ill, Henry was designated to take his place _____ (*pro tem.*). While at college, he excelled in a number of difficult subjects, _____ (*e.g.*), entomology, calculus, and metaphysics, _____ (*i.e.*), a branch of philosophy. His thesis was entitled "Larvae of the Leopard-Moth," in which he showed how trees became infected, the nature of tree diseases, _____ (*etc.*). He also indicated _____ _____ (*op. cit.*) a method of treatment, _____ _____ (*viz.*), spraying with a rarely used chemical. _____ _____ (*Ibid.*) he formulated a very interesting theory of insect control which may soon be put into practice.

Lesson 81—COLLEGE MOTTOES

University of Michigan
Artes, scientia, veritas, The arts, knowledge, truth

University of Florida
Civium in moribus rei publicae salus, In the character of its citizens lies the welfare of the state

University of Chicago
Crescat scientia, vita excolatur, Let knowledge grow, let life be enriched

University of Texas
Disciplina praesidium civitatis, Training, the defense of the state

University of the South
Ecce quam bonum, Behold how good

Brown University
In Deo speramus, In God we trust

Columbia University
In lumine tuo videbimus lumen, In thy light we shall see light

University of Nebraska
Litteris dedicata et omnibus artibus, Dedicated to letters and all the arts

University of North Dakota
Lux et lex, Light and law

Yale University
Lux et veritas, Light and truth

University of New Mexico
Lux hominum vita, Light, the life of men

University of Washington
Lux sit, Let there be light

University of Oregon
Mens agitat molem, Mind moves the mass

Hunter College
Mihi cura futuri, My anxiety is for the future

Brooklyn College
Nil sine magno labore, Nothing without great effort

Tulane University
Non sibi, sed suis, Not for herself, but for her own

New York University
Perstare et praestare, To persevere and surpass

Trinity College
Pro ecclesia et patria, For church and country

City College of New York
Respice, adspice, prospice, Look back, look to the present, look to the future

University of Missouri
Salus populi, The welfare of the people

Fordham University
Sapientia et doctrina, Wisdom and knowledge

215

Delaware College
Scientia sol mentis, Knowledge, the sun of the mind

University of Vermont
Studiis et rebus honestis, To honorable pursuits and deeds

Amherst College
Terras irradient, Let them illumine the earth

Harvard University
Veritas, Truth

Johns Hopkins University
Veritas vos liberabit, The truth will set you free

University of Mississippi
Virtute et armis, By valor and arms

Dartmouth College
Vox clamantis in deserto, The voice of one crying in the wilderness

EXERCISES

A. Give the meaning of the following college mottoes:

1. Lux et lex _____

2. Salus populi _____

3. In Deo speramus _____

4. Pro ecclesia et patria _____

5. Scientia sol mentis _____

6. Lux sit _____

7. Perstare et praestare _____

8. Veritas vos liberabit _____

9. Lux et veritas _____

10. Mens agitat molem _____

B. Complete the following college mottoes:

1. Ecce quam _____

2. Nil sine magno _____

3. _____ irradient

4. Respice, _____, prospice

5. _____ clamantis in deserto

6. In lumine tuo _____ lumen

7. Lux _____ vita

8. _____ et doctrina

9. Virtute et _____

10. Mihi _____ futuri

216

Lesson 82—STATE MOTTOES

Kansas
Ad astra per aspera, To the stars through difficulties

Wyoming
Cedant arma togae, Let arms yield to the toga (peace)

New Mexico
Crescit eundo, It grows as it goes

Maine
Dirigo, I point the way

Arizona
Ditat Deus, God enriches

South Carolina
Dum spiro, spero, While there's life, there's hope

Massachusetts
Ense petit placidam sub libertate quietem, With the sword she seeks calm peace under liberty

United States
E pluribus unum, Out of many, one

North Carolina
Esse quam videri, To be rather than to seem

Idaho
Esto perpetua, May it last forever

New York
Excelsior, Ever upward

District of Columbia
Iustitia omnibus, Justice to all

Oklahoma
Labor omnia vincit, Toil overcomes all obstacles

West Virginia
Montani semper liberi, Mountaineers are always free

Colorado
Nil sine numine, Nothing without divine guidance

Connecticut
Qui transtulit sustinet, He who transplanted, sustains

Arkansas
Regnat populus, The people rule

Missouri
Salus populi suprema lex esto, The welfare of the people shall be the supreme law

Maryland
Scuto bonae voluntatis Tuae coronasti nos, With the shield of Thy good-will Thou hast covered us

Virginia
Sic semper tyrannis, Thus ever to tyrants

217

Michigan

Si quaeris paeninsulam amoenam circumspice, If you seek a pleasant peninsula, look about you

Mississippi

Virtute et armis, By valor and arms

EXERCISES

A. Give the meaning of the following state mottoes:

1. Regnat populus _____

2. Labor omnia vincit _____

3. Dirigo _____

4. Iustitia omnibus _____

5. Cedant arma togae _____

6. Dum spiro, spero _____

7. Sic semper tyrannis _____

8. Ad astra per aspera _____

9. Excelsior _____

10. E pluribus unum _____

B. Complete the following state mottoes:

1. Montani semper _____

2. _____ sine numine

3. Ditat _____

4. _____ quam videri

5. Salus _____ suprema lex esto

6. Si quaeris paeninsulam amoenam _____

7. Qui transtulit _____

8. Ense petit placidam sub _____ quietem

9. _____ bonae voluntatis Tuae coronasti nos

10. _____ eundo

Lesson 83—REVIEW OF CIVILIZATION AND CULTURE

A

Underline the word or expression that best completes each of the following statements:

1. The Romans generally referred to the Mediterranean as Mare (1) Africānum (2) Magnum (3) Nostrum (4) Lātum.

2. When the Etruscans marched on Rome, the bridge over the Tiber was defended by (1) Cato (2) Horatius (3) Romulus (4) Tarquinius.

3. Much information about Roman life has been obtained from the excavations at (1) Naples (2) Ostia (3) Brundisium (4) Pompeii.

4. The man who first tried to fly was the famous artisan (1) Daedalus (2) Argus (3) Hercules (4) Midas.

5. Up to about 500 B.C., Rome was ruled by (1) consuls (2) kings (3) emperors (4) dictators.

6. A consul was elected for (1) one year (2) two years (3) five years (4) life.

7. "And so forth" is represented by the abbreviaton (1) e.g. (2) i.e. (3) q.v. (4) etc.

8. The legendary founder of Rome was (1) Jupiter (2) Hercules (3) Romulus (4) Horatius.

9. The Saturnalia was a holiday period roughly comparable to (1) Easter (2) Christmas (3) Thanksgiving (4) Memorial Day.

10. Mercury was the gods' (1) blacksmith (2) king (3) messenger (4) warrior.

B

Underline the word or expression that best completes each of the following statements:

1. A magazine article which speaks of "Our Sea" as the cradle and grave of empires is referring to the (1) Aegean Sea (2) Black Sea (3) Caspian Sea (4) Mediterranean Sea.

2. The chief official in the Roman Republic was the (1) consul (2) praetor (3) quaestor (4) censor.

3. Ashes from Mount Vesuvius buried the city of (1) Naples (2) Rome (3) Brundisium (4) Pompeii.

4. The chief official of the Roman religion was the (1) consul (2) pontifex maximus (3) imperator (4) quaestor.

5. The race track in Rome was called the (1) Palatine (2) Forum (3) Circus Maximus (4) Colosseum.

6. The Roman equivalent for a modern club house was the (1) Campus Martius (2) Capitoline (3) thermae (4) basilica.

7. An architectural form perfected by the Romans was the (1) pointed arch (2) Doric columns (3) rounded arch (4) Ionic columns.

8. An aqueduct is a (1) reservoir (2) water pipe (3) waterfall (4) road.

9. "Note well" or "Pay close attention" is represented by the abbreviation (1) N.B. (2) A.D. (3) A.M. (4) P.S.

10. Chariot races were held in the (1) Forum (2) Via Appia (3) Circus Maximus (4) Colosseum.

C

Underline the word or expression that best completes each of the following statements:

1. The chief god of the Romans was (1) Mars (2) Apollo (3) Jupiter (4) Juno.

2. Of the following abbreviations, the one that means "compare" is (1) e.g. (2) N.B. (3) cf. (4) viz.

3. Our word "candidate" derives its meaning from the fact that Roman office seekers were accustomed to (1) give candy (2) appear candid (3) wear pure white togas (4) carry candles.

4. One of the most famous bathing establishments in Rome was named after (1) Caesar (2) Caracalla (3) Cato (4) Cincinnatus.

5. The Roman who was nicknamed "Scaevola," because he had thrust his right hand into a fire, was (1) Mucius (2) Horatius (3) Porsena (4) Remus.

6. The last of the seven kings was (1) Romulus (2) Augustus (3) Tullus Hostilius (4) Tarquinius Superbus.

7. The Roman road that was known as the Rēgīna Viārum was the Via (1) Aurēlia (2) Flāminia (3) Appia (4) Latīna.

8. The messenger of the gods was (1) Apollo (2) Mercury (3) Mars (4) Neptune.

9. Products bearing the name Venus emphasize their (1) size (2) strength (3) color (4) beauty.

10. Remus was the twin brother of (1) Romulus (2) Tarquinius (3) Horatius (4) Brutus.

D

Underline the word or expression that best completes each of the following statements:

1. A Roman consul obtained his office by (1) being appointed (2) being elected (3) seizing power (4) heredity.

2. An ancient hero much admired for his strength was (1) Orpheus (2) Caesar (3) Hercules (4) Cato.

3. The Latin abbreviation meaning "and others" is (1) e.g. (2) i.e. (3) q.v. (4) et al.

4. The motto of New York State is (1) Lux (2) Lex (3) Excelsior (4) Superior.

5. The Roman deity who was the guardian of the doorways was (1) Juno (2) Janus (3) Vesta (4) Apollo.

6. The Roman who left his farm to lead the army was (1) Cincinnatus (2) Scaevola (3) Fabricius (4) Decius Mus.

7. The senatorial order in Rome was known as the (1) Equitēs (2) Plēbs (3) Populārēs (4) Optimātēs.

8. For outdoor living, the Roman family particularly enjoyed the (1) ātrium (2) peristȳlium (3) tablīnum (4) trīclīnium.

9. The planet Neptune is named after the god of (1) fire (2) war (3) the sea (4) the harvest.

10. To assure a good grape harvest, the Romans would pray to (1) Jupiter (2) Juno (3) Mercury (4) Bacchus.

E

Underline the word or expression that best completes each of the following statements:

1. Tarquin the Proud was expelled from Rome because of his (1) dishonesty (2) despotism (3) disloyalty (4) bribery.

2. The Greek cities of southern Italy were defended by (1) Pyrrhus (2) Alexander (3) Hannibal (4) Attalus.

3. The Latin word *forum* has given us the English word (1) foreign (2) forage (3) fortune (4) forensic.

4. The Romans used olive oil for many purposes, among them as a (1) drink (2) drug (3) fuel (4) soap.

5. Caesar invaded Gaul, Germany, and (1) Britain (2) Africa (3) Greece (4) Spain.

6. The usual number of laps to a chariot race was (1) 3 (2) 5 (3) 7 (4) 9.

7. The Romans did not have in their diet (1) olives (2) tomatoes (3) grapes (4) figs.

8. The Campus Martius was used for (1) chariot racing (2) gladiatorial combats (3) swimming events (4) military training.

9. Temples and altars to the gods were built by (1) private enterprise (2) priests (3) religious societies (4) the government.

10. The Julian calendar was further changed by Pope (1) John (2) Pius (3) Gregory (4) Clement.

Unit XIII—Latin Words and Expressions for Oral Classroom Use

I. QUESTION WORDS

ENGLISH	LATIN
who	quis
what	quid
why	cūr
where (in what place)	ubi
where (to what place)	quō
where (from what place)	unde
when	quandō, quō tempore
how	quō modō
how long	quam diū
how many	quot

II. VOCABULARY FOR CLASSROOM CONVERSATION

ENGLISH	LATIN
answer	respōnsum
assignment	pēnsum
blackboard	tabula
book	liber
bookcase	armārium
chalk	crēta
clock	hōrologium
door	iānua, porta
eraser	ērāsūra
locker	capsa
map	tabula geōgraphica
paper	charta
pen	penna
pencil	stilus
picture	pīctūra
principal	prīnceps
principal's office	locus prīncipis
pupil	discipulus (discipula)
question	interrogātiō
room	camera, cella
school	lūdus, schola
seat	sella
story	fābula
table	mēnsa
teacher	magister (magistra)
window	fenestra
word	verbum

III. CLASSROOM DIRECTIONS

ENGLISH	LATIN
come in, enter	inī (inīte); venī (venīte); intrā (intrāte)
go out, leave	exī (exīte)
go	ī (īte)
come here	venī (venīte) hūc
stand up	surge (surgite)

221

sit down	cōnsīde (cōnsīdite)
open the door	aperī iānuam
close the door	claude iānuam
listen	attende (attendite); audī (audīte)
be quiet	tacē (tacēte)
go on, continue	perge (pergite)
stop that	mitte haec
look here, here is	ecce
put down	pōne
come on	age
take	cape, sūme
read	lege
recite, read aloud	recitā
repeat	repete
answer in English	respondē Anglicē
answer in Latin	respondē Latīnē
translate into English	verte Anglicē
translate into Latin	verte Latīnē

IV. COMMON EXPRESSIONS

ENGLISH	LATIN
hello, good morning (afternoon)	salvē (salvēte)
good-bye	valē (valēte)
how are you?	quid agis?
pretty well	satis bene
yes	sīc; ita; vērō; certē
no	minimē
please	quaesō; si tibi placet
thank you	tibi grātiās agō
excuse me	mihi īgnōsce
sir	domine
madame (ma'am)	domina
what time is it?	quota hōra est?
how is the weather today?	quaenam est tempestās hodiē?
the sun is shining	sōl lūcet
it is raining	pluit
it is snowing	ningit
I shall say it in Latin	Latīnē dīcam
let's talk Latin	Latīnē colloquāmur
you have answered correctly	rēctē respondistī
all right	fīat; licet

V. SAMPLE DIALOGUE

QUESTION OR STATEMENT	ANSWER
Salvēte, discipulī!	Salvē, magister.
Ubi est Mārcus?	Hīc ego sum; adsum.
Ubi est Anna?	Anna abest.
Quis est Paulus?	Ego sum Paulus.
Quae rēs est, Carole?	Est iānua, fenestra, etc.
Estne hic liber?	Ita, est liber.
Estne haec penna?	Minimē, est crēta.
Scrībe in tabulā, Philippe.	In tabulā scrībō.
Claude iānuam, quaesō.	Iānuam claudō.
Ubi est Italia?	Italia in Eurōpā est.

EXERCISES

A. Answer the following questions orally in complete Latin sentences:

1. Quod est tuum nōmen?

2. Habēsne patrem mātremque?

3. Quot frātrēs et sorōrēs habēs?

4. Quod est praenōmen tuī frātris?

5. Quod est praenōmen tuae sorōris?

6. Quid agis?

7. Quaenam est tempestās hodiē?

8. Ubi est terra Italia?

9. Estne Italia longa aut lāta?

10. Ubi est urbs Rōma?

B. Formulate questions orally in Latin to which the following statements are answers:

1. Vērō, Mārcus est meus amīcus.

2. Hodiē sōl lūcet.

3. Maria abest.

4. Haec est fenestra.

5. Scrībō in tabulā.

6. Liber Latīnus in meā manū est.

7. Ita, puella est parva.

8. Magistrum meum videō.

9. Multam pecūniam nōn habeō.

10. Amāmus nostram patriam.

C. Give full-sentence commands orally in Latin in accordance with the following directions:

1. Use the verb *scrībere* addressing one person.

2. Use the verb *legere* addressing your father.

3. Use the verb *claudere* addressing Sextus.

4. Use the verb *aperīre* addressing Julia.

5. Use the verb *surgere* addressing several people.

6. Use the expression *vertere Anglicē* addressing Marcus.

7. Use a verb of motion addressing Quintus and Cornelia.

8. Greet your friend.

9. Bid good-bye to your friends.

10. Ask your teacher to please give you chalk.

Unit XIV—Vocabularies

LATIN MASTERY LIST

NOUNS

aciēs, -ēī (f.), line of battle
adventus, -ūs (m.), arrival, approach
aestās, -ātis (f.), summer
ager, agrī (m.), field, land
agricola, -ae (m.), farmer
amīcitia, -ae (f.), friendship
amīcus, -ī (m.), friend
animus, -ī (m.), mind, spirit
annus, -ī (m.), year
aqua, -ae (f.), water
arma, -ōrum (n. pl.), arms
auxilium, -ī (n.), aid
bellum, -ī (n.), war
caput, -itis (n.), head
castra, -ōrum (n. pl.), camp
causa, -ae (f.), cause, reason
celeritās, -ātis (f.), speed, swiftness
cīvis, -is (m.), citizen
cīvitās, -ātis (f.), state, citizenship
cōnsilium, -ī (n.), plan, advice
cōpia, -ae (f.), supply, abundance; (pl.), troops
corpus, -oris (n.), body
diēs, -ēī (m.), day
domus, -ūs (f.), house, home
dux, ducis (m.), leader, general
eques, -itis (m.), horseman
exercitus, -ūs (m.), army
fēmina, -ae (f.), woman
fidēs, -eī (f.), faith, trust
fīlia, -ae (f.), daughter
fīlius, -ī (m.), son
fīnis, -is (m.), end, boundary; (pl.), territory
flūmen, -inis (n.), river
frāter, -tris (m.), brother

frūmentum, -ī (n.), grain
fuga, -ae (f.), flight
gladius, -ī (m.), sword
hiems, -emis (f.), winter
homō, -inis (m.), man, person
hōra, -ae (f.), hour
hostis, -is (m.), enemy
imperātor, -ōris (m.), general
imperium, -ī (n.), command, rule
īnsula, -ae (f.), island
iter, itineris (n.), march, journey, route
lēx, lēgis (f.), law
liber, -brī (m.), book
locus, -ī (m.); (pl.), loca, -ōrum (n.), place
lūx, lūcis (f.), light
manus, -ūs (f.), hand, band
mare, -is (n.), sea
māter, -tris (f.), mother
memoria, -ae (f.), memory
mīles, -itis (m.), soldier
modus, -ī (m.), manner, way
mōns, montis (m.), mountain
mors, mortis (f.), death
multitūdō, -inis (f.), multitude, crowd
nātūra, -ae (f.), nature
nauta, -ae (m.), sailor
nāvis, -is (f.), ship
nōmen, -inis (n.), name
nox, noctis (f.), night
numerus, -ī (m.), number
oppidum, -ī (n.), town
pars, partis (f.), part
passus, -ūs (m.), pace, step
pater, -tris (m.), father
patria, -ae (f.), country, native land

pāx, pācis (f.), peace
pecūnia, -ae (f.), money
perīculum, -ī (n.), danger
pēs, pedis (m.), foot
poena, -ae (f.), punishment
pōns, pontis (m.), bridge
populus, -ī (m.), people
porta, -ae (f.), gate
praemium, -ī (n.), reward, prize
praesidium, -ī (n.), protection, guard
prīnceps, -ipis (m.), chief, leader
proelium, -ī (n.), battle
prōvincia, -ae (f.), province
puella, -ae (f.), girl
puer, puerī (m.), boy
rēgnum, -ī (n.), kingdom, rule
rēs, reī (f.), thing, matter
rēx, rēgis (m.), king
senātus, -ūs (m.), senate
servus, -ī (m.), slave
signum, -ī (n.), signal, standard
silva, -ae (f.), forest
socius, -ī (m.), ally, comrade
soror, -ōris (f.), sister
spēs, speī (f.), hope
tempus, -oris (n.), time
terra, -ae (f.), land
timor, -ōris (m.), fear
urbs, urbis (f.), city
via, -ae (f.), way, road, street
victōria, -ae (f.), victory
vīlla, -ae (f.), country house, farm
vir, virī (m.), man
virtūs, ūtis (f.), courage
vīta, -ae (f.), life
vulnus, -eris (n.), wound

ADJECTIVES AND PRONOUNS

ācer, ācris, ācre, sharp, fierce
altus, -a, -um, high, deep
amīcus, -a, -um, friendly
bonus, -a, -um, good
brevis, -e, short
celer, -eris, -ere, swift
certus, -a, -um, certain, sure
ego, I; (pl.) nōs, we

facilis, -e, easy
fīnitimus, -a, -um, neighboring
fortis, -e, brave, strong
hic, haec, hoc, this, he, she, it
īdem, eadem, idem, the same
ille, illa, illud, that, he, she, it
ipse, ipsa, ipsum, -self, very
is, ea, id, this, that, he, she, it

līber, -era, -erum, free
longus, -a, -um, long
magnus, -a, -um, great, large
malus, -a, -um, bad, evil
meus, -a, -um, my, mine
miser, -era, -erum, wretched, poor
multus, -a, -um, much, many

224

noster, -tra, -trum, our, ours
novus, -a, -um, new, strange
omnis, -e, all, every
parvus, -a, -um, small, little
paucī, -ae, -a, few

potēns, powerful
quī, quae, quod, who, which, that
quis?, quid?, who?, what?
suī, of himself, herself, itself, themselves

suus, -a, -um, his (her, its, their) own
tū, you; (pl.) vōs, you
tuus, -a, -um, your, yours
vester, -tra, -trum, your, yours

VERBS

accipiō, -ere, -cēpī, -ceptus, receive
agō, -ere, ēgī, āctus, drive, do
amō, -āre, -āvī, -ātus, love, like
appellō, -āre, -āvī, -ātus, name
audiō, -īre, -īvī, -ītus, hear
capiō, -ere, cēpī, captus, take, seize
cognōscō, -ere, -nōvī, -nitus, find out, learn
cōnficiō, -ere, -fēcī, -fectus, finish
cōnstituō, -ere, -stituī, -stitūtus, decide, station
contendō, -ere, -tendī, -tentus, hasten, fight
conveniō, -īre, -vēnī, -ventus, come together, assemble
cupiō, -ere, īvī, -ītus, wish, desire
dēbeō, -ēre, -uī, -itus, owe, ought
dēfendō, -ere, -fendī, -fēnsus, defend
dēligō, -ere, -lēgī, -lēctus, choose
dīco, -ere, dīxī, dictus, say, speak
discēdō, -ere, -cessī, -cessus, leave, depart
dō, dare, dedī, datus, give

dūcō, -ere, dūxī, ductus, lead
exīstimō, -āre, -āvī, -ātus, think
faciō, -ere, fēcī, factus, make, do
gerō, -ere, gessī, gestus, carry on, wage
habeō, -ēre, -uī, -itus, have
iaciō, -ere, iēcī, iactus, throw
incipiō, -ere, -cēpī, -ceptus, begin
interficiō, -ere, -fēcī, -fectus, kill
iubeō, -ēre, iussī, iussus, order
labōrō, -āre, -āvī, -ātus, work
laudō, -āre, -āvī, -ātus, praise
līberō, -āre, -āvī, -ātus, free
maneō, -ēre, mānsī, mānsūrus, remain, stay
mittō, -ere, mīsī, missus, send
moneō, -ēre, -uī, -itus, advise, warn
moveō, -ēre, mōvī, mōtus, move
mūniō, -īre, -īvī, -ītus, fortify, build
nāvigō, -āre, -āvī, -ātus, sail
nūntiō, -āre, -āvī, -ātus, announce
occupō, -āre, -āvī, -ātus, seize
parō, -āre, -āvī, -ātus, prepare
perveniō, -īre, -vēnī, -ventus, arrive
petō, -ere, -īvī, -ītus, seek, ask

pōnō, -ere, posuī, positus, put, place
portō, -āre, -āvī, -ātus, carry
possum, posse, potuī, be able, can
prohibeō, -ēre, -uī, -itus, hold back, prevent
pugnō, -āre, -āvī, -ātus, fight
putō, -āre, -āvī, -ātus, think
relinquō, -ere, -līquī, -lictus, leave, abandon
respondeō, -ēre, -spondī, -spōnsus, reply
sciō, -īre, -īvī, -ītus, know
scrībō, -ere, scrīpsī, scrīptus, write
servō, -āre, -āvī, -ātus, save, keep
spectō, -āre, -āvī, -ātus, look at
sum, esse, fuī, futūrus, be
superō, -āre, -āvī, -ātus, defeat, surpass
temptō, -āre, -āvī, -ātus, try
teneō, -ēre, -uī, hold, keep
timeō, -ēre, -ui, fear
trādō, -ere, -didī, -ditus, surrender, hand over
veniō, -īre, vēnī, ventus, come
videō, -ēre, vīdī, vīsus, see
vincō, -ere, vīcī, victus, conquer
vocō, -āre, -āvī, -ātus, call
vulnerō, -āre, -āvī, -ātus, wound

ADVERBS, CONJUNCTIONS, PREPOSITIONS, ENCLITICS

ā, ab (with abl.), from, by
ad (with acc.), to, toward, near
ante (with acc.), before, in front of
cum (with abl.), with
cūr?, why?
dē (with abl.), down from, concerning, about
diū, for a long time
ē, ex (with abl.), out of, from
et, and; et . . . et, both . . . and

ibi, there
in (with abl.), in, on; (with acc.), into
inter (with acc.), between, among
itaque, and so, therefore
-ne, sign of a question
nōn, not
nunc, now
ob (with acc.), on account of
per (with acc.), through
post (with acc.), after, behind

prō (with abl.), before, for
propter (with acc.), because of
-que, and
quod, because
sed, but
sine (with abl.), without
sub (with acc. and abl.), under
trāns (with acc.), across
tum, then
ubi?, where?

LATIN MASTERY LIST

NUMERALS

CARDINAL	ORDINAL
ūnus, -a, -um, one	**prīmus, -a, -um,** first
duo, duae, duo, two	**secundus, -a, -um,** second
trēs, tria, three	**tertius, -a, -um,** third
quattuor, four	**quārtus, -a, -um,** fourth
quīnque, five	**quīntus, -a, -um,** fifth
sex, six	**sextus, -a, -um,** sixth
septem, seven	**septimus, -a, -um,** seventh
octō, eight	**octāvus, -a, -um,** eighth
novem, nine	**nōnus, -a, -um,** ninth
decem, ten	**decimus, -a, -um,** tenth
vīgintī, twenty	
centum, one hundred	
mīlle, one thousand	

EXERCISES

A. In the space before each word in column *A*, write the letter of the English equivalent in column *B*.

Column A	Column B
_____ **1.** domus	*a.* remain
_____ **2.** proelium	*b.* throw
_____ **3.** incipiō	*c.* war
_____ **4.** moneō	*d.* time
_____ **5.** diū	*e.* home
_____ **6.** praesidium	*f.* begin
_____ **7.** bellum	*g.* reward
_____ **8.** iter	*h.* between
_____ **9.** iaciō	*i.* battle
_____ **10.** praemium	*j.* a long time
_____ **11.** parvus	*k.* guard
_____ **12.** tempus	*l.* warn
_____ **13.** paucī	*m.* small
_____ **14.** inter	*n.* few
_____ **15.** maneō	*o.* journey

B. Underline the English word that best translates the Latin word.

1. *eques:* equal, horse, horseman, army

2. *līber:* book, free, freedom, set free

3. *cupiō:* wish, take, make, throw

4. *ibi:* where, why, on account of, there

5. *quīntus:* five, fifth, fourth, four

6. *animus:* friend, friendly, mind, year

7. *mūniō:*   fortify, warn, remain, move

8. *īdem:*   self, that, the same, this

9. *cōnsilium:*   guard, danger, aid, plan

10. *pōns:*   mountain, punishment, bridge, part

11. *virtūs:*   man, courage, safety, life

12. *putō:*   seek, carry, think, put

13. *vincō:*   conquer, come, see, call

14. *multus:*   great, bad, much, crowd

15. *fīnitimus:*   end, neighboring, territory, final

16. *aestās:*   summer, winter, equal, battle line

17. *rēs:*   king, kingdom, thing, foot

18. *caput:*   time, camp, river, head

19. *dūcō:*   say, do, lead, owe

20. *cōnficiō:*   learn, finish, decide, hasten

C. Underline the word that does *not* belong in each group. Explain why.

1. fēmina, frāter, caput, homō

----

2. diēs, rēs, diū, aestās

----

3. annus, mīlle, decimus, sex

----

4. trāns, post, ob, et

----

5. noster, tū, suus, tuus

----

6. ōrdō, mittō, iubeō, moveō

----

7. gladius, manus, caput, pēs

----

8. videō, audiō, sciō, faciō

----

9. prōvincia, pater, patria, locus

----

10. exercitus, populus, fīlius, multitūdō

----

11. eques, mīles, imperātor, agricola

227

12. frūmentum, mors, pecūnia, pōnō

- -

13. aciēs, castra, flūmen, arma

- -

14. omnis, malus, fortis, celeritās

- -

15. dēbeō, contendō, mūniō, vincō

- -

D. Underline the word in parentheses that best completes the meaning of each sentence.

1. Dux castra (dedit, scrīpsit, posuit).

2. Puerī perterritī sunt (propter, quod, itaque) perīculum.

3. Multī nōn labōrant (itinere, aestāte, oppidō).

4. Servī nōn sunt (amīcī, līberī, fīnitimī).

5. Sextus est mīles. Est in (adventū, celeritāte, exercitū).

6. Multitūdō iam (occupāverat, convēnerat, potuerat).

7. Mārcus pecūniam nōn habet. Est (malus, certus, miser).

8. (Inter, Ob, Sed) oppida erat flūmen.

9. Hostēs pugnāvērunt magnā cum (morte, virtūte, cīvitāte).

10. Mīlitēs (sub, ante, diū) mānsērunt.

LATIN-ENGLISH VOCABULARY

ā, ab (with abl.), from, by

absum, -esse, āfuī, āfutūrus, be away, be absent

accipiō, -ere, -cēpī, -ceptus, receive

ācer, ācris, ācre, sharp, fierce

aciēs, -ēī (f.), line of battle

ācriter, sharply, fiercely

ad (with acc.), to, toward, near

addūcō, -ere, -dūxī, -ductus, lead to, influence

adsum, -esse, -fuī, -futūrus, be near, be present

adventus, -ūs (m.), arrival, approach

aequus, -a, -um, equal, level, fair

aestās, -ātis (f.), summer

ager, agrī (m.), field, land

agō, -ere, ēgī, āctus, drive, do

agricola, -ae (m.), farmer

altitūdō, -inis (f.), height, depth

altus, -a, -um, high, deep

amīcitia, -ae (f.), friendship

amīcus, -a, -um, friendly

amīcus, -ī (m.), friend

āmittō, -ere, -mīsī, -missus, send away, lose

amō, -āre, -āvī, -ātus, love, like

animus, -ī (m.), mind, spirit

annus, -ī (m.), year

ante (with acc.), before, in front of

anteā, previously, formerly

appellō, -āre, -āvī, -ātus, name

appropinquō, -āre, -āvī, -ātus, approach

apud (with acc.), among, in the presence of, near

aqua, -ae (f.), water

arbor, -oris (f.), tree

arma, -ōrum (n. pl.), arms

atque (ac), and, and especially

auctōritās, -ātis (f.), influence, authority

audiō, -īre, -īvī, -ītus, hear

aut, or; aut . . . aut, either . . . or

autem, however, but, moreover

auxilium, -ī (n.), aid

barbarus, -a, -um, foreign, uncivilized, savage

barbarus, -ī (m.), barbarian, native, foreigner

bellum, -ī (n.), war

bene, well

beneficium, -ī (n.), benefit, favor, kindness

bonus, -a, -um, good

brevis, -e, short

campus, -ī (m.), plain, field

capiō, -ere, cēpī, captus, take, seize, capture

caput, -itis (n.), head

castra, -ōrum (n. pl.), camp

causa, -ae (f.), cause, reason

cēdō, -ere, cessī, cessus, move, yield

celer, -eris, -ere, swift

celeritās, -ātis (f.), speed, swiftness

celeriter, quickly

centum, one hundred

certus, -a, -um, certain, sure

circumveniō, -īre, -vēnī, -ventus, surround

cīvis, -is (m.), citizen

cīvitās, -ātis (f.), state, citizenship

cognōscō, -ere, -nōvī, -nitus, find out, learn

cōgō, -ere, coēgī, coāctus, compel, collect

collis, -is (m.), hill

committō, -ere, mīsī, -missus, join, entrust

commoveō, -ēre, -mōvī, -mōtus, move deeply, alarm

commūnis, -e, common

comparō, -āre, -āvī, -ātus, get together, prepare

condiciō, -ōnis (f.), terms, agreement

cōnficiō, -ere, -fēcī, -fectus, finish

cōnfīrmō, -āre, -āvī, -ātus, encourage, strengthen

coniciō, -ere, -iēcī, -iectus, hurl

cōnscrībō, -ere, -scrīpsī, -scrīptus, enlist, enroll

cōnservō, -āre, -āvī, -ātus, preserve, keep

cōnsilium, -ī (n.), plan, advice

cōnstituō, -ere, -stituī, -stitūtus, decide, station

cōnsuētūdō, -inis (f.), custom, habit

cōnsul, -is (m.), consul

contendō, -ere, -tendī, -tentus, hasten, fight

contineō, -ēre, -tinuī, -tentus, hold together, hem in

conveniō, -īre, -vēnī, -ventus, come together, assemble

cōpia, -ae (f.), supply, abundance; (pl.), troops

cornū, -ūs (n.), horn, wing (of an army)

corpus, -oris (n.), body

cum (with abl.), with

cupiditās, -ātis (f.), desire

cupidus, -a, -um, desirous, eager

cupiō, -ere, -īvī, -ītus, wish, desire, want

cūr?, why?

dē (with abl.), down from, concerning, about

dēbeō, -ēre, -uī, -itus, owe, ought

decem, ten

decimus, -a, -um, tenth

dēfendō, -ere, -fendī, -fēnsus, defend

dēficiō, -ere, -fēcī, -fectus, fail, revolt

dēligō, -ere, -lēgī, -lēctus, choose

dēmōnstrō, -āre, -āvī, -ātus, point out, show

deus, -ī (m.), god

dexter, -tra, -trum, right

dīcō, -ere, dīxī, dictus, say, speak

diēs, -ēī (m.), day

difficilis, -e, hard, difficult

difficultās, -ātis (f.), difficulty

dīligentia, -ae (f.), care, diligence

dīmittō, -ere, -mīsī, -missus, send away, let go

discēdō, -ere, -cessī, -cessus, leave, depart

diū, for a long time

dō, dare, dedī, datus, give

doceō, -ēre, -uī, -tus, teach, explain

dominus, -ī (m.), master

domus, -ūs (f.), house, home

dubitō, -āre, -āvī, -ātus, doubt, hesitate

dūcō, -ere, dūxī, ductus, lead

duo, duae, duo, two
dux, ducis (*m.*), leader, general

ē, ex (*with abl.*), out of, from
ego, I
ēgregius, -a, -um, outstanding, remarkable
enim, for
ēnūntiō, -āre, -āvī, -ātus, declare, announce
eques, -itis (*m.*), horseman
equitātus, -ūs (*m.*), cavalry
equus, -ī (*m.*), horse
et, and; **et . . . et,** both . . . and
etiam, even, also
excēdō, -ere, -cessī, -cessus, go out, depart
exercitus, -ūs (*m.*), army
exīstimō, -āre, -āvī, -ātus, think
expōnō, -ere, -posuī, -positus, put out, set forth
exspectō, -āre, -āvī, -ātus, wait (for), expect

facile, easily
facilis, -e, easy
faciō, -ere, fēcī, factus, make, do
factum, -ī (*n.*), deed, act
facultās, -ātis (*f.*), ability, opportunity
fēmina, -ae (*f.*), woman
fidēs, -eī (*f.*), faith, trust
fīlia, -ae (*f.*), daughter
fīlius, -ī (*m.*), son
fīnis, -is (*m.*), end, boundary; (*pl.*), territory
fīnitimus, -a, -um, neighboring
flūmen, -inis (*n.*), river
fortis, -e, brave, strong
fortiter, bravely
fortūna, -ae (*f.*), fortune, luck
forum, -ī (*n.*), forum, marketplace
frāter, -tris (*m.*), brother
frūmentum, -ī (*n.*), grain
fuga, -ae (*f.*), flight

genus, -eris (*n.*), race, birth, kind
gerō, -ere, gessī, gestus, carry on, wage
gladius, -ī (*m.*), sword
grātia, -ae (*f.*), gratitude, favor
gravis, -e, heavy, severe, serious

habeō, -ēre, -uī, -itus, have

hic, haec, hoc, this, he, she, it
hiems, -emis (*f.*), winter
hodiē, today
homō, -inis (*m.*), man, person
hōra, -ae (*f.*), hour
hostis, -is (*m.*), enemy

iaciō, -ere, iēcī, iactus, throw
iam, already, soon, now
ibi, there
īdem, eadem, idem, the same
idōneus, -a, -um, suitable
ille, illa, illud, that, he, she, it
imperātor, -ōris (*m.*), general
imperium, -ī (*n.*), command, rule
in (*with abl.*), in, on; (*with acc.*), into
incipiō, -ere, -cēpī, -ceptus, begin
inimīcus, -a, -um, unfriendly
inīquus, -a, -um, unequal, uneven, unfavorable
iniūria, -ae (*f.*), injury, wrong, injustice
inopia, -ae (*f.*), lack, scarcity
īnstruō, -ere, -strūxī, -strūctus, draw up, arrange
īnsula, -ae (*f.*), island
inter (*with acc.*), between, among
interficiō, -ere, -fēcī, -fectus, kill
interim, meanwhile
intermittō, -ere, -mīsī, -missus, stop, discontinue
inveniō, -īre, -vēnī, -ventus, find, come upon
ipse, ipsa, ipsum, -self, very
is, ea, id, this, that, he, she, it
itaque, and so, therefore
iter, itineris (*n.*), march, journey, route
iubeō, -ēre, iussī, iussus, order
iūs, iūris (*n.*), right, law

labōrō, -āre, -āvī, -ātus, work
lātitūdō, -inis (*f.*), width
lātus, -a, -um, wide
laudō, -āre, -āvī, -ātus, praise
legō, -ere, lēgī, lēctus, choose, read
levis, -e, light, mild
lēx, lēgis (*f.*), law
liber, -brī (*m.*), book
līber, -era, -erum, free
līberī, -ōrum (*m. pl.*), children
līberō, -āre, -āvī, -ātus, free, set free

lībertās, -ātis (*f.*), liberty, freedom
lingua, -ae (*f.*), tongue, language
locus, -ī (*m.*); (*pl.*), **loca, -ōrum** (*n.*), place
longus, -a, -um, long
lūdō, -ere, lūsī, lūsus, play
lūna, -ae (*f.*), moon
lūx, lūcis (*f.*), light

magis, more
magister, -trī (*m.*), teacher
magnitūdō, -inis (*f.*), greatness, size
magnopere, greatly
magnus, -a, -um, great, large
malus, -a, -um, bad, evil
maneō, -ēre, mānsī, mānsūrus, remain, stay
manus, -ūs (*f.*), hand, band
mare, -is (*n.*), sea
maritimus, -a, -um, maritime, of the sea
māter, -tris (*f.*), mother
maximē, most of all, especially
memoria, -ae (*f.*), memory
mēns, mentis (*f.*), mind
mēnsis, -is (*m.*), month
merīdiēs, -ēī (*m.*), noon
meus, -a, -um, my, mine
mīles, -itis (*m.*), soldier
mīlle, one thousand
miser, -era, -erum, wretched, poor
mittō, -ere, mīsī, missus, send
modus, -ī (*m.*), manner, way
moneō, -ēre, -uī, -itus, advise, warn
mōns, montis (*m.*), mountain
mors, mortis (*f.*), death
moveō, -ēre, mōvī, mōtus, move
multitūdō, -inis (*f.*), multitude, crowd
multus, -a, -um, much, many
mūniō, -īre, -īvī, -ītus, fortify, build

nam, for
nātūra, -ae (*f.*), nature
nauta, -ae (*m.*), sailor
nāvigō, -āre, -āvī, -ātus, sail
nāvis, -is (*f.*), ship
-ne (sign of a question)
nē . . . quidem, not even
necessārius, -a, -um, necessary
negōtium, -ī (*n.*), business, task

neque (nec), and not, nor; neque . . . neque, neither . . . nor

nōbilis, -e, noble, famous

nōmen, -inis (n.), name

nōn, not

nōnus, -a, -um, ninth

nōs, we

noster, -tra, -trum, our, ours

nōtus, -a, -um, known, famous

novem, nine

novus, -a, -um, new, strange

nox, noctis (f.), night

numerus, -ī (m.), number

nunc, now

nūntiō, -āre, -āvī, -ātus, announce

ob (with acc.), on account of

obtineō, -ēre, -tinuī, -tentus, hold, possess

occupō, -āre, -āvī, -ātus, seize

octāvus, -a, -um, eighth

octō, eight

ōlim, once, formerly

omnis, -e, all, every

oppidum, -ī (n.), town

ōrātiō, -ōnis (f.), speech

ōrdō, -inis (m.), order, rank

ostendō, -ere, -dī, -tus, show, display

pār, equal, like

parātus, -a, -um, prepared, ready

parō, -āre, -āvī, -ātus, prepare

pars, partis (f.), part

parvus, -a, -um, small, little

passus, -ūs (m.), pace, step

pater, -tris (m.), father

patria, -ae (f.), country, native land

paucī, -ae, -a, few

pāx, pācis (f.), peace

pecūnia, -ae (f.), money

pellō, -ere, pepulī, pulsus, drive, rout

per (with acc.), through

perficiō, -ere, -fēcī, -fectus, finish

perīculum, -ī (n.), danger

permittō, -ere, -mīsī, -missus, allow, entrust

permoveō, -ēre, -mōvī, -mōtus, move deeply, arouse

perterreō, -ēre, -uī, -itus, terrify

pertineō, -ēre, -tinuī, reach, extend, pertain

perveniō, -īre, -vēnī, -ventus, arrive

pēs, pedis (m.), foot

petō, -ere, -īvī, -ītus, seek, ask

poena, -ae (f.), punishment

poēta, -ae (m.), poet

pōnō, -ere, posuī, positus, put, place

pōns, pontis (m.), bridge

populus, -ī (m.), people

porta, -ae (f.), gate

portō, -āre, -āvī, -ātus, carry

possum, posse, potuī, be able, can

post (with acc.), after, behind

posteā, afterwards

potēns, powerful

potestās, -ātis (f.), power

praemittō, -ere, -mīsī, -missus, send ahead

praemium, -ī (n.), reward, prize

praesidium, -ī (n.), protection, guard

praesum, -esse, -fuī, -futūrus, be in command

premō, -ere, pressī, pressus, press, oppress

prīmus, -a, -um, first

princeps, -ipis (m.), chief, leader

prō (with abl.), before, for

prōdūcō, -ere, -dūxī, -ductus, lead forth

proelium, -ī (n.), battle

prohibeō, -ēre, -uī, -itus, hold back, prevent, keep from

propinquus, -a, -um, near, neighboring

prōpōnō, -ere, -posuī, -positus, set forth, offer

propter (with acc.), because of

prōvincia, -ae (f.), province

prūdēns, foreseeing, wise

pūblicus, -a, -um, public

puella, -ae (f.), girl

puer, puerī (m.), boy

pugna, -ae (f.), fight, battle

pugnō, -āre, -āvī, -ātus, fight

putō, -āre, -āvī, -ātus, think

quam, how, as, than

quārtus, -a, -um, fourth

quattuor, four

-que, and

quī, quae, quod, who, which, that

quidem, indeed, in fact

quīnque, five

quīntus, -a, -um, fifth

quis?, quid?, who?, what?

quod, because

quot, how many?, as many as

ratiō, -ōnis (f.), method, plan, reason

recēns, recent, fresh

reddō, -ere, -didī, -ditus, give back, return

rēgīna, -ae (f.), queen

rēgnum, -ī (n.), kingdom, rule

relinquō, -ere, -līquī, -lictus, leave, abandon

reliquus, -a, -um, remaining, rest of

remittō, -ere, -mīsī, -missus, send back

removeō, -ēre, -mōvī, -mōtus, move back, withdraw

renūntiō, -āre, -āvī, -ātus, bring back word, report

rēs, reī (f.), thing, matter

rēs pūblica, reī pūblicae (f.), republic, government

respondeō, -ēre, -spondī, -spōnsus, reply

rēx, rēgis (m.), king

rīpa, -ae (f.), bank of a river

sagitta, -ae (f.), arrow

satis, enough

sciō, -īre, -īvī, -ītus, know

scrībō, -ere, scrīpsī, scrīptus, write

secundus, -a, -um, second

sed, but

senātus, -ūs (m.), senate

sentiō, -īre, sēnsī, sēnsus, feel, perceive

septem, seven

septimus, -a, -um, seventh

servō, -āre, -āvī, -ātus, save, keep

servus, -ī (m.), slave

sex, six

sextus, -a, -um, sixth

sī, if

signum, -ī (n.), signal, standard

silva, -ae (f.), forest

similis, -e, similar, like

sine (with abl.), without

sinister, -tra, -trum, left

socius, -ī (m.), ally, comrade

sōl, sōlis (m.), sun

soror, -ōris (f.), sister

LATIN-ENGLISH VOCABULARY

spatium, -ī (n.), space, distance
spectō, -āre, -āvī, -ātus, look at
spēs, speī (f.), hope
sub (with acc. and abl.), under
suī, of himself, herself, itself, themselves
sum, esse, fuī, futūrus, be
superō, -āre, -āvī, -ātus, defeat, surpass
sustineō, -ēre, -tinuī, -tentus, hold up, withstand
suus, -a, -um, his (her, its, their) own

tamen, however, still, yet
temptō, -āre, -āvī, -ātus, try
tempus, -oris (n.), time
teneō, -ēre, -uī, hold, keep
terra, -ae (f.), land
terreō, -ēre, -uī, -itus, frighten
tertius, -a, -um, third

timeō, -ēre, -uī, fear
timidus, -a, -um, fearful, timid
timor, -ōris (m.), fear
toga, -ae (f.), toga
trādō, -ere, -didī, -ditus, surrender, hand over
trāns (with acc.), across
trēs, tria, three
tū, you
tuba, -ae (f.), trumpet
tum, then
tuus, -a, -um, your, yours

ubi?, where?
ūnus, -a, -um, one
urbs, urbis (f.), city

veniō, -īre, vēnī, ventus, come
verbum, -ī (n.), word
vērō, in truth, indeed

vērus, -a, -um, true
vester, -tra, -trum, your, yours
via, -ae (f.), way, road, street
victor, -ōris (m.), conqueror, victor
victōria, -ae (f.), victory
videō, -ēre, vīdī, vīsus, see
vīgintī, twenty
vīlla, -ae (f.), country house, farm
vincō, -ere, vīcī, victus, conquer
vir, virī (m.), man
virtūs, -ūtis (f.), courage
vīs, vīs (f.), force, violence, strength
vīta, -ae (f.), life
vocō, -āre, -āvī, -ātus, call
vōs, you (pl.)
vōx, vōcis (f.), voice, word
vulnerō, -āre, -āvī, -ātus, wound
vulnus, -eris (n.), wound

EXERCISES

A. Underline the English word that best translates the Latin word.

1. doceō: say, teach, give, do
2. ratiō: method, race, kingdom, rest
3. tamen: once, time, each, however
4. coniciō: learn, come together, hurl, prepare
5. lūdō: praise, play, read, work
6. vīs: man, road, voice, force
7. pār: equal, part, through, pace
8. collis: collar, column, hill, ditch
9. cōnsuētūdō: plan, custom, terms, consulship
10. ēgregius: exit, Greek, selfish, outstanding
11. remittō: give back, report, send back, send out
12. līberī: books, children, freedom, set free
13. genus: birth, nation, wise, general
14. etiam: for, even, but, greatly
15. iūs: just, right, force, fair

B. In each of the following sentences, one or two Latin words have been used. Show that you understand their meaning by underlining the correct word in parentheses needed to complete the sentence.

1. If a person has *inopia pecūniae*, he is (rich, poor, miserly).
2. One would expect a *pōns* to be located over a (river, mountain, farm).
3. If someone is *propinquus*, he is your (friend, enemy, neighbor).
4. If you traveled *magnum spatium*, you would be going (slowly, swiftly, far).
5. If a student did not *perficere* a job, he might be (praised, punished, deceived).
6. In the expression *vīgintī equī*, reference is made to the (number, size, swiftness) of horses.
7. A *sagitta* could be used for (writing, shooting, swimming).
8. If I came upon a *collis*, I might (climb it, swim it, cut it).
9. A king with *satis potestās* would be (scheming, content, disappointed).
10. If a person were to *trādere*, it would indicate for him (victory, defeat, business).

C. In the space before each word in column *A*, write the letter of the English equivalent in column *B*.

	Column A		Column B
-------	**1.** deus	*a.*	be in command
-------	**2.** mēns	*b.*	day
-------	**3.** negōtium	*c.*	kindness
-------	**4.** praesum	*d.*	feel
-------	**5.** sustineō	*e.*	be away
-------	**6.** diēs	*f.*	order
-------	**7.** propinquus	*g.*	month
-------	**8.** sentiō	*h.*	god
-------	**9.** mēnsis	*i.*	collect
-------	**10.** prūdēns	*j.*	hold up
-------	**11.** cōgō	*k.*	lack
-------	**12.** absum	*l.*	near
-------	**13.** ōrdō	*m.*	wise
-------	**14.** inopia	*n.*	business
-------	**15.** beneficium	*o.*	mind

D. Underline the word that does *not* belong in each group. Explain why.

1. novem, novus, mīlle, nōnus

----

2. renūntiō, removeō, permoveō, commoveō

----

3. posteā, tum, iam, prō

----

4. cēdō, moveō, nūntiō, nāvigō

----

5. ratiō, sagitta, arma, gladius

----

6. dux, prīnceps, mīles, imperātor

----

7. vērō, vērus, quidem, certē

----

8. rēs pūblica, lēx, cōnsul, inopia

----

9. respondeō, pōnō, nūntiō, dīcō

----

10. victōria, vincō, rēx, superō

E. Below is a list of 50 vocabulary words. Some words refer to *parts of the body*, some are *military terms*, some are words denoting *time*, and some denote *place*. Indicate in which category each word belongs by putting a check in the appropriate column.

	PARTS OF THE BODY	MILITARY TERMS	TIME	PLACE
1. manus	--------	--------	--------	--------
2. aciēs	--------	--------	--------	--------
3. īnsula	--------	--------	--------	--------
4. aestās	--------	--------	--------	--------
5. eques	--------	--------	--------	--------
6. terra	--------	--------	--------	--------
7. castra	--------	--------	--------	--------
8. lingua	--------	--------	--------	--------
9. diēs	--------	--------	--------	--------
10. ager	--------	--------	--------	--------
11. oppidum	--------	--------	--------	--------
12. imperātor	--------	--------	--------	--------
13. tuba	--------	--------	--------	--------
14. merīdiēs	--------	--------	--------	--------
15. rīpa	--------	--------	--------	--------
16. rēgnum	--------	--------	--------	--------
17. dux	--------	--------	--------	--------
18. nox	--------	--------	--------	--------
19. silva	--------	--------	--------	--------
20. caput	--------	--------	--------	--------
21. sagitta	--------	--------	--------	--------
22. mare	--------	--------	--------	--------
23. tempus	--------	--------	--------	--------
24. gladius	--------	--------	--------	--------
25. locus	--------	--------	--------	--------
26. exercitus	--------	--------	--------	--------
27. pēs	--------	--------	--------	--------
28. campus	--------	--------	--------	--------
29. flūmen	--------	--------	--------	--------
30. prīnceps	--------	--------	--------	--------
31. cīvitās	--------	--------	--------	--------
32. patria	--------	--------	--------	--------
33. signum	--------	--------	--------	--------
34. mīles	--------	--------	--------	--------
35. collis	--------	--------	--------	--------
36. forum	--------	--------	--------	--------
37. cōpiae	--------	--------	--------	--------
38. via	--------	--------	--------	--------
39. hōra	--------	--------	--------	--------
40. urbs	--------	--------	--------	--------
41. prōvincia	--------	--------	--------	--------
42. annus	--------	--------	--------	--------
43. arma	--------	--------	--------	--------
44. pōns	--------	--------	--------	--------
45. hiems	--------	--------	--------	--------
46. mōns	--------	--------	--------	--------
47. corpus	--------	--------	--------	--------
48. equitātus	--------	--------	--------	--------
49. mēnsis	--------	--------	--------	--------
50. fīnēs	--------	--------	--------	--------

able (be), possum, posse, potuī
about, dē (with abl.)
absent (be), absum, -esse, āfuī, āfutūrus
abundance, cōpia, -ae (f.)
across, trāns (with acc.)
advice, cōnsilium, -ī (n.)
advise, moneō, -ēre, -uī, -itus
after, post (with acc.)
afterwards, posteā
aid, auxilium, -ī (n.)
alarm, commoveō, -ēre, -mōvī, -mōtus
all, omnis, -e
allow, permittō, -ere, -mīsī, -missus
ally, socius, -ī (m.)
already, iam
also, etiam
among, apud (with acc.)
and, et
and not, neque
and so, itaque
announce, nūntiō, -āre, -āvī, -ātus
approach, appropinquō, -āre, -āvī, -ātus
arms, arma, -ōrum (n. pl.)
army, exercitus, -ūs (m.)
arouse, permoveō, -ēre, -mōvī, -mōtus
arrival, adventus, -ūs (m.)
arrive, perveniō, -īre, -vēnī, -ventus
arrow, sagitta, -ae (f.)
ask, petō, -ere, -īvī, -ītus
assemble, conveniō, -īre, -vēnī, -ventus
authority, auctōritās, -ātis (f.)
away (be), absum, -esse, āfuī, āfutūrus

bad, malus, -a, -um
bank, rīpa, -ae (f.)
barbarian, barbarus, -ī (m.)
battle, proelium, -ī (n.)
be, sum, esse, fuī, futūrus
be in command, praesum, -esse, -fuī, -futūrus
be near, adsum, -esse, -fuī, -futūrus
be present, same as **be near**
because, quod
because of, propter (with acc.)

before, ante (with acc.)
begin, incipiō, -ere, -cēpī, -ceptus
behind, post (with acc.)
benefit, beneficium, -ī (n.)
between, inter (with acc.)
body, corpus, -oris (n.)
book, liber, -brī (m.)
both . . . and, et . . . et
boundary, fīnis, -is (m.)
boy, puer, puerī (m.)
brave, fortis, -e
bravely, fortiter
bridge, pōns, pontis (m.)
brother, frāter, -tris (m.)
business, negōtium, -ī (n.)
but, sed
by, ā, ab (with abl.)

call, vocō, -āre, -āvī, -ātus
camp, castra, -ōrum (n. pl.)
can, possum, posse, potuī
capture, capiō, -ere, cēpī, captus
carry, portō, -āre, -āvī, -ātus
carry on, gerō, -ere, gessī, gestus
cause, causa, -ae (f.)
cavalry, equitātus, -ūs (m.)
certain, certus, -a, -um
chief, prīnceps, -ipis (m.)
children, līberī, -ōrum (m. pl.)
choose, dēligō, -ere, -lēgī, -lēctus
citizen, cīvis, -is (m.)
city, urbs, urbis (f.)
collect, cōgō, -ere, coēgī, coāctus
come, veniō, -īre, vēnī, ventus
come together, conveniō, -īre, -vēnī, -ventus
command, imperium, -ī (n.)
common, commūnis, -e
compel, cōgō, -ere, coēgī, coāctus
comrade, socius, -ī (m.)
concerning, dē (with abl.)
conquer, vincō, -ere, vīcī, victus
conqueror, victor, -ōris (m.)
consul, cōnsul, -is (m.)
country, patria, -ae (f.)
country house, vīlla, -ae (f.)
courage, virtūs, -ūtis (f.)
crowd, multitūdō, -inis (f.)
custom, cōnsuētūdō, -inis (f.)

danger, perīculum, -ī (n.)
daughter, fīlia, -ae (f.)
day, diēs, -ēī (m.)
death, mors, mortis (f.)

decide, cōnstituō, -ere, -stituī, -stitūtus
deed, factum, -ī (n.)
deep, altus, -a, -um
defeat, superō, -āre, -āvī, -ātus
defend, dēfendō, -ere, -fendī, -fēnsus
depart, discēdō, -ere, -cessī, -cessus
depth, altitūdō, -inis (f.)
desire, cupiditās, -ātis (f.)
desire, cupiō, -ere, -īvī, -ītus
desirous, cupidus, -a, -um
difficult, difficilis, -e
difficulty, difficultās, -ātis (f.)
diligence, dīligentia, -ae (f.)
display, ostendō, -ere, -dī, -tus
distance, spatium, -ī (n.)
distant (be), absum, -esse, āfuī, āfutūrus
do, faciō, -ere, fēcī, factus
doubt, dubitō, -āre, -āvī, -ātus
down from, dē (with abl.)
draw up, īnstruō, -ere, -strūxī, -strūctus
drive, agō, -ere, ēgī, āctus

easily, facile
easy, facilis, -e
eight, octō
eighth, octāvus, -a, -um
either . . . or, aut . . . aut
encourage, cōnfīrmō, -āre, -āvī, -ātus
end, fīnis, -is (m.)
enemy, hostis, -is (m.)
enlist, cōnscrībō, -ere, -scrīpsī, -scrīptus
enough, satis
enroll, same as **enlist**
entrust, permittō, -ere, -mīsī, -missus
equal, aequus, -a, -um
especially, maximē
even, etiam; **not even,** nē . . . quidem
every, omnis, -e
evil, malus, -a, -um
expect, exspectō, -āre, -āvī, -ātus
extend, pertineō, -ēre, -tinuī

fair, aequus, -a, -um
faith, fidēs, -eī (f.)
famous, nōtus, -a, -um

farm, vīlla, -ae (*f.*)
farmer, agricola, -ae (*m.*)
father, pater, -tris (*m.*)
favor, beneficium, -ī (*n.*)
fear, timor, -ōris (*m.*)
fear, timeō, -ēre, -uī
feel, sentiō, -īre, sēnsī, sēnsus
few, paucī, -ae, -a
field, ager, agrī (*m.*)
fierce, ācer, ācris, ācre
fiercely, ācriter
fifth, quīntus, -a, -um
fight, pugna, -ae (*f.*)
fight, pugnō, -āre, -āvī, -ātus
find, inveniō, -īre, -vēnī, -ventus
find out, cognōscō, -ere, -nōvī, -nitus
finish, cōnficiō, -ere, -fēcī, -fectus
first, prīmus, -a, -um
five, quīnque
flight, fuga, -ae (*f.*)
foot, pēs, pedis (*m.*)
for, enim
for, prō (*with abl.*)
for a long time, diū
force, vīs, vīs (*f.*)
forest, silva, -ae (*f.*)
formerly, anteā
fortify, mūniō, -īre, -īvī, -ītus
fortune, fortūna, -ae (*f.*)
forum, forum, -ī (*n.*)
four, quattuor
fourth, quārtus, -a, -um
free, līber, -era, -erum
free, līberō, -āre, -āvī, -ātus
freedom, lībertās, -ātis (*f.*)
friend, amīcus, -ī (*m.*)
friendly, amīcus, -a, -um
friendship, amīcitia, -ae (*f.*)
frighten, terreō, -ēre, -uī, -itus
from, ā, ab (*with abl.*)

gate, porta, -ae (*f.*)
general, imperātor, -ōris (*m.*)
get together, comparō, -āre, -āvī, -ātus
girl, puella, -ae (*f.*)
give, dō, dare, dedī, datus
give back, reddō, -ere, -didī, -ditus
go out, excēdō, -ere, -cessī, -cessus
god, deus, -ī (*m.*)
good, bonus, -a, -um
government, rēs pūblica, reī pūblicae (*f.*)
grain, frūmentum, -ī (*n.*)
gratitude, grātia, -ae (*f.*)

great, magnus, -a, -um
greatly, magnopere
greatness, magnitūdō, -inis (*f.*)
guard, praesidium, -ī (*n.*)

hand, manus, -ūs (*f.*)
hand over, trādō, -ere, -didī, -ditus
hard, difficilis, -e
hasten, contendō, -ere, -tendī, -tentus
have, habeō, -ēre, -uī, -itus
he, is, ea, id
head, caput, -itis (*n.*)
hear, audiō, -īre, -īvī, -ītus
heavy, gravis, -e
height, altitūdō, -inis (*f.*)
hem in, contineō, -ēre, -tinuī, -tentus
hesitate, dubitō, -āre, -āvī, -ātus
high, altus, -a, -um
hill, collis, -is (*m.*)
his (her, its, their) own, suus, -a, -um
hold, teneō, -ēre, -uī
hold back, prohibeō, -ēre, -uī, -itus
hold together, contineō, -ēre, -tinuī, -tentus
hold up, sustineō, -ēre, -tinuī, -tentus
home, domus, -ūs (*f.*)
hope, spēs, speī (*f.*)
horn, cornū, -ūs (*n.*)
horse, equus, -ī (*m.*)
horseman, eques, -itis (*m.*)
hour, hōra, -ae (*f.*)
house, domus, -ūs (*f.*)
however, tamen
how many?, quot?
hundred, centum
hurl, iaciō, -ere, -iēcī, iactus

I, ego
if, sī
in, in (*with abl.*)
indeed, vērō
in fact, quidem
influence, auctōritās, -ātis (*f.*)
influence, addūcō, -ere, -dūxī, -ductus
in front of, ante (*with acc.*)
injury, iniūria, -ae (*f.*)
injustice, iniūria, -ae (*f.*)
in the presence of, apud (*with acc.*)

into, in (*with acc.*)
in truth, vērō
island, īnsula, -ae (*f.*)

join, committō, -ere, -mīsī, missus
journey, iter, itineris (*n.*)

keep, teneō, -ēre, -uī
kill, interficiō, -ere, -fēcī, -fectus
kind, genus, -eris (*n.*)
kindness, beneficium, -ī (*n.*)
king, rēx, rēgis (*m.*)
kingdom, rēgnum, -ī (*n.*)
know, sciō, -īre, -īvī, -ītus

lack, inopia, -ae (*f.*)
land, terra, -ae (*f.*)
language, lingua, -ae (*f.*)
large, magnus, -a, -um
law, lēx, lēgis (*f.*)
lead, dūcō, -ere, dūxī, ductus
lead forth, prōdūcō, -ere, -dūxī, -ductus
lead to, addūcō, -ere, -dūxī, -ductus
leader, dux, ducis (*m.*)
learn, cognōscō, -ere, -nōvī, -nitus
leave, discēdō, -ere, -cessī, -cessus
left, sinister, -tra, -trum
let go, dīmittō, -ere, -mīsī, -missus
level, aequus, -a, -um
liberty, lībertās, -ātis (*f.*)
life, vīta, -ae (*f.*)
light, levis, -e
light, lūx, lūcis (*f.*)
like, similis, -e
like, amō, -āre, -āvī, -ātus
line of battle, aciēs -ēī (*f.*)
little, parvus, -a, -um
long, longus, -a, -um
long time, diū
look at, spectō, -āre, -āvī, -ātus
lose, āmittō, -ere, -mīsī, -missus
love, amō, -āre, -āvī, -ātus
luck, fortūna, -ae (*f.*)

make, faciō, -ere, fēcī, factus
man, vir, virī (*m.*)
manner, modus, -ī (*m.*)
many, multī, -ae, -a
march, iter, itineris (*n.*)
march, iter facere
maritime, maritimus, -a, -um
master, dominus, -ī (*m.*)
matter, rēs, reī (*f.*)

meanwhile, interim
memory, memoria, -ae (f.)
method, ratiō, -ōnis (f.)
mind, animus, -ī (m.)
mine, meus, -a, -um
money, pecūnia, -ae (f.)
month, mēnsis, -is (m.)
moon, lūna, -ae (f.)
more, magis
moreover, autem
most of all, maximē
mother, māter, -tris (f.)
mountain, mōns, montis (m.)
move, moveō, -ēre, mōvī, mōtus
move back, removeō, -ēre, -mōvī, -mōtus
move deeply, permoveō, -ēre, -mōvī, -mōtus
much, multus, -a, -um
multitude, multitūdō, -inis (f.)
my, meus, -a, -um

name, nōmen, -inis (n.)
name, appellō, -āre, -āvī, -ātus
native land, patria, -ae (f.)
nature, nātūra, -ae (f.)
near, propinquus, -a, -um
necessary, necessārius, -a, -um
neighboring, fīnitimus, -a, -um
neither . . . nor, neque . . . neque
new, novus, -a, -um
night, nox, noctis (f.)
nine, novem
ninth, nōnus, -a, -um
noble, nōbilis, -e
noon, merīdiēs, -ēī (m.)
nor, neque
not, nōn
not even, nē . . . quidem
now, nunc
number, numerus, -ī (m.)

offer, prōpōnō, -ere, -posuī, -positus
on, in (with abl.)
on account of, propter (with acc.)
once, ōlim
one, ūnus, -a, -um
opportunity, facultās, -ātis (f.)
oppress, premō, -ere, pressī, pressus
or, aut
order, ōrdō, -inis (m.)
order, iubeō, -ēre, iussī, iussus
ought, dēbeō, -ēre, -uī, -itus
our, ours, noster, -tra, -trum

out of, ē, ex (with abl.)
outstanding, ēgregius, -a, -um
owe, dēbeō, -ēre, -uī, -itus

pace, passus, -ūs (m.)
part, pars, partis (f.)
peace, pāx, pācis (f.)
people, populus, -ī (m.)
perceive, sentiō, -īre, sēnsī, sēnsus
pertain, pertineō, -ēre, -tinuī
place, locus, -ī (m.); (pl.), loca, -ōrum (n.)
place, pōnō, -ere, posuī, positus
plain, campus, -ī (m.)
plan, cōnsilium, -ī (n.)
play, lūdō, -ere, lūsī, lūsus
poet, poēta, -ae (m.)
point out, dēmōnstrō, -āre, -āvī, -ātus
poor, miser, -era, -erum
possess, obtineō, -ēre, -tinuī, -tentus
power, potestās, -ātis (f.)
powerful, potēns
praise, laudō, -āre, -āvī, -ātus
prepare, parō, -āre, -āvī, -ātus
prepared, parātus, -a, -um
preserve, cōnservō, -āre, -āvī, -ātus
press, premō, -ere, pressī, pressus
prevent, prohibeō, -ēre, -uī, -itus
previously, anteā
prize, praemium, -ī (n.)
protection, praesidium, -ī (n.)
province, prōvincia, -ae (f.)
public, pūblicus, -a, -um
punishment, poena, -ae (f.)
put, pōnō, -ere, posuī, positus
put out, expōnō, -ere, -posuī, -positus

queen, rēgīna, -ae (f.)

race, genus, -eris (n.)
rank, ōrdō, -inis (m.)
reach, pertineō, -ēre, -tinuī
read, legō, -ere, lēgī, lēctus
ready, parātus, -a, -um
reason, causa, -ae (f.)
receive, accipiō, -ere, -cēpī, -ceptus
recent, recēns
remain, maneō, -ēre, mānsī, mānsūrus
remaining, reliquus, -a, -um
remarkable, ēgregius, -a, -um

reply, respondeō, -ēre, -spondī, -spōnsus
report, renūntiō, -āre, -āvī, -ātus
republic, rēs pūblica, reī pūblicae (f.)
rest (of), reliquus, -a, -um
return, reddō, -ere, -didī, -ditus
revolt, dēficiō, -ere, -fēcī, -fectus
reward, praemium, -ī (n.)
right, dexter, -tra, -trum
right, iūs, iūris (n.)
river, flūmen, -inis (n.)
road, via, -ae (f.)
route, iter, itineris (n.)
rule, rēgnum, -ī (n.)

sail, nāvigō, -āre, -āvī, -ātus
sailor, nauta, -ae (m.)
same, īdem, eadem, idem
savage, barbarus, -a, -um
save, servō, -āre, -āvī, -ātus
say, dīcō, -ere, dīxī, dictus
scarcity, inopia, -ae (f.)
sea, mare, -is (n.)
second, secundus, -a, -um
see, videō, -ēre, vīdī, vīsus
seek, petō, -ere, -īvī, -ītus
seize, occupō, -āre, -āvī, -ātus
-self, ipse, -a, -um
self (reflexive), sē
senate, senātus, -ūs (m.)
send, mittō, -ere, mīsī, missus
send ahead, praemittō, -ere, -mīsī, -missus
send away, dīmittō, -ere, -mīsī, -missus
send back, remittō, -ere, -mīsī, -missus
serious, gravis, -e
set forth, prōpōnō, -ere, -posuī, -positus
seven, septem
seventh, septimus, -a, -um
severe, gravis, -e
sharp, ācer, ācris, ācre
sharply, ācriter
she, ea
ship, nāvis, -is (f.)
short, brevis, -e
show, dēmōnstrō, -āre, -āvī, -ātus
signal, signum, -ī (n.)
similar, similis, -e
sister, soror, -ōris (f.)
six, sex
sixth, sextus, -a, -um
size, magnitūdō, -inis (f.)

ENGLISH-LATIN VOCABULARY

slave, servus, -ī (*m.*)
small, parvus, -a, -um
soldier, mīles, -itis (*m.*)
son, fīlius, -ī (*m.*)
soon, iam
space, spatium, -ī (*n.*)
speak, dīcō, -ere, dīxī, dictus
speech, ōrātiō, -ōnis (*f.*)
speed, celeritās, -ātis (*f.*)
spirit, animus, -ī (*m.*)
standard, signum, -ī (*n.*)
state, cīvitās, -ātis (*f.*)
station, cōnstituō, -ere, -stituī, -stitūtus
stay, maneō, -ēre, mānsī, mānsūrus
step, passus, -ūs (*m.*)
still, tamen
stop, intermittō, -ere, -mīsī, -missus
strange, novus, -a, -um
street, via, -ae (*f.*)
strength, vīs, vīs (*f.*)
strengthen, cōnfīrmō, -āre, -āvī, -ātus
strong, fortis, -e
suitable, idōneus, -a, -um
summer, aestās, -ātis (*f.*)
sun, sōl, sōlis (*m.*)
supply, cōpia, -ae (*f.*)
sure, certus, -a, -um
surpass, superō, -āre, -āvī, -ātus
surrender, trādō, -ere, -didī, -ditus
surround, circumveniō, -īre, -vēnī, -ventus
swift, celer, -eris, -ere
swiftness, celeritās, -ātis (*f.*)
sword, gladius, -ī (*m.*)

take, capiō, -ere, -cēpī, captus
task, negōtium, -ī (*n.*)
teach, doceō, -ēre, -uī, -tus
teacher, magister, -trī (*m.*)
ten, decem

tenth, decimus, -a, -um
terms, condiciō, -ōnis (*f.*)
terrify, perterreō, -ēre, -uī, -itus
territory, fīnēs, -ium (*m. pl.*)
than, quam
that, ille, illa, illud
that, quī, quae, quod
then, tum
there, ibi
therefore, itaque
thing, rēs, reī (*f.*)
think, putō, -āre, -āvī, -ātus
third, tertius, -a, -um
this, hic, haec, hoc
thousand, mīlle
three, trēs, tria
through, per (*with acc.*)
throw, iaciō, -ere, iēcī, iactus
time, tempus, -oris (*n.*)
timid, timidus, -a, -um
to, toward, ad (*with acc.*)
today, hodiē
toga, toga, -ae (*f.*)
tongue, lingua, -ae (*f.*)
town, oppidum, -ī (*n.*)
tree, arbor, -oris (*f.*)
troops, cōpiae, -ārum (*f. pl.*)
true, vērus, -a, -um
trumpet, tuba, -ae (*f.*)
trust, fidēs, -eī (*f.*)
try, temptō, -āre, -āvī, -ātus
twenty, vīgintī
two, duo, duae, duo

under, sub (*with acc. and abl.*)
unequal, inīquus, -a, -um
uneven, inīquus, -a, -um
unfavorable, inīquus, -a, -um
unfriendly, inimīcus, -a, -um

very, ipse, ipsa, ipsum
victor, victor, -ōris (*m.*)
victory, victōria -ae (*f.*)
violence, vīs, vīs (*f.*)

voice, vōx, vōcis (*f.*)

wage, gerō, -ere, gessī, gestus
wait (for), exspectō, -āre, -āvī, -ātus
war, bellum, -ī (*n.*)
warn, moneō, -ēre, -uī, -itus
water, aqua, -ae (*f.*)
way, modus, -ī (*m.*)
we, nōs
well, bene
what?, quid?
where?, ubi?
which, quī, quae, quod
who, quī, quae, quod
who?, quis?
why?, cūr?
wide, lātus, -a, -um
width, lātitūdō, -inis (*f.*)
wing, cornū, -ūs (*n.*)
winter, hiems, -emis (*f.*)
wise, prūdēns
wish, cupiō, -ere, -īvī, -ītus
with, cum (*with abl.*)
withdraw, removeō, -ēre, -mōvī, -mōtus
without, sine (*with abl.*)
withstand, sustineō, -ēre, -tinuī, -tentus
woman, fēmina, -ae (*f.*)
word, verbum, -ī (*n.*)
work, labōrō, -āre, -āvī, -ātus
wound, vulnus, -eris (*n.*)
wound, vulnerō, -āre, -āvī, -ātus
wretched, miser, -era, -erum
write, scrībō, -ere, scrīpsī, scrīptus
wrong, iniūria, -ae (*f.*)

year, annus, -ī (*m.*)
yet, tamen
yield, cēdō, -ere, cessī, cessus
you, tū; (*pl.*), vōs
your, tuus, -a, -um; vester, -tra, -trum

EXERCISES

A. Underline the Latin word that best translates the English word.

1. *there* cūr, ubi, tum, ibi
2. *think* petō, sciō, putō, parō
3. *arrival* adventus, celeritās, cīvitās, passus
4. *battle* bellum, proelium, poena, praemium
5. *sharp* celer, potēns, ācer, fortis
6. *warn* mūniō, moveō, maneō, moneō
7. *come* vincō, veniō, videō, gerō
8. *wound* vulnus, tempus, timor, praesidium
9. *kingdom* rēx, imperium, rēgnum, rēs
10. *same* ipse, ille, suus, īdem

B. In the space before each word in column *A*, write the letter of the Latin equivalent in column *B*.

	Column A		Column B
-------	**1.** plan	*a.*	interim
-------	**2.** order	*b.*	auxilium
-------	**3.** therefore	*c.*	spectō
-------	**4.** short	*d.*	dux
-------	**5.** throw	*e.*	dēbeō
-------	**6.** aid	*f.*	iubeō
-------	**7.** remaining	*g.*	quis
-------	**8.** river	*h.*	cōnsilium
-------	**9.** easy	*i.*	sine
-------	**10.** look at	*j.*	facilis
-------	**11.** without	*k.*	brevis
-------	**12.** ought	*l.*	iaciō
-------	**13.** who	*m.*	flūmen
-------	**14.** leader	*n.*	reliquus
-------	**15.** meanwhile	*o.*	itaque

C. Underline the correct Latin word to be used in each of the following sentences:

1. (addūcō, auctōritās)   He will *influence* his pupils.
2. (adventus, appropinquō)   They awaited his *approach*.
3. (post, posteā)   *After* the war came lasting peace.
4. (timeō, timor)   He does not *fear* death.
5. (levis, lūx)   The baggage was *light*.
6. (amō, similis)   He was *like* his mother.
7. (appellō, nōmen)   They will *name* him Marcus.
8. (dexter, iūs)   He attacked on the *right* flank.
9. (iubeō, ōrdō)   To *order* is to obey.
10. (quī, quis)   He was the man *who* came to dinner.

D. Underline the word in parentheses that best completes the meaning of each sentence.

1. A year has twelve (mēnsēs, mentēs, manūs).
2. Caesar drew up a (timōrem, adventum, aciem).
3. The boy was happy because he received a (modum, beneficium, perīculum).
4. The signal for battle (datum est, pugnātum est, victum est).
5. The enemy was overcome by (rīpā, vī, portā) of arms.
6. This reward is mine; that one is (tum, tū, tuum).
7. The battle was fought on the right (exercitū, equitibus, cornū).
8. Both generals presented terms (pācis, ducis, gladī).
9. September is the (novem, nōnus, novus) month.
10. Fighting was the (difficultās, merīdiēs, cōnsuētūdō) of the Germans.

Unit XV—Model Examinations

A. ONE PERIOD EXAMINATION

I. Translate into English. [30]

    a. Hīs rēbus cognitīs, imperātor cum omnibus cōpiīs in Galliam celeriter contendit.
    b. Propter perīculum magnum mīlitēs locum castrīs idōneum dēligent.
    c. Quis dīxit puerōs ad īnsulam cum suō magistrō iam nāvigāre?
    d. Dux iussit equitēs in oppidō omnēs equōs ad aquam dūcere.
    e. Magnitūdine et altitūdine hoc mare illud flūmen superat.

II. Write all the specified forms. [20]

    a–b. ablative singular of *adventus celer*
    c–d. accusative plural of *hic fīnis*
    e–f. nominative plural of *magnum iter*
    g–l. synopsis in the indicative third plural of *possum*
    m–n. present and perfect active infinitives of *cupiō*
    o–p. perfect passive participle of *gerō, relinquō*
    q. pluperfect indicative passive third singular of *dō*
    r. comparative of *bene*
    s–t. superlative of *novus, parvus*

III. In each sentence below, select the word or expression in parentheses that makes the sentence grammatically correct. [10]

    a. Ubi sunt (līberī, līberōs)?
    b. Mīlitēs in (castrīs, castra) vēnērunt.
    c. Lēgēs in forō (cōnstitūtī, cōnstitūtae) sunt.
    d. Sine (timōre, timōrem) pugnant.
    e. (Tubā, Cum tubā) signum dedit.

IV. Translate the italicized words into Latin. [10]

    a. Erat aequus frātrī *in courage.*
    b. *After the town had been captured,* sēsē in fugam dedit.
    c. Puer patrem *cannot see.*
    d. Erant inimīcī *for five years.*
    e. *In an unfavorable place* castra posuērunt.

V. For each word in column *A,* find the synonym in column *B.* [10]

Column A	Column B
a. dux	1. vir
b. iter	2. pellō
c. pugnō	3. exīstimō
d. agō	4. pār
e. animus	5. pugna
f. spectō	6. imperātor
g. homō	7. mēns
h. putō	8. contendō
i. aequus	9. videō
j. proelium	10. via

VI. In each sentence below, (1) write a Latin word with which the italicized word is associated by derivation, and (2) choose the word or expression in the accompanying list that best expresses the meaning of the italicized word. [10]

    a. A *malediction* came from his lips.
       (1) prayer (2) curse (3) blessing (4) sigh

b. The satellite exerted *centrifugal* force as it sped around the earth.
   (1) central   (2) directed from the center   (3) directed toward the center   (4) maximum
c. The couple tried to *abduct* the infant.
   (1) kidnap   (2) adopt   (3) rear   (4) desert
d. He suffered a *mortal* wound.
   (1) severe   (2) slight   (3) painful   (4) deadly
e. His sons lacked *virile* qualities.
   (1) moral   (2) manly   (3) tactful   (4) mental

VII. Select the word or expression that best completes each statement below.   [10]

a. A person appointed in times of extreme public danger was called a (1) tribune (2) consul (3) dictator (4) praetor.
b. The wealthy class in ancient Rome was called the (1) Equitēs (2) Optimātēs (3) Plēbs (4) freedmen.
c. The basilica was a (1) temple (2) speaker's platform (3) hill (4) law court.
d. The name "Marcus" was a common (1) nōmen (2) praenōmen (3) cognōmen (4) nickname.
e. The boy who flew too near the sun and drowned in the sea was called (1) Icarus (2) Daedalus (3) Pyramus (4) Orpheus.

B. ONE PERIOD EXAMINATION

I. Translate into English.   [40]

a. Post multōs annōs Rōmānī iūra cīvitātis omnibus dedērunt.
b. Rēge interfectō, mīlitēs ex oppidō celeriter excessērunt.
c. Ille puer et aestāte et hieme in agrīs labōrābat.
d. Pāx amīcitiaque cum cīvitātibus fīnitimīs ā Rōmānīs cōnfīrmātae sunt.
e. Hic eques omnem exercitum virtūte et celeritāte superat.
f. Diū et ācriter inter Rōmānōs hostēsque pugnātum est.
g. Imperātor nūntiāvit omnēs cōpiās ā Rōmānīs fortissimīs victās esse.
h. Parvīs nāvibus Germānī trāns flūmen sē in fugam dederant.

II. Translate the italicized words into Latin.   [10]

a. *With his brother* iter fēcit.
b. Puer *to the river* contendit.
c. Ab magistrō *he had been praised*.
d. Nautae celeriter *will come*.
e. *For three hours* pugnāvērunt.

III. In each sentence below, select the word or expression in parentheses that makes the sentence grammatically correct.   [10]

a. (Longus, Diū) nōn labōrābit.
b. Puer (armīs, ab armīs) pressus est.
c. (Sociī, Sociōs) in oppidō esse scīvit.
d. In (locum, locō) mānsērunt.
e. Eī hominēs erant (miserī, miserōs).

IV. Write all the specified forms.   [25]

a–b. ablative singular of *id tempus*
c–d. nominative plural of *nauta bonus*
e–f. accusative singular of *ille eques*
g–h. superlative of *fortis, bene*
i.   comparative of *magnus*
j–o. principal parts of *moneō, pellō*
p–u. synopsis in the indicative active third plural of *mittō*
v–w. present infinitive passive of *mūniō, pōnō*
x–y. present and future indicative passive first plural of *teneō*

V. In each sentence below, (1) write a Latin word with which the italicized word is associated by derivation, and (2) choose the word or expression in the accompanying list that best expresses the meaning of the italicized word. [10]

    a. The words "shall" and "have" are *auxiliary* verbs.
        (1) compound   (2) helping   (3) transitive   (4) intransitive
    b. He plans to *accelerate* his studies.
        (1) hasten   (2) finish   (3) drop   (4) neglect
    c. The sounds were *inaudible*.
        (1) loud   (2) clear   (3) peculiar   (4) unable to be heard
    d. Congress finally *convened*.
        (1) recessed   (2) adjourned   (3) met   (4) voted
    e. They *collaborated* with the enemy.
        (1) fought   (2) worked   (3) departed   (4) remained

VI. Select the word or expression that best completes each statement below. [5]

    a. The legendary hero who slew the sea monster was (1) Jason (2) Hercules (3) Perseus (4) Ulysses.
    b. The Latin abbreviation for "namely" is (1) ibid. (2) q.v. (3) et al. (4) viz.
    c. The Roman god of the sea was (1) Mars (2) Neptune (3) Vulcan (4) Jupiter.
    d. The Latin expression that means "make haste slowly" is (1) in toto (2) ipso facto (3) ex officio (4) festina lente.
    e. The Latin word "excelsior" is a (1) symbol of authority (2) battle cry (3) state motto (4) warning sign.

C. ONE PERIOD EXAMINATION

I. Translate into English. [30]

    a. Propter timōrem hostium Rōmānī ex castrīs eō diē nōn excessērunt.
    b. Oppidō captō, mīlitēs decem mīlia passuum in Galliam iter fēcērunt.
    c. Quis dīxit omnia praemia puerīs ā magistrō data esse?
    d. Sine vulnere dux nāve parvā trāns flūmen sēsē in fugam dederat.
    e. Vīdēruntne līberī hodiē montēs altissimōs in īnsulā fīnitimā?

II. Write all the specified forms. [20]

    a–b. ablative singular of *illud tempus*
    c–d. accusative plural of *vir fortis*
    e–f. ablative plural of *ea rēs*
    g–l. synopsis in the indicative active third plural of *petō*
    m–n. present active and passive infinitives of *respondeō*
    o–p. perfect passive participle of *premō, agō*
    q. perfect indicative passive third singular of *dēfendō*
    r. adverb from *brevis*
    s–t. superlative of *ācer, magnus*

III. Select the expression in parentheses that makes the sentence correct. [10]

    a. Puerī in (silvam, silvā) mānsērunt.
    b. Librum (puellae, ad puellam) dabit.
    c. Mīlitēs (manibus, cum manibus) pugnant.
    d. Putāvit cōnsulēs in oppidō (erant, esse).
    e. Omnēs viae fuērunt (malae, malās).

IV. Translate the italicized words into Latin. [10]

    a. Pugnāvērunt *for many days.*
    b. Erat fīlius *of the friendly sailor.*
    c. Frūmentum in oppidum *had been carried.*
    d. *To that island* contendit.
    e. *With his father* manet.

V. For each word in column *A*, find the word in column *B* which is most nearly *opposite* in meaning. [10]

Column A	Column B
a. cum	1. parvus
b. paucī	2. pāx
c. āmittō	3. labōrō
d. magnus	4. difficilis
e. socius	5. multī
f. bellum	6. sine
g. lūdō	7. cōnficiō
h. facilis	8. gravis
i. incipiō	9. hostis
j. levis	10. inveniō

VI. In each sentence below, (1) write a Latin word with which the italicized word is associated by derivation, and (2) choose the word or expression in the accompanying list that best expresses the meaning of the italicized word. [10]

a. His accomplishments were *multifarious*.
   (1) ordinary   (2) many   (3) unbelievable   (4) insufficient
b. He demonstrated the theory of *centripetal* force.
   (1) tremendous   (2) central   (3) directed from the center   (4) directed toward the center
c. The scientist used a *propellant* in the test.
   (1) onward force   (2) trial balloon   (3) test tube   (4) dual oar
d. Your explanation is far from *lucid*.
   (1) complete   (2) clear   (3) correct   (4) detailed
e. She was known for her *brevity* of expression.
   (1) clearness   (2) power   (3) shortness   (4) frequency

VII. Select the word or expression that best completes each statement below. [10]

a. The abbreviation N.B. means (1) not below (2) note well (3) that is (4) never binding.
b. The goddess of the chase was (1) Minerva (2) Diana (3) Juno (4) Vesta.
c. To express the idea of "without limit," one says (1) ad nauseam (2) in toto (3) per se (4) ad infinitum.
d. The ātrium in a Roman house was the (1) courtyard (2) private study (3) front hall (4) water basin.
e. Our *most* important debt to the Romans was in the field of (1) architecture (2) politics (3) engineering (4) language and literature.

D. TWO PERIOD EXAMINATION

I. Translate into English. [20]

[War with the Sabines]

Rōma prīmō multōs virōs, paucās fēminās habēbat. Rōmulus, rēx Rōmānōrum, hoc cōnsilium cēpit. Fīnitimī Rōmānīs erant fīnēs Sabīnōrum. Sabīnī multās fīliās habēbant. Rōmulus Sabīnōs cum fēminīs līberīsque ad pūblicōs lūdōs (games) invītāvit. Sabīnī, et virī et fēminae et līberī, ad urbem novam lībenter (gladly) vēnērunt. Neque arma neque gladiōs portābant. Omnēs in Forō lūdōs spectābant.

Signum ā Rōmulō celeriter datum est. Signō datō, Rōmānī puellās Sabīnās cēpērunt et domum contendērunt. Patrēs frātrēsque Sabīnī magnopere permovēbantur, sed sine armīs pugnāre nōn poterant. Posteā erat bellum inter Rōmānōs Sabīnōsque.

II. In each sentence below, select the word or expression in parentheses that makes the sentence grammatically correct. [10]

a. Dux gladium (mīlitī, ad mīlitem) dedit.
b. Fīliī cōnsulis sunt (bonōs, bonī).

c. Mīlitēs in (castra, castrīs) contendērunt.
d. (Gladiō, Cum gladiō) fortiter pugnat.
e. (Ab servō, Servō) vulnerātus est.
f. Virī (hieme, in hieme) labōrābant.
g. Puellae (servātī sunt, servātae sunt).
h. Puer sorōrem (altitūdine, in altitūdine) superat.
i. Vīcērunt sine (pugnā, pugnam).
j. Puerī poterant (lūdunt, lūdere).

III. Read the following passage through carefully several times, and then answer in English the questions below. [10]

[The Battle of Marathon]

Antīquīs temporibus Graecī cum Persīs prō lībertāte contendērunt. Dārīus, rēx Persārum, magnās cōpiās et multās nāvēs comparāvit. Trāns mare nāvigāvit, et in plānitiē (plain) Marathōniā, quae vīgintī sex mīlia passuum ab Athēnīs aberat, castra posuit. Athēniēnsēs quoque (also) bellum parāvērunt, et decem mīlia mīlitum coēgērunt. Proelium in plānitiē commissum est. Athēniēnsēs hostēs vīcērunt, et eōs in fugam dedērunt.

Inter mīlitēs Athēniēnsēs erat adulēscēns Phīdippidēs. Hic post proelium iter longum inter Marathōna et Athēnās magnā cum celeritāte paucīs hōrīs fēcit. Ad urbem pervēnit et victōriam nūntiāvit. Tum exanimātus (out of breath), ē vītā excessit.

a. For what did the Greeks fight?
b. Who was Darius?
c. What did he bring together besides troops?
d. Where did he pitch camp?
e. How far was Marathon from Athens?
f. How many soldiers did the Athenians have?
g. After the Athenians won the battle, what did they do to the Persians?
h. How long did it take Phidippides to make the trip from Marathon to Athens?
i. For what purpose did he make the trip?
j. Then what happened to him?

IV. In each sentence below, select the correct translation for the italicized word or expression. [10]

a. The *farmer's* fields were destroyed.
    (1) agricola   (2) agricolae   (3) agricolārum
b. The slaves *are captured*.
    (1) capiunt   (2) capient   (3) capiuntur
c. These girls are *unhappy*.
    (1) miserae   (2) miserās   (3) miseram
d. *They will praise* the winner.
    (1) laudābant   (2) laudābunt   (3) laudant
e. The boat sailed *with the soldiers*.
    (1) mīlitibus   (2) cum mīlitibus   (3) cum mīlite
f. He hurried *to his father*.
    (1) patrī   (2) patris   (3) ad patrem
g. The Gauls *had been conquered*.
    (1) victī sunt   (2) victī erant   (3) victī erunt
h. They ran *into the forest*.
    (1) in silvam   (2) in silvīs   (3) in silvā
i. The soldier was defended *by the leader*.
    (1) ab ducibus   (2) ab duce   (3) duce
j. The enemy *arrived* quickly.
    (1) perveniunt   (2) perveniēbant   (3) pervēnērunt

V. Rewrite the sentences below, making *all* changes required by the directions in parentheses. [10]

a. Homō **est** dux.   (change to **petit**)
b. **Mīles** sagittās iacit.   (change to the plural)
c. **Puerī** commōtī sunt.   (substitute *girls*)

d. Nautae in aquam **contendunt.**   (substitute the equivalent form of **esse**)

e. Nostrī **fīliī** mānsērunt.   (change to the singular)

f. Dux equitibus **dīcet.**   (substitute the equivalent form of **contendere**)

g. **Gladiō** pugnāvit.   (substitute *his friend*)

h. Virī scrībunt.   (insert **possunt** after **Virī**)

i. Excēdunt **propter** perīculum.   (substitute *without*)

j. Dominus līberōs docet.   (express the same idea in the passive)

VI. Write the specified verb forms.   [20]

a–f. principal parts of *iaciō* and *mittō*

g–l. synopsis in the indicative active third person plural of *vincō*

m–n. present infinitive active and passive of *petō*

o–p. present active and perfect passive participle of *videō*

q. perfect indicative third singular passive of *dūcō*

r. future indicative first plural active of *pōnō*

s–t. present and imperfect indicative third plural of *possum*

VII. For each of the following sentences, (1) write a Latin word with which the italicized word is associated by derivation, and (2) choose the word or expression in the accompanying list that best expresses the meaning of the italicized word.   [10]

a. The sailor acted in a *puerile* fashion.
(1) selfish   (2) mature   (3) childish   (4) noble

b. They ran into *pecuniary* difficulties.
(1) financial   (2) family   (3) slight   (4) serious

c. He *dominated* the club.
(1) organized   (2) joined   (3) avoided   (4) ruled

d. She was famous for her *magnanimity.*
(1) loyalty   (2) generosity   (3) intelligence   (4) ability

e. They entered a *subterranean* passage.
(1) dark   (2) underground   (3) narrow   (4) dangerous

f. The *gravity* of the situation convinced the general.
(1) hopelessness   (2) closeness   (3) seriousness   (4) study

g. They were unable to *suppress* the revolt.
(1) support   (2) put down   (3) begin   (4) detect

h. The senator was known for his *veracity.*
(1) truthfulness   (2) stubbornness   (3) wit   (4) fighting spirit

i. *Agrarian* laws were finally passed.
(1) stern   (2) money   (3) land   (4) housing

j. He gave *cogent* reasons for his action.
(1) weak   (2) forceful   (3) truthful   (4) simple

VIII. For each incomplete statement below, select the word or expression that best completes the statement.   [10]

a. The Latin abbreviation that means "at pleasure" is (1) i.e. (2) cf. (3) e.g. (4) ad lib.

b. When Congress adjourns "sine die," it does so (1) immediately (2) indefinitely (3) without debate (4) for one day.

c. The Greek hero who slew the Minotaur was (1) Theseus (2) Ulysses (3) Perseus (4) Hercules.

d. The mother of the famous Gracchi brothers was (1) Calpurnia (2) Medea (3) Proserpina (4) Cornelia.

e. Ceres was the goddess of (1) love (2) wisdom (3) the chase (4) agriculture.

f. The god identified with fire was (1) Janus (2) Mars (3 Saturn (4) Vulcan.

g. The master's study or office in a Roman house was the (1) tablīnum (2) ātrium (3) peristȳlium (4) impluvium.

h. The Colosseum was used chiefly for (1) gladiatorial combats (2) chariot races (3) plays (4) elections.

i. The short-sleeved undergarment worn indoors by the Romans was called a (1) toga (2) stola (3) tunica (4) palla.

j. The given name of a Roman was called the (1) nōmen (2) praenōmen (2) cognōmen (4) nickname.

I. Translate into English.   [20]

[Aeneas, the Trojan]

Aenēās erat Trōiānus quī cum Graecīs proeliīs multīs pugnābat. Nē ille quidem patriam servāre potuit. Graecī cum magnīs cōpiīs Trōiam occupāvērunt.

Trōiā captā, Aenēās domum relīquit et, spē adductus, prīmō in Macedoniam vēnit. Post multōs diēs cum amīcīs ad Siciliam pervēnit, et ab Siciliā paucīs nāvibus ad Italiam Trōiānī vēnērunt. Ibi in Latiō rēx erat Latīnus. Proelium inter Trōiānōs mīlitēsque Latīnī commissum est. Posteā pāx cōnfīrmāta est, et Aenēās socius ab rēge Latīnō acceptus est. Latīnus etiam fīliam Laviniam Aenēae in mātrimōnium dedit. Trōiānī oppidum condidērunt (founded) quod Aenēās ab nōmine Laviniā Lavinium appellāvit. Nepōtēs (descendants) Aenēae fuērunt Rōmulus et Remus.

II. Translate the italicized words into Latin.   [10]

a. Praemium *to the boy* dedit.
b. Contendērunt *into the water*.
c. *With a sword* vulnerātus est.
d. Auxilium *they had sent*.
e. *At that time* parātī sunt.

f. *Very quickly* labōrāvit.
g. Sine *arms* vēnērunt.
h. *He will be praised* ab duce.
i. Iter fēcit *with his friend*.
j. *Camp* posuērunt.

III. Read the following passage through carefully several times, and then answer in English the questions below.   [10]

[Regulus and the Serpent]

Rōmānī ōlim bellum cum Poenīs (Carthaginians) gerēbant. Post multōs annōs cōnstitūtum est in Africam, Rēgulō duce, cōpiās Rōmānās mittere. Castrīs Rōmānīs in Africā positīs, mīlitēs novō perīculō perterritī sunt. Nam serpēns magnus in castrīs vīsus est. Tum Rēgulus virtūtem maximam ostendit. Animōs permōtōs mīlitum cōnfīrmāvit. Suōs iussit lapidēs (stones) in serpentem iacere. Hōc modō mōnstrum, quod centum vīgintī pedēs longum esse dīcēbātur, facillimē interfectum est.

a. Who was the leader of the Romans?
b. How long was the war fought?
c. What did the Romans decide to do?
d. Where did the Romans pitch their camp?
e. What was the new danger that confronted the Romans?
f. How did the soldiers react to this danger at first?
g. What did Regulus do to their spirits?
h. What order did he give them?
i. How big was the serpent said to be?
j. What finally happened to it?

IV. In each sentence below, select the word or expression in parentheses that makes the sentence grammatically correct.   [10]

a. Puerī in (aquā, aquam) sunt.
b. Dīxit (virī, virōs) venīre.
c. Mīlitēs trāns (flūmine, flūmen) contendērunt.
d. Castra circumventa (est, sunt).
e. (Puerīs, Ad puerōs) dīcunt.
f. Equus (cum sagittā, sagittā) vulnerātus est.
g. Līberī (aestāte, in aestāte) lūdunt.
h. Virōs (fortis, fortēs) laudāvit.
i. Sine (timōre, timōrem) pugnāvērunt.
j. Celeriter (scrībunt, scrībere) possunt.

V. Write all the specified forms.   [10]

a–b. accusative plural of *flūmen altum*
c–d. dative singular of *hic homō*
e–f. ablative singular of *gladius levis*

g–h. accusative singular of *senātus melior*
i–j. superlative of *gravis, celeriter*

VI. Write the specified verb forms.   [20]

a–i. principal parts of *pōnō, nūntiō, scrībō*
j–o. synopsis in the indicative active third plural of *dūcō*
p–q. present infinitive active and passive of *capiō*
r–s. perfect passive participle of *mittō, faciō*
t.   pluperfect indicative passive third singular of *moveō*

VII. In each group below, (1) write a Latin word with which the italicized word is associated by derivation, and (2) choose the word in the accompanying list that best expresses the meaning of the italicized word.   [10]

a. *locate*   neglect, license, descend, situate
b. *vital*   artificial, essential, popular, current
c. *spectacle*   display, cycle, planet, anecdote
d. *deity*   vitamin, tool, god, exile
e. *virile*   glossy, pompous, futile, manly
f. *pugnacious* quarrelsome, sufficient, native, unanimous
g. *inimical*   hostile, loose, friendly, biased
h. *copious*   jealous, copied, ample, feverish
i. *portal*   wine, sparrow, recital, entrance
j. *counsel*   officer, advice, table, request

VIII. In the following passage, ten words are italicized and repeated in the questions below. Underline the alternative that best explains each italicized word as it is used in the passage.   [10]

The history of Rome in its early stages is made up largely of traditions based upon some elements of truth. Rome in fact was located on a *river*, it was built on *hills*, and it had a *seaport* sixteen miles away. However, the *date* of its founding and the *founders* themselves are legendary. The area in which Rome was situated was called Latium, whence the word Latin.

The smallest group of Roman society was the family, which the early Romans regarded as the most sacred of all human institutions. At its head was the household *father*. A number of families descended from a common ancestor formed a *clan*, bound together by common religious rites.

The earliest gods worshipped by the Romans were *Jupiter* and *Mars* on the Capitoline Hill. The sacred fire was forever kept burning in a *temple* dedicated for that purpose. In peace and in war the Romans lived in the presence of the gods, and remembered them by worship and festivals.

a. *river*
  (1) Po   (3) Seine
  (2) Tiber   (4) Marne

b. *hills*
  (1) 3   (3) 7
  (2) 5   (4) 9

c. *seaport*
  (1) Ostia   (3) Antium
  (2) Pisa   (4) Appia

d. *date*
  (1) 509 B.C. (3) 1000 B.C.
  (2) 27 B.C.   (4) 753 B.C.

e. *founders*
  (1) Castor and Pollux
  (2) Romulus Augustulus
  (3) Romulus and Remus
  (4) Marius and Sulla

f. *father*
  (1) pontifex maximus
  (2) paterfamilias
  (3) tribunus plebis
  (4) dictator

g. *clan*
  (1) gens   (3) familia
  (2) genus   (4) comitium

h. *Jupiter*
  (1) Cronus   (3) Hermes
  (2) Zeus   (4) Apollo

i. *Mars*
  (1) god of the sea (3) god of war
  (2) god of fire   (4) god of the harvest

j. *temple*
  (1) Apollo   (3) Concord
  (2) Saturn   (4) Vesta

F. TWO PERIOD EXAMINATION

I. Translate into English.   [20]

[Theseus and the Minotaur]

Ōlim Crētensēs cum Athēniēnsibus diū bellum gerēbant. Athēniēnsēs, bellō superātī, quotannīs (every year) dare septem puerōs septemque puellās ā victōribus iussī sunt. Patrēs mātrēsque līberōrum magnō dolōre (grief) permovēbantur, quod fīliōs fīliāsque posteā spectāre nōn poterant. Mīnōs, rēx Crētae, līberōs in Labyrinthum iaciēbat, in quō erant viae multae et tortuōsae (winding). Ibi līberī perterritī Mīnōtaurum, mōnstrum terribile, vidēbant. Hoc mōnstrum, quī caput taurī (of a bull), corpus hominis habuit, līberōs Athēniēnsium facile interfēcit.

Tamen Thēseus, fīlius rēgis Athēniēnsis, mōnstrum vincere et līberōs līberāre cōnstituit.

II. Read the continuation of the story carefully, but do *not* write a translation. Below the passage you will find five incomplete Latin statements. Complete each statement by selecting one of the three choices given.   [10]

Thēseus ad īnsulam Crētam cum sex puerīs et septem puellīs nāvigāvit. Scīvit magnitūdinem perīculī neque timēbat. Nāvis cum līberīs ad īnsulam appropinquāvit. Multī hominēs in rīpā nāvem spectābant. Inter eōs erat Ariadnē, fīlia rēgis Crētēnsis, quī Thēseum amāvit. Illa eī auxilium dare cōnstituit. Ad portam Labyrinthī Ariadnē Thēseum exspectāvit, et eī gladium et glomus (ball of yarn) dedit.

"Hōc gladiō," dīxit Ariadnē, "Mīnōtaurum interficiēs, hōc glomere viam inveniēs." Tum Thēseus sine timōre in Labyrinthum contendit. Mōnstrum vīdit et cum eō diū et ācriter pugnāvit. Mīnōtaurus, multīs vulneribus acceptīs, interfectus est. Thēseus et Ariadnē ad Graeciam sēsē in fugam dedērunt. Puerī puellaeque Graeciae servātī sunt.

a. Thēseus ad īnsulam Crētam nāvigāvit.
  (1) perīculum timēns.
  (2) perīculum sciēns.
  (3) magnopere perterritus.
b. Hominēs in rīpā nāvem appropinquantem
  (1) vidēbant.
  (2) timēbant.
  (3) sciēbant.
c. Ariadnē Thēseō auxilium dedit quod
  (1) erat fīlia rēgis.
  (2) gladium habēbat.
  (3) eum amābat.

d. Thēseus Mīnōtaurum interficere potuit
  (1) gladiō.
  (2) glomere.
  (3) timōre.
e. Mīnōtaurō interfectō, Thēseus Ariadnēque
  (1) in Labyrinthum contendērunt.
  (2) ad Graeciam contendērunt.
  (3) multa vulnera accēpērunt.

III. Select the expression that makes the sentence correct.   [10]

a. Pater (ad fīlium, fīliō) pecūniam dedit.
b. Nauta fīliōs suōs amat quod (ēgregiī, ēgregiōs) sunt.
c. Urbs (ā cīvibus, cīvibus) capta est.
d. (Ūnam hōram, Ūna hōra) labōrāvit.
e. Virī in (oppidum, oppidō) sunt.
f. Puella (cum mātre, mātre) vēnit.
g. Oppidum (armīs, cum armīs) dēfendunt.
h. Puer (oppidō, ad oppidum) contendit.
i. Dīcit (līberī, līberōs) in aquā esse.
j. Mīlitēs (virtūte, in virtūte) omnēs superant.

IV. In each sentence below, select the correct translation for the italicized word or expression.   [10]

a. The *consul's* house is large.
  (1) cōnsul   (2) cōnsulis   (3) cōnsulum
b. They attacked the *men*.
  (1) virōs   (2) virīs   (3) virum
c. He told the *boys* a story.
  (1) puerōs   (2) puerīs   (3) puerōrum
d. The sailor *had captured* the boat.
  (1) cēpit   (2) cēperat   (3) cēperit

248

e. The camp *is* near the river.
    (1) est (2) erat (3) sunt
  f. The town *was defended* by the soldiers.
    (1) dēfendēbat (2) dēfendēbātur (3) dēfendunt
  g. The horseman was *very brave*.
    (1) fortis (2) fortior (3) fortissimus
  h. The girl saw *her own* father.
    (1) suum (2) suam (3) eius
  i. A *very large* horse was built by the Trojans.
    (1) plūrimus (2) maximus (3) optimus
  j. The man wounded *himself*.
    (1) suī (2) sē (3) sibi

V. Write the specified forms. [10]

  a–b. ablative singular of *idem tempus*
  c–d. accusative plural of *illud flūmen*
  e–f. nominative plural of *omnis rēs*
  g–h. genitive singular of *bonus exercitus*
  i.   comparative of *fortiter*
  j.   superlative of *parvus*

VI. Write the specified verb forms. [20]

  a–f. principal parts of *faciō, iubeō*
  g–l. synopsis in the indicative third plural active of *capiō*
  m–n. present infinitive active and passive of *audiō*
  o–p. perfect passive participle of *moveō* and *sentiō*
  q–r. future indicative passive third singular of *servō* and *gerō*
  s–t. perfect indicative active and passive first singular of *dūcō*

VII. In each sentence below, (1) write a Latin word with which the italicized word is associated by derivation, and (2) choose the word or expression in the accompanying list that best expresses the meaning of the italicized word. [10]

  a. *Amity* was the keynote of his speech.
    (1) hope (2) friendship (3) pleasure (4) pity
  b. He finally met his *paternal* uncle.
    pertaining to a (1) father (2) country (3) brother (4) mother
  c. His ambitions were very *laudable*.
    (1) undesirable (2) excessive (3) loud (4) praiseworthy
  d. He received a new *appellation*.
    (1) gift (2) suit (3) name (4) assignment
  e. He was amazed by the *paucity* of applicants.
    (1) small number (2) multitude (3) appearance (4) noise
  f. We arranged for the *itinerary*.
    (1) departure (2) welcome (3) plan of a trip (4) arrival
  g. His record was a *potent* factor in the election.
    (1) unusual (2) powerful (3) unimportant (4) indefinite
  h. The price of the car was *prohibitive*.
    (1) very low (2) unknown (3) not shown (4) forbidding
  i. She acted in an *ostentatious* manner.
    (1) shy (2) showy (3) disreputable (4) elegant
  j. They used *belligerent* means for settling their differences.
    (1) peaceful (2) inadequate (3) warlike (4) diplomatic

VIII. Complete each statement below by selecting the word or expression that best completes the statement. [10]

  a. Supreme authority, symbolized by a bundle of rods with an ax, was indicated by the Roman (1) cognōmen (2) rōstra (3) fascēs (4) thermae.
  b. The Roman god of the sun was (1) Apollo (2) Vulcan (3) Mars (4) Mercury.

249

c. The abbreviation e.g. means (1) that is (2) and so forth (3) in the same place (4) for example.

d. The king whose name is associated with a monster, half-man and half-bull, was (1) Priam (2) Midas (3) Croesus (4) Minos.

e. Horatius was famous for defending a (1) camp (2) river (3) town (4) bridge.

f. "A slip of the tongue" is expressed in Latin by the words (1) festina lente (2) in toto (3) lapsus linguae (4) corpus delicti.

g. Tenement houses in Rome were called (1) vigilēs (2) thermae (3) īnsulae (4) rōstra.

h. The official motto of the United States of America is (1) Excelsior (2) E pluribus unum (3) Iustitia omnibus (4) Sic semper tyrannis.

i. The expression "cursus honōrum" referred to the (1) order of office (2) courts at Rome (3) gladiatorial rewards (4) Roman roads.

j. The meal eaten by the Romans around noon was called the (1) cēna (2) ientāculum (3) trīclīnium (4) prandium.